Convoy Peewit

Dedication
For Zoë

Convoy Peewit

August 8, 1940:
The First Day of the Battle of Britain?

Andy Saunders

Grub Street • London

Published by
Grub Street
4 Rainham Close
London
SW11 6SS

British Library Cataloguing in Publication Data
Saunders, A. D.
   Convoy Peewit : August 8, 1940 – the first day of the
   Battle of Britain?.
   1. World War, 1939-1945 – Campaigns – English Channel.
   2. World War, 1939-1945 – Naval operations, British.
   3. World War, 1939-1945 – Naval operations, German.
   4. World War, 1939-1945 – Aerial operations, British.
   5. World War, 1939-1945 – Aerial operations, German.
   6. Britain, Battle of, Great Britain, 1940.
   I. Title
   940.5'4211-dc22

ISBN-13: 9781906502676

Cover design by Sarah Driver

Design by Roy Platten, Eclipse, Hemel Hempstead
roy.eclipse@btopenworld.com

Printed and bound by MPG Ltd, Bodmin, Cornwall

Grub Street Publishing only uses
FSC (Forest Stewardship Council) paper for its books.

Contents

Foreword

GIVEN THE shelf-groaning number of books on the Battle of Britain published during the past 60-odd years, it is no easy task to produce a new slant on that hard-fought series of actions. But Andy Saunders succeeds with this book.

He centres on a single day's fighting, that which took place over and around Convoy Peewit as it headed westwards through the English Channel on 8 August 1940. This action occurred near the end of the first phase of the Battle of Britain, during which the Luftwaffe had concentrated its attacks on the merchant shipping that plied the waters round the British Isles. And, painstaking researcher that he is, Andy has assembled an account of that day's actions that goes far beyond any that has appeared previously.

'Peewit' set sail from Southend early on the morning of 7 August, bound for Weymouth Bay. It comprised twenty-four small coasters, the largest being a tad under 1,600 tons and the six smallest having a displacement of less than 400 each. Most of the vessels were laden with coal from pits in the north of England, intended for power stations, industrial concerns and domestic use in the West Country. Other ships were loaded with raw materials and foodstuffs. The small Royal Navy force escorting the convoy comprised two destroyers and ten smaller ships.

On the afternoon of 7 August the convoy rounded North Foreland and plodded at 8 knots into the English Channel. The action opened during the early morning darkness of 8 August, when four E-Boats (fast motor torpedo boats) of the German navy ambushed the convoy as it sailed past Beachy Head. They sank three coasters and inflicted damage on several others.

From mid-morning to mid-afternoon on the 8th the Luftwaffe launched three major attacks on the convoy involving 188 sorties by Junkers 87 Stuka dive bombers. Escorting them was a large number of Messerschmitt Bf 109 and Bf 110 fighters. The first attack missed the main convoy and spent its fury against six coasters that had intended to join Peewit as it sailed past the Isle of Wight. Two of those coasters were sunk and the remaining four suffered serious damage. The RAF went into action in force against this attack and a series of dogfights ensued. Soon after noon came the second attack, which sank one of the coasters and damaged three more. Again there were fierce dogfights. Due to poor visibility the third attack failed to connect with the main convoy, though one of the Royal Navy escorts damaged previously was finished off.

The actions around Peewit were the largest so far to take place in the Battle of Britain. The ferocity of that air fighting is borne out by the scale of the losses suffered on each side. All told the Luftwaffe counted around twenty aircraft destroyed that day, while RAF Fighter Command lost a similar number. Most of those losses, though not all, were inflicted in the vicinity of Convoy Peewit.

The losses inflicted on the convoy itself amounted to six coasters and one Royal Navy escort sunk and several ships damaged and requiring repair.

Convoy Peewit is a good story, well told. I hope it achieves the success it deserves.

Dr. Alfred Price

Introduction

NOT UNREASONABLY one might consider the timings for any battles fought throughout the history of modern warfare to be quite straightforward to determine. Certainly one might expect that the attacking side would have no difficulty in setting out what those dates actually were, but in the case of the Battle of Britain the defenders determined the dates of battle whilst the attackers themselves remained singularly ambivalent about whether a battle, *per se*, had actually taken place. It fell to the leader of RAF Fighter Command, Air Chief Marshal Sir Hugh C T Dowding, to set the stage for later debate when he wrote on 10 September 1946:

"It is difficult to fix the exact date on which the Battle of Britain can be said to have begun. Operations of various kinds merged into one another almost insensibly, and there are grounds for choosing the date of 8 August, on which was made the first attack in force against laid objectives in this country, as the beginning of the Battle."

When, some six years earlier, His Majesty's Stationery Office had published the Air Ministry information booklet on the Battle of Britain it did so by setting down the period of that battle using 8 August as the start date, with the battle ending on 31 October 1940. Six years after that publication, and in his September 1946 dispatch for *The London Gazette*, Dowding returned again to the question of commencement of battle and referred specifically to that date but then went on to change it.

Clearly, and whilst there had been sporadic air attacks against the British Isles since September

Dowding's dispatch to *The London Gazette* of 10 September 1946.

1939, these attacks had not hitherto been sustained, nor had they yet been mass assaults. With the British withdrawal from France and subsequent German preparations for the invasion and occupation of Great Britain, the pace of Luftwaffe air operations intensified, with July 1940 seeing a steady increase in tempo. Indeed, by the beginning of August the Luftwaffe had already carried out such a degree of extensive and sustained reconnaissance around the perimeter of the British Isles that they must have known, for instance, a great deal about the assembly and movements of shipping, where and when it was most easily found and when it was most vulnerable to attack. During 6 and 7 August the Germans had operated on only a relatively small scale and virtually confined themselves to reconnaissance flights over the North Sea and English Channel.

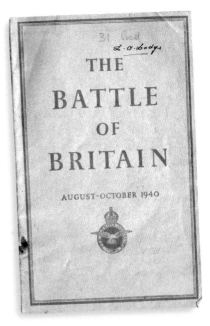

The 1941 Air Ministry booklet on the Battle of Britain, setting the start date of 8 August.

Initially, they made no attempt to interfere with a large westbound convoy which passed through the Straits of Dover (Convoy CW9 'Peewit') during the afternoon of 7 August. They were not, though, indifferent to its passage and plotted its course carefully and accurately. Before dawn the next day, 8 August, the convoy was attacked by German E-Boats off Beachy Head and Newhaven, causing some losses and hindering and breaking up the procession of ships. Later in the day, as the convoy reached the Isle of Wight, it (and the shipping associated with it) came under repeated air attacks and RAF fighters intercepted and engaged the enemy forces.

The fierce air battles that ensued were the heaviest air fighting that the war had yet seen. This, coupled with repeated and mass air attacks that day, doubtless led the Air Ministry to decide that 8 August was the first day of the Battle of Britain. That said, of course, it is a fact that most battles have very clearly defined parameters; an established start and end date, being fought on a clearly defined geographic ground and, usually, ending up with the conclusive defeat of one of the two combatant sides. As Dowding recognised, none of these can be said to apply to the Battle of Britain and thus it was that historians in the Air Ministry retrospectively 'set' the dates of that battle.

For the Germans, of course, there was no such thing as the Battle of Britain – it was merely a continuation of air operations against Britain that had commenced with the declaration of war and had merely carried on through different phases into the night bombing of 1940 and 1941 and then beyond and into various other attack strategies. So, there was no agreement on the part of the two combatant nations as to the dates the battle was fought. It was up to the Air Ministry to decide and it did so by settling upon 8 August 1940.

With the benefit of hindsight – and as Dowding acknowledged – it was not an unreasonable date to set as the 'official' commencement of the Battle of Britain although post-war that date of commencement was revised and back-dated. Indeed, having 'adjusted' the start date of the Battle of Britain back from 8 August when writing his dispatch to *The London Gazette* of September 1946, Air Chief Marshal Sir Hugh C T Dowding further set out his reasoning for that change:

"...On the other hand, the heavy attacks made against our Channel convoys probably constituted, in fact, the beginning of the German offensive; because the weight and scale of the attack indicates that the primary object was rather to bring out Fighters to battle than to destroy the hulls and cargoes of the small ships engaged in the coastal trade. While we were fighting in Belgium and France, we suffered the disadvantage that even the temporary stoppage of an engine involved the loss of pilot and aircraft, whereas, in similar circumstances, the German pilot might be fighting again the same day, and his aircraft airborne in a matter of hours.

"In fighting over England these considerations were reversed, and the moral and material disadvantages of fighting over enemy country may well have determined the Germans to open the attack with a phase of fighting in which the advantages were more evenly balanced. I have, therefore, somewhat arbitrarily, chosen the events of 10 July as the opening of the battle. Although many attacks had previously been made on convoys, and even land objectives such as Portland, 10 July saw the employment by the Germans of the first really big formation (seventy aircraft) intended primarily to bring our Fighter Defence to battle on a large scale."

So it was that at a stroke of the pen the first day of the Battle of Britain was declared to be 10 July 1940, although Dowding did concede that this was a "somewhat arbitrary" decision. That it was arbitrary is something that Squadron Leader George Lott, commanding officer of 43 Squadron during July 1940, would have surely agreed with. Shot down during a head-on attack against a Messerschmitt 110 near The Needles on 9 July 1940, and baling out of his stricken Hurricane near Tangmere after having been permanently blinded in one eye, Lott was out of the war. By just one day he was denied the coveted 'membership' that would qualify him as a Battle of Britain pilot and entitle him to wear the Battle of Britain clasp on the ribbon of his 1939-45 Star.

As George Lott would later point out: "Nobody had told the Germans that the Battle of Britain hadn't started yet!" It just served to illustrate that declaring any specific day as the start of the Battle of Britain was going to be invidious. Just as much as there might have been grounds for selecting 10 July, so too might there have even been grounds for settling on 4 July. On the other hand Dowding had also thought that there were grounds for choosing 8 August 1940. Indeed there were, and for some years it was the date considered to be the first day of the Battle of Britain.

Preamble –
How This Book Came To Be Written

DURING 1990 I chanced upon contact with a retired Royal Navy officer, Arthur Hague RD, who recounted a lively tale of his involvement with the barrage balloon vessels protecting south-coast convoys during 1940. His story and his photo collection were quite remarkable – and a fascinating 'snapshot' of one previously untold element of the Battle of Britain. However, since my primary sphere of interest lay within the history of aerial warfare, and specifically the minutiae of RAF and Luftwaffe participation during 1940, I filed away Arthur Hague's material and almost forgot about its existence for nigh on twenty years. True, the story he told certainly *involved* the RAF and the Luftwaffe although his specific account rather fell outside my particular focus at that time.

Towards the end of 2008 I was approached by television producer John Hayes-Fisher with whom I had previously worked on a TV documentary about Mick Mannock VC for BBC Timewatch. John was seeking ideas for a BBC television documentary series to be aired in 2010 to mark the 70th anniversary of the Battle of Britain. Commissioned by 360 Productions to come up with ideas, I set about drawing together around thirty detailed and potentially workable stories that ultimately might be built into three projected documentaries; a mini-series called 'Dig 1940'. The remit was to find subjects that would tell the story of 1940 through a journey of discovering relics and artefacts from that period – and this was to cover land, sea and air. After all, the Battle of Britain and the story of 1940 generally had not only been about air fighting.

In putting forward a range of ideas that encompassed the recovery of aircraft wrecks, the exploration of the Dunkirk beaches and personal stories of individual pilots amongst a plethora of other possibilities, there was one particular story amongst them all that stood out for John Hayes-Fisher; Convoy Peewit and Arthur Hague's balloon ship. Ultimately, the series of programmes were commissioned for BBC 1 television and I eventually found myself during the August of 2009 bobbing about in the English Channel on a small dive boat together with TV presenter Jules Hudson, a diving team and a camera crew whilst an exploratory dive was made to film the wreck of Arthur Hague's sunken vessel. When they returned to the surface the divers brought with them tangible relics of Convoy Peewit.

These small artefacts were a direct link back to that day in 1940 and I realised that the story of so many interlinking events on 8 August had never been properly told. What *had* been written about CW9 Peewit was consistently inaccurate in many respects and this had been repeated in almost countless published sources, many of them respected histories of the Battle of Britain. My mind was made up. The account by Arthur Hague was just a small part of a much bigger picture and I resolved that the tale of Peewit needed to be fully researched and told. It is my hope that this book will stand as a comprehensive record of just one aspect of the Battle of Britain.

This is the story of the men of Convoy CW9 Peewit.

Author's note: *For the sake of clarity and uniformity all times quoted in this book are BST. All times used in contemporaneous German records have therefore been converted from Central European Time (CET) to BST.*

Acknowledgements

A GREAT MANY friends and colleagues assisted in varying degrees with the preparation of this book, and without their contribution it would be a poorer work.

I must, in particular, single out three people who have made a significant input to my research and without whom my task would have been very much harder. They gave freely of their time, expertise, knowledge and advice and I am eternally grateful to them. They are: Peter Cornwell, Chris Goss and Winston Ramsey. Peter was supremely patient as I ran a veritable barrage of questions past him, one after the other, seeking clarification on a range of Luftwaffe operational issues for 7 and 8 August 1940. He was continually helpful in unravelling some of the mysteries of contemporary Luftwaffe records, and in making sense of contradictory or mystifying statements made within those records. Often, they turned out to be typographical errors on the part of some German clerk – but Peter always came up trumps in providing answers. Thank you, Peter! Chris Goss was ever helpful by freely giving his valued advice, and in providing many photographs and eye-witness accounts etc as well as providing one or two useful snippets of data that would have otherwise escaped me. Winston Ramsey, who has been a good friend for over thirty years, has always been enthusiastic about my various projects and in this context he hardly had to be asked for information, sources of detail or photographs – even kindly offering to visit certain locations that were of interest to me in order to take photographs. These three have been vital in making this book what I hope it is!

I must next thank Dave Wendes, master of the dive ship *Wight Spirit*, who so enthusiastically and willingly furnished me with masses of detail relating to the wrecks of Convoy CW9. The experience of going out with him to the wreck of HMS *Borealis* and seeing tangible artefacts from CW9 recovered up onto the deck was utterly fascinating and for me brought the whole story to life with a real sense of immediacy.

I must also thank John Hayes-Fisher, producer of the BBC1 television documentary series 'Dig 1940' who re-kindled my interest in CW9 and, in effect, kick started the project that became this book.

Next, a very special thank you to Karl Scheuch who helped me with countless pieces of detail relating to the operation of German E-Boats on the night of 7/8 August 1940. Karl was a gem of a find for me during my writing of this book, and without him it would have been very difficult to piece together aspects of that attack or, more importantly, to understand properly how the E-Boats operated.

I must also thank Dr Alfred Price for generously writing the foreword to this book. As the very doyen of studies into specific days during the Battle of Britain, and arguably Britain's foremost historic aviation writer, I consider it an honour to have him connected to my work. The very modest part I played, some years ago, in the production of Alfred's books on 18 August and 15 September 1940 was an inspiration to do something similar and many years later this book is the result. Unfortunately, the passage of years has meant that there are no longer the witnesses and participants available as they were during the research for Alfred's works but by great good fortune many had left behind detailed testimonies and accounts of 8 August 1940. Others I had fortunately managed to contact and interview many years ago. Thank you again, Alfred, for your kind words and assistance.

John Williams cannot be forgotten as he helpfully came to this land-lubber's assistance with various nautical charts. I apologise, for causing offence by calling them maps! John was most useful in helping me to plot courses, estimate the convoy's time at set points and to compute its relative speed and positions and generally to help me get a better grasp of things nautical.

Others who helped me are legion and whether it was by providing photographs or bits of detail that I did not have all those who gave me their assistance were equally important to this project. In no particular order, and certainly not in any order of merit, I must mention the following:

Simon Muggleton, Cees Broere, Norman Franks, Dennis Knight, Peter C. Smith, Martin Mace, Danny Burt, Phyllis Will, Rosie Williams, Virginia Feeney, Dean Sumner, Paul Baillie, Paul Cole, Ross McNeil, Dave Robbins, Mark Kirby, Mary Wellspring, Michael Wellspring, Gerry Burke, Richard Smith, Ian Hutton, Philippa Wheeler and Ted Bowen.

My sincerest thanks go to John Davies, Sarah Driver, Sophie Campbell and Emer Hogan and all the team at Grub Street for guiding this project to fruition. As ever, it has been a pleasure to work with you all and I look forward to future projects.

Lastly, I must give the biggest thank you of them all to Zoë. Without her support none of this would have happened and she has put up with me being shut away for long hours and almost being a stranger to the family during its production. Thank you again, Zoë!

My thanks go out to all who helped, one way or another, in getting this book into print. If I have forgotten anyone then do please forgive the unintentional oversight.

CHAPTER 1

Opening Shots

Convoy: Admiralty Definitions – 'Convoy' refers to escorting force. 'In Convoy' refers to ships escorted. Ships proceeding in a group but not escorted are not in convoy.

"In the present situation of belligerent rights, numbers of English men-of-war must be employed in convoying merchantmen."   HM ADMIRALTY 1862

Peewit: (lat: *Vanellus vanellus*) otherwise more commonly known as the Lapwing – a name used to describe its wavering passage of flight.

"The call of the Peewit is, to me, most happily associated with August on the Yorkshire Moors, but in the summer of 1940 it was a different story."
ARTHUR HAGUE RD RN (RETD) CAPTAIN HMS *BOREALIS*,
CONVOY CW9 PEEWIT, 8 AUGUST 1940.

Long before the Germans had even launched their 'Blitzkrieg' attacks in the West during May 1940 British merchant shipping in the English Channel had been scrutinised by the Luftwaffe. As early as March 1940 such shipping had also come under attack. At this stage of the war Channel shipping was not directly threatened by land-based enemy aircraft operating from occupied France and the Low Countries or from long-range guns, although it was nonetheless at some risk from German long-range bombers flying armed maritime reconnaissance operations. German naval craft were a clear and present threat from the very outset of the war and might strike against British merchant shipping assets at any time. They were certainly the greatest threat during 1939 and into the early months of 1940.

To protect shipping against attack, and primarily from surface or submarine attack, as early as 26 August 1939 merchant shipping was placed under the control of the Admiralty with authority to place merchant ships in convoy. Not *all* merchant shipping, though, was under the protection of convoy – especially at this stage of the war when Britain's economic survival surely depended upon the continuation of international trade. Merchant shipping was still a privately owned industry, able to determine its own cargoes or routes – although the latter were severely restricted in home waters by the establishment of British 'declared' minefields and the allocation of what were narrow war-sailing channels. With Britain's very lifeline for survival being the sea, however, it was only to be expected that the Germans should attach such importance to merchant shipping and to associated ports and harbour installations throughout the duration of the war.

So it was that during the late evening of 20 March 1940 a Heinkel He 111H of the Korpsführungskette, FliegerKorps X, droned westwards along the English Channel. Quite likely it was already approaching the very limit of its endurance when it spotted an east-bound merchant vessel three miles south-west of Beachy Head. Although two Hurricanes of 3 Squadron (flown by Sqn Ldr Gifford and Fg Off Ball) were up from Croydon patrolling the coast between Bexhill-on-Sea and Beachy Head, both pilots saw explosions but were unable to locate the enemy aircraft. Shortly after 10.30pm a stick of bombs straddled the ship (the explosions seen by Gifford and Ball) with one of the bombs striking and penetrating

Sqn Ldr Pat Gifford DFC was one of two Hurricane pilots of 3 Squadron who came close to intercepting the attacker of the SS *Barn Hill* over the English Channel on the night of 20 March 1940. He is pictured here whilst flying Spitfires with 603 Squadron during October 1939.

her deck plating and exploding in the No.4 hold, killing four members of the crew outright and injuring several others. The ship, bound from Halifax, Nova Scotia, to London was the SS *Barn Hill*.

Built in Canada during 1921 as the *Canadian Challenger* for the Montreal, Australia & New Zealand Line she was a two-deck steamer with a passenger certificate but upon outbreak of war had been renamed the *Barn Hill* and transferred to another line, Counties Ship Management Co. Ltd of London. No longer plying the passenger routes, the vessel now carried cargoes between Canada and Britain and on the fateful night of 20 March she was headed for the port of London loaded with a general cargo, comprising timber, carbide, tinned food, cheeses, tissue paper, typewriters, waders, and cardboard along with metal ingots of copper, zinc and aluminium. Some of the cargo, notably the timber and carbide, had violently ignited when the bomb struck the ship and almost at once the vessel's triple-expansion engines ground to a halt as she took on a pronounced list to starboard. Below decks, the fire raged out of control and it soon became clear that the *Barn Hill* was doomed. Distress calls were put out, with an unknown Dutch ship coming to her aid and taking off eighteen men.

On shore at Eastbourne, and only a few miles distant, many watchers including the coastguard had seen and heard the explosions and could now observe the raging fire from the blazing ship as she drifted helplessly just a relatively short distance offshore. Inexplicably, it was not until 23.15pm that the Eastbourne lifeboat, *Jane Holland*, was called out to attend – not being launched until almost a full hour after the attack.

The SS *Barn Hill* ablaze and adrift after the bombing attack off Beachy Head with the Eastbourne lifeboat and a Newhaven tug alongside.

When the *Jane Holland*, under the charge of Coxswain Michael Hardy, finally arrived on the scene at 01.40 the *Barn Hill* was drifting at 30°34′ N, 0°2′ W and well ablaze, with frequent explosions coming from below decks. Clearly there was nothing that could be done to save the ship, and after taking off the eighteen survivors from the Dutch vessel the *Jane Holland* drew alongside and took off another ten men from *Barn Hill*. When Coxswain Hardy had satisfied himself that all survivors had been accounted for he returned to shore with his human cargo, although it quickly became apparent that a further six crewmen were still missing. Of the twenty-eight crew members landed by Hardy, seven were injured and one of them would die later in Eastbourne's Princess Alice hospital – but it was now a race to return to the burning and listing ship to look for the unaccounted-for crew.

The *Jane Holland*, though, was beaten to the burning ship by *Foremost*, a Newhaven tug, whose crew were surprised to hear the ship's bell ringing. Scanning the tangled wreckage of the ship the tug's crew could see the crumpled form of a man lying on the forecastle of the *Barn Hill*, the lanyard of the ship's bell gripped firmly between his teeth. By now, the ship was rolling heavily and flames were shooting up to at least 90ft into the air. Despite this harrowing scene there was little that *Foremost* could do to get alongside, but the arrival of *Jane Holland* enabled the lifeboat to close in for a hazardous rescue attempt.

Pitching, rolling and burning, the *Barn Hill* presented a fearsome spectacle and a grave danger to the smaller lifeboat whose size, in any event, did not lend itself to the easy transfer on-board of any would-be rescuers. In the event, however, Lifeboatmen Alec Huggett and Thomas Allchorn volunteered to board the stricken merchantman and managed to do so at great personal risk. Picking their way along the shattered and nearly red-hot deck, the master of *Foremost* played his fire hose around the two intrepid rescuers to douse the flames and dissipate the heat as the two lifeboatmen finally discovered the casualty, the badly injured master of the *Barn Hill*, Captain Michael O'Neill. With severe burns, a punctured lung, concussion, a double fracture of the arm, a broken collar bone and five broken ribs he had somehow managed to half crawl, half roll along the deck to the ship's bell in order to attract attention. He was the last survivor on board, the other missing crew all having died in the attack or its immediate aftermath; the casualty who died in hospital and one other recovered body (Chief Steward Charles Adams and 2nd Engineer Officer Douglas Bertram) were buried ashore whilst the other three were never found and are remembered on the Merchant Shipping Memorial at Tower Hill, London.

Eventually, the shattered hulk of the *Barn Hill* was towed inshore finally to run aground at Langney Point, Eastbourne, where it broke into two, spewing much of its surviving cargo into the sea and out onto adjacent beaches. Here, the flotsam and jetsam provided rich pickings for the local population. The attack on the SS *Barn Hill* had witnessed the first air assault on a merchant vessel in the English Channel and had resulted in the loss of the ship, its cargo and five lives. It was a portent of things to come. It had also demonstrated the vulnerability of shipping to air attack in home waters. Whilst its cargo was doubtless valuable in the greater scheme of the overall war effort, the cargoes of many of the merchant shipping losses that would follow in the English Channel would be far more valuable: Coal.

Eventually the SS *Barn Hill* was run aground at Langney Point where she broke her back. At low tide, wreckage of the *Barn Hill* may still be seen protruding above the waves.

CHAPTER 2

A Disgraceful Episode

AS THE Germans settled into the occupation of northern France after the British evacuations from Dunkirk, their forces rolled up to the coast and immediately set about laying plans to wrest control of the English Channel. Its control, if not its closure, to all but the German military was vitally important in the furtherance of German war aims. Although peace overtures were made and Hitler issued his 'Last Appeal To Reason' they were, of course, ignored, much as the Germans had no doubt expected they would be. On 4 July 1940 the Luftwaffe struck what might be considered its first major blow towards securing air supremacy in the English Channel with a two-pronged Junkers 87 Stuka attack against a convoy off Portland (OA 178) and on the Portland naval base itself. Officially, and as Dowding would later decide, there were still six days to go before the Battle of Britain began. Officially at least, this was not yet the Battle of Britain.

Whilst OA 178 was a convoy taking its passage through the English Channel, it was not a Channel convoy *per se*. This in fact was an 'Outbound Atlantic' convoy numbered 178 – hence OA 178. These OA convoys, at this stage of the war at least, were escorted to the Western Approaches where the ships then dispersed for their onward voyages, although the English Channel attacks had resulted in OA convoys being re-routed from July 1940 after the attack on OA 178. To avoid running the gauntlet of E-Boats and Stukas, OAs were later sailed northwards around Scotland after congregating and departing from Methil. However, the convoys with which the subject of this book is *specifically* concerned were those that had no choice but to traverse the English Channel since their very ports of destination or departure were in the English Channel. These were the Channel Eastbound (CE) and Channel Westbound (CW) convoys, more of which later. For the present then, let us look at OA 178 and the related events of 4 July 1940.

With long-range fighter cover provided by the Messerschmitt 110s of V./(Z)LG 1 and Messerschmitt 109s of two staffeln of I./JG 1 (re-designated as III./JG 27 the following day), the Junkers 87 dive bombers of III./St.G 51 (also re-designated as II./St .G 1 two days later) struck Portland at shortly after 08.15, bombing the harbour, harbour installations and the ships within it. Twenty-six dive bombers took part in the raid, and one of the vessels hit was HMS *Foylebank*, an anti-aircraft ship converted from a pre-war freighter and stationed at Portland from 9 June 1940 to defend this important naval base against air attack.

Mounted on the *Foylebank* were four twin four-inch high angle guns, multiple two-

The anti-aircraft ship HMS *Foylebank* was hit and sunk by Stukas in Portland Harbour on 4 July 1940.

Ablaze and sinking, the attack on *Foylebank* resulted in a terrible loss of life. Unfortunately, there was no RAF Fighter Command presence to counter the attack and this led to Churchill tetchily asking whether the air force had "…contributed effectively".

pounder quick firing Pom-Pom guns and 0.5inch calibre machine guns. The Stukas dived on *Foylebank* before the gun crews on board properly had time to react to the "Action Stations!" alert, and unlike many of the Stukas, later shipping targets in the English Channel she was a sitting duck – stationary within the harbour. There was no question of this vessel taking avoiding action, nor that the Stuka pilots needed to resolve sighting issues on a moving, twisting or turning target. In the onslaught, a good many bombs struck the *Foylebank* with direct hits; 500kg, 250kg and 50kg missiles all rained down in salvos of four at a time – 104 in total being dropped. Other bombs fell very close to *Foylebank*, causing blast and splinter damage to the ship. One of them scored a direct hit and blew to matchwood the *Foylebank*'s own tender tied up alongside. On board the anti-aircraft ship herself it was sheer mayhem and carnage. One who was there described the ghastly scenes on deck as being like "…a cross between a butcher's shop and a scrap metal yard".

In a few short minutes, no less than 176 Royal Navy sailors had been killed and the *Foylebank* was sent to the bottom of the harbour. In the moments before she finally succumbed to the German attack, however, some of the gunners had reached their stations and had begun to ready themselves to fire back at the Stukas. Such was the surprise of the attack however, and so quickly was it all over, that only the ship's 'Y' four-inch gun was able to fire, managing to get off twenty-seven rounds from the port barrel and twenty-eight from the starboard. Meanwhile, Leading Seaman Jack Mantle was battling to get his set of Pom-Pom guns to bear.

In his diving attacks the Stuka pilot's usually adopted method was to dive as steeply as possible, and sometimes at up to 90°, towards the stern of the ship. At around 1,500ft the angle was decreased to 45° and the pilot's Revi gunsight was lined up on the target ship's stern as the pilot fired his twin forward 7.92mm MG 17 machine guns, mounted one in each wing. Gradually, the hail of bullets would move along the length of the ship and when the pilot saw his bullets striking the water ahead of the ship's bow, so the bombs were released. In this way, the machine-gun fire was an aid to sighting the bombs and had the additional effect of keeping down the heads of any would-be defenders who might be firing back.

In addition, the altimeter was set to local altitude above mean sea level and when passing the set altitude for bomb release a loud warning horn sounded to tell the pilot to press the bomb release and pull out of his dive. As the Stuka pulled out and drew away from the target, so the rear gunner would take over the machine gunning to maintain anti-aircraft fire suppression. So, when the Stukas dived on *Foylebank* they were raking her with high explosives and bullets almost continuously for several minutes – and just at the moment gun crews were racing along exposed decks and gangways, and up ladders, to get to their stations. Some were lucky to escape, but many were cut down by machine-gun bullets or flying shrapnel – or literally caught in bomb blasts from direct hits.

Standing in his exposed gun position, Jack Mantle was having difficulty with the change-over lever on top of the gun. Either through blast or gunfire it had become slightly bent, although he had managed to get away some rounds. Already, Mantle had been hit and badly wounded in the leg and was losing a great deal of blood but instead of seeking the medical attention that he so clearly desperately needed he stayed at his post. Just as he had won his battle with the damaged lever, so a further wave of attacking Stukas came in over

The Mole by Portland's South Ship Channel. As Jack Mantle opened up, so did the pilot of the diving Stuka in his attacking-come-sighting burst of gunfire and the sailor fell across his gun, mortally wounded. He had been hit across the chest with machine-gun bullets. Lifted gently down from his bullet and shrapnel spattered station, and soaked in his own blood, Mantle was taken to Portland hospital where the twenty-three-year-old seaman died later that same day. The captain of HMS *Foylebank*, Captain H P Wilson, reported on Mantle's behaviour to the C-in-C Portsmouth who, on receiving Wilson's report, was moved to record that Mantle had "…..behaved too magnificently for words". It was behaviour that, ultimately, would lead to the posthumous award of a Victoria Cross for Leading Seaman Jack Mantle. His citation was fulsome in its praise:

> "Between his bursts of fire he had time to reflect on the grievous injuries of which he was soon to die; but his great courage bore him up till the end of the fight when he fell by the gun he had so valiantly served."

Notwithstanding Jack Mantle's courage, nothing that might be called an effective defence was put up by HMS *Foylebank*. Although she was an anti-aircraft ship she had been sunk by the very kind of attack against which she was designed to defend. Other defences that day were impotent also.

During the attack on Portland, the Messerschmitt 110s and 109s had circled protectively overhead to ward off the anticipated interfering RAF fighters. However, there was absolutely no response from RAF Fighter Command who had been taken by surprise as much as the Royal Navy

Leading Seaman Jack Mantle was a gunner on board *Foylebank* during the attack and continued to man his guns despite mortal wounds. If the VC awarded to Flt Lt James Nicolson during the Battle of Britain could perhaps be seen as a wider recognition for the bravery of 'the Few' then Mantle's VC might be seen as representing the outstanding courage of Royal Navy gunners in the English Channel during the 1940 battle of the convoys. Mantle's VC is currently on loan to the Royal Navy Museum, Portsmouth.

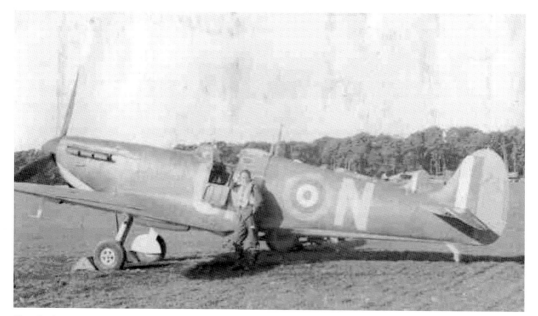

Sgt Arthur Kearsey was the only RAF pilot over Portland during the air attack on 4 July 1940 – albeit accidentally! Kearsey later transferred to 152 Squadron flying Spitfires which is when this photograph of him was taken.

– so much so that a solitary Fairey Battle of No.10 Bombing and Gunnery School from RAF Warmwell had not been recalled but instead found itself virtually caught up in the dive-bombing attack on Portland. It was also the *only* RAF aircraft anywhere in the vicinity. Piloting the aircraft (K9429) was Sgt A W Kearsey* who was steadily approaching the practice bombing range at nearby Chesil Beach when he noticed bombs falling off to his left at Portland with "…an angry swarm of bees above". He called to his two trainee aircrew to man the defensive Vickers 'K' gun before it dawned on him that it had been taken out for airfield defence. Feeling somewhat vulnerable in such close proximity to a mass of Stukas, and with enemy fighters circling overhead, Kearsey beat a hasty and judicious retreat back to Warmwell. To quote Kearsey: "I was going downhill, balls-out, and as fast as I could!"

As smoke was still rising over Portland, a single Junkers 88 reconnaissance aircraft of 1.(F)/123 set out to check on the progress of OA 178 and reporting the shipping now south-west of Portland, an immediate strike was ordered and carried out by twenty-four Junkers 87s of I./St.G 2 flying from Falaise, with an escort of a single staffel of I./JG 1. This attack was followed very shortly afterwards by another from the hastily re-armed III./St.G 51 who sent out a further twenty-three Stukas.

To some of those on board ships of the convoy it seemed that they were sailing perilously close to the French coast. The Isle of Wight had looked a very long way away when they had passed by, whilst further on in the journey Cap La Hague, the Channel Islands and the whole coast of France had seemed alarmingly close. Of course, the passage of OA 178 had

*Note: Sgt Arthur W Kearsey transferred to RAF Fighter Command during August 1940 and flew Spitfires with 152 Squadron for the remainder of the Battle of Britain.

not escaped the attention of the 1.(F)/123 Junkers 88, and the Stuka strike was duly ordered, although in reality the closeness or otherwise to the French coast of the OA 178 convoy was not a significant factor in the attack being implemented.

When the Stukas pounced they hit the merchant vessels *Dallas City, Flimston, Deucalion* and *Antonio*. Of these, *Dallas City* was badly damaged and on fire. Eventually she would sink, but not before colliding with *Flimston* – the two vessels being locked together by the collision for an agonising fifteen minutes. On board the *Dallas City*, her gunner gave more than a good account of himself as he stood his ground, firing resolutely at the diving Stukas as they in turn machine-gunned him. Meanwhile, *Flimston* and *Antonio* had managed to limp, both of them badly damaged, into the bomb-shattered wreckage that had been Portland Harbour and where the *Foylebank* was still sinking.

Again, there had been no interference with the attack on OA 178 from RAF Fighter Command, although two Stukas of 7./St.G 51 had been lost during the attacks to anti-aircraft fire; Lt Wilhelm Schwarze and Uffz Julius Dörflinger were killed when their Junkers 87 B-1 crashed into the English Channel south of Portland after its engine exploded. The crew of another 7 Staffel machine was rescued from the sea off the Cotentin Peninsula. In addition, one Messerschmitt 109 of I./JG 1 had returned damaged and crashed on landing at Théville, its pilot unhurt. Out in the Channel the convoy was now in disarray and four of its ships had been lost. As night time approached there was another danger: E-Boats.

From their home port of Boulogne on the French coast, four motor torpedo boats of the 1.S-Flottille were put to sea (S19, S20, S24 and S26) and headed for the already battered OA 178 where, just before midnight, the SS *Elmcrest* was struck on the port side by a torpedo. The attack had come out of the dark of the night, and with complete surprise. Listing, and clearly in a sinking state, the crew of *Elmcrest* were ordered to abandon ship. As they did so, the E-Boat came in to deliver a final blow and fired another torpedo into the starboard side. Unfortunately, this coincided with the moment that the lifeboat was pulling away from the stricken ship and the torpedo passed directly under the boat causing it to capsize and throwing all the survivors into the water. Sixteen men drowned.

Moments later, another E-Boat put two more torpedoes into the merchant ship SS *British Corporal* and the crew abandoned what they believed to be a sinking vessel. Miraculously, she remained afloat and was later towed into harbour with two of her crew dead. The *Hartlepool* was also torpedoed and abandoned in what also seemed to be a sinking condition, although she too was salvaged and later beached at Weymouth. The nocturnal attackers had been S19, S20, S24 and S26, captained by Oblt.z.See Töniges, Lt.z.See von Mirbach, Oblt.z.See Detlefsen and Oblt.z.See Fimmen respectively. Also aboard the S24 was Kapt Lt Birnbacher, the flotilla commander. (Author's note: this will not be the last time we meet two of these German boats and some of these captains in the eventually unfolding saga of 7 and 8 August 1940.)

Prime Minister Winston Churchill had been sufficiently alarmed by events in the English Channel on 4 July 1940 that he felt it necessary to issue an 'Action This Day' memo to the Admiralty:

"Could you let me know on one sheet of paper what arrangements you are making about the Channel convoys now that the Germans are all along the French coast? The attacks on the convoy yesterday, both from the air and by E-Boats, were very serious, and I should like to be assured this morning that the situation is in hand and that the Air is contributing effectively."

Of course, in respect of "Air" involvement on 4 July 1940 there had not been any, effective *or* otherwise. The only RAF presence, and that only by accident, had been Arthur Kearsey's lumbering Fairey Battle. Whilst it was decided that the OA convoys should be routed differently after the debacle and massacre of 4 July it still remained the case that the CE and CW convoys needed to ply the English Channel. Clearly it was imperative that, so far as reasonably practicable, they should continue do so under protective cover of RAF fighter patrols or any other defensive measures against air attack that could be usefully employed.

Of the events on 4 July, Admiral Max Horton of the Royal Navy Northern Patrol was scathing, and called it: "A disgraceful episode…" Whilst the earlier attack on *Barn Hill* had illustrated the vulnerability of Channel traffic to bomber aircraft, so the events of 4 July 1940 had been a clear demonstration of German military power in the English Channel with the virtual inability of the Royal Navy and Royal Air Force, thus far, to do very much about it.

The Stukas and E-Boats had been demonstrated as a deadly combined force against the coasters and merchant ships running the Channel. If lessons had been learned from 4 July it would yet still be the case that further convoys would come under the same sort of punishing attacks; Stukas by day, E-Boats by night. These elements of attacks on Channel convoys became commonly recurring themes. It is also a theme that has a rich vein running through it; the utterly magnificent courage of Royal Navy gunners who were defending valiantly against air attack. Time and again their heroism shines out of the dark story of these convoy attacks. It was a special kind of courage, and a courage epitomised by that of Leading Seaman Jack Mantle VC. Courage during the Battle of Britain would not uniquely be the domain of RAF fighter pilots or civilians.

CHAPTER 3 — The Indestructible Highway

S PART of the Luftwaffe's reconnaissance of British coastal waters a lone Dornier 17 Z of KG 2 followed its assigned patrol course during the early morning of 7 August 1940 by beginning its 'sweep' somewhere south of Dungeness and heading north-eastwards up towards Dover in what was decreasing visibility. Aside from an MTB off Dungeness and a couple of what were described as "sentry boats" off Dover, there was little activity of any significance to report in the English Channel by the time the Dornier had rounded North Foreland at about 06.00. Here, and fifteen miles to the east of Margate, the crew spotted two minesweepers on a westerly heading before the Dornier crew set a course northwards and up into the North Sea. The two minesweepers, with their sweeping apparatus deployed, were looking for mines laid overnight in the Thames estuary by four German He 115s of Ku.Fl.Gr 106. A clear and safe channel needed to be assured for imminent British shipping movements down the estuary. Unknown to the Luftwaffe crew as they passed North Foreland the most interesting activity might have been seen some twenty-five miles or so westwards and down the Thames estuary towards London.

Here, just off Southend-on-Sea, an assembly of well over twenty merchant ships and naval escort vessels were preparing to weigh anchor and move off down towards the mouth of the estuary and North Foreland. As boilers were fired and black smoke belched and billowed from a collection of variously coloured merchant funnels the activity might have been seen had the Dornier ventured further westwards, although visibility was deteriorating quite badly at that moment. If witnessed, it would have been a sight that indicated the hurried preparations of a convoy about to set sail.

The cargo carried on board most of those merchant vessels was as much the life-blood for Britain as was petrol, and the interruption of its supply chain could have had a significant effect on the war effort. That commodity, of course, was coal and its importance in 1940 cannot be underestimated; it fuelled factories, railways, power stations and provided the majority of domestic heating. Without coal the nation would quite literally have ground to a halt. As such, it was a vital ingredient in the winning of the Battle of Britain. And it had to be delivered to where it was needed and when it was needed – along the sea routes that surrounded the British Isles. Not without good reason did those routes become known as The Indestructible Highway.

Historically, vast quantities of coal had been transported by coastal collier ships from the north east of England, and other mining areas, and taken to distribution centres around the entire coastline of Britain for decades, if not longer. From the coastal ports it could more easily be distributed locally by road or rail after off-loading at coal wharves and depots and, in some cases, delivered almost to the front door of coal-fired power stations. Quite simply, the road and rail networks in the wartime British Isles could not have coped with moving around such huge quantities of coal and on such a regular basis.

In any event, wartime consumption to cope with demand from the war effort both industrial and military, had significantly increased the demand for the fuel to way above its pre-war levels. Equally, the transport of other goods – including military supplies and personnel – also had to be moved by road and rail within the country. Quite simply, and

The life-line is firm
thanks to the
MERCHANT NAVY

notwithstanding the inherent dangers from enemy attack, coal had to continue to be moved by shipping. There was simply no other way. It was a huge undertaking, and a possibly conservative estimate reckoned that no less than 40,000 tons of coal per week was required in south-east England alone and the collier ships, on average, carried around 1,000 tons each. Consideration had to be given as to exactly how best to continue these essential deliveries; more importantly, how to effect them in the safest manner. Of course, and whilst it was a vitally important commodity, coal was not the only critical cargo being carried by sea to (or around) the British Isles.

Food, fuel and raw materials needed to be brought in from overseas if the nation was to survive and continue the fight and as several previous wars had demonstrated, the safest means to affect this was to implement a protective convoy system, which, as described earlier, was implemented on 26 August 1939. This way, merchant ships could be shepherded and better protected by both naval and air assets. It was the duty of the trade division of the Admiralty to organise routes and escorts and set down sailing orders, all of this coming under the remit of the Naval Control Service which had established offices in all ports used by merchant vessels. Of course, the requirements applied equally to the deep-sea ocean-going convoys as much as they did to the coastal convoys of colliers – although the danger to south coast shipping from land-based aircraft, long-range guns and E-Boats operating out of France were difficult to foresee or even imagine as early as August 1939.

The attack on the SS *Barn Hill* by an aircraft in the English Channel during March 1940, however, highlighted the danger and the ship's vulnerability was exposed, long before France had fallen. Admiralty minds were now concentrated and merchant seamen could be left in no doubt as to the perils they faced in home waters. Indeed, as early as 7 October 1939 one Thomas Sidney Johnston, an Edinburgh merchant seaman, had felt moved to write to the First Lord of The Admiralty, Winston Churchill, complaining about the lack of protection for small merchant ships that were sailing the coasts of Britain. In his letter, Johnston railed at the shipping owners who, often, had failed to provide adequate equipment and safety measures for men in an already hazardous occupation but now exposed to war operations. He went on:

"It appears that the merchant ships and their crews are of no account so far as the British Government are concerned – and this would be all right if the enemy thought otherwise. Unfortunately, this is not the case, and it will be of no surprise if the enemy makes a sudden attack by sea or air one of these days or nights, and some of these small merchant ships, with no protection whatsoever, will perish along with their crews. Being below a certain tonnage we are compelled to sail at night, like rats, and seek safety during hours of daylight."

As things would turn out, and following the loss of the SS *Barn Hill*, night was no guarantee of protection from attack, either. However, Johnston certainly had a point and at the time his letter was written the convoy protection system was generally in place to protect longer-range ocean-going and larger merchant vessels than Johnston's. It was not that the smaller merchant vessels were of "no account" as he supposed, but rather that no thought had thus far been given to protecting coastal merchant vessels in convoy. The need, somehow, had just not seemed so pressing. As the war took its course, so the thinking changed. These small merchant ships were most certainly of some considerable account, whatever Johnston thought. In particular, the value of the colliers could not be over estimated, and so the convoy system was ultimately extended to include their sailings.

In the context of this book we are, of course, concerned only with convoy operations in the English Channel area although that is not in any way to belittle the dangers and perils faced, equally, by merchant shipping around the entire British coastline. Indeed, the east coast routes were, in particular, extremely dangerous to the wartime merchant mariner. In the south, however, the nominated convoy assembly area was in the Thames estuary off Southend-on-Sea, where the Naval Control Service established its headquarters at the Palace Hotel, in the houses of Royal Terrace and on the world famous pier – the various locations collectively becoming HMS *Leigh* for the duration of hostilities. From here, orders were issued to the masters of all merchant ships in the assembled convoy, escort vessels took up station, and the appointed RN convoy commodore briefed the masters of the rag-tag procession that he would ultimately direct along the English Channel. The commodores, who sailed aboard one of the vessels under their 'command', were generally either retired naval officers or experienced merchant captains who often held a rank in the Royal Navy Reserve. As such, the latter group of officers understood well the way the merchant ships worked and had clear knowledge, too, of the protocols and operating procedures of the Royal Navy.

The commodore's role, within the convoy system, was vital to help ensure discipline in convoy, that correct sailing channels were being followed, navigation was accurate, that sailing speeds and stations were maintained and to provide liaison with naval escorts. After the convoy had assembled off Southend-on-Sea the individual masters would be brought ashore by tug to be briefed.

In an account set out in the official HMSO publication on the Merchant Navy's coasters (*British Coaster 1939-1945*) we can get a picture of how events ashore at Southend-on-Sea during the early morning of 7 August 1940 would have unfolded:

"If a coastal convoy was due to depart about dawn, then the ships would come down-river on the previous afternoon tide. Masters and the commodore's signalmen went ashore to attend the convoy conference. Some of the masters would be absent because their ships were late arriving or because, having attended so many similar conferences and being supplied with written orders, they had found other urgent business. In the conference room, decorated with posters concerning caution at sea, sketches of E-Boats, blackboards, tables of instructions and charts and the like, it was easy to pick out the masters who knew the route from those who did not. The former had the patient look of men performing a duty without any expectation of being entertained; the latter were as attentive as model pupils. Some of the masters were in uniform; many, probably the majority, were not, for except on his own bridge the coaster master, even in war, is a little shy of parading a uniform.

"The base convoy officer or his representative, always a naval officer, opens the proceedings. He runs through the orders, stressing certain points. The commodore of the convoy, usually a merchant captain, follows; he says a word or two about the way he likes things done. There is no verbosity; there may or may not be questions from the masters. Two points, however, are seldom omitted: although he is in convoy and under the commodore's orders, 'the master is held responsible for the safety of his ship'; and 'ships must be navigated – there must be no follow-my-leader stuff in each other's wake.' As the masters are taken back to their ships in a tug, talk is concerned largely with the idiosyncrasies of that particular commodore and, of course, with tides."

Such, then, was the scene at Southend-on-Sea as Convoy CW9 readied itself to sail. It was already a tried and tested procedure and, as we have seen, this was by no means the first such convoy of coasters and colliers that would ply its dangerous course through the English Channel. Since the sinking of the *Barn Hill*, though, the situation had changed somewhat with the fall of France and the experience of Convoy OA 178 was ample evidence of that. Now, the danger was not just from some long-range opportunist German bomber that might chance upon the ships – but instead from the might of the Luftwaffe that currently ranged only a few short miles away beyond the French coast.

Clearly, everything that went on in the Channel was being keenly observed by the Germans, and radar and long-range guns were also being set up around Cap Gris-Nez. As if all of that was not enough to contend with, fast motor torpedo attack boats, S-Boats, were now stationed at ports along the French Channel coast. (Author's note: To the Germans these were S-Boots, standing for *Schnell Boot* (Fast Boat) but to the British they were always E-Boats, standing for Enemy Boats.) Already, and as we have seen, convoys passing through the English Channel during July had come under heavy attack, and there had been significant losses to air and surface intervention. So, the convoy preparations on that morning of 7 August 1940 were not for anything that was out of the ordinary. And the masters and their crews knew only too well what they may be facing.

Back on board their ships the masters opened their sealed orders which contained details of sailing times, speeds and their position within the convoy. Of course, all of this had been studied at the briefing but each master had a detailed set of instructions that would be an *aide-memoire* for the voyage, with notes of signals, identities of other ships and the like, and would be retained by the master on the bridge or about his person or locked in a safe if he left for comfort breaks, rest etc. For now, and with sailing time approaching, the master went about his business on board making sure all was ready with the crew and his vessel. On board, too, would be one or two Royal Navy ratings – and that was certainly a departure from the peacetime days. These sailors were DEMS personnel; Defence Equipment Merchant Shipping. All those naval gunners involved with the convoy whose passage forms the basis of this book were nominally attached to HMS *President III*.

The role of DEMS gunners, as the title suggested, was the close-defence of the ship against air or surface attack and using a motley selection of speedily assembled weaponry of sometimes doubtful efficacy. Hastily trained and deployed in the hectic days of 1940 the efficacy, too, of the DEMS ratings themselves might also be questioned – both as gunners *and* as mariners! That said, and like the merchant seamen themselves, they displayed undoubted courage and fortitude in the face of terrible danger. Indeed, the record shows that the courage of the DEMS gunners during the actions of 7 and 8 August was exemplary. It would not be over stating the case to say that in many instances it was above and beyond the call of duty.

Incredibly, and in relation to the arming of merchant vessels, international law required that merchantmen could only be fitted with 'defensive' weaponry and convention required that such weapons could only be positioned aft. This harked backed to the age of sail, where a fleeing merchant ship could be allowed to fire from her stern at a pursuer. Place her defensive guns anywhere else and she would be considered in the same league as a man-of-war. So, to position weapons anywhere else on a Second World War merchant vessel (even during total war where the sinking of merchant ships by U-Boat, for example, was pretty much indiscriminate) would have contravened international maritime laws and rendered ships fitted with such 'offensive' weapons to be interned should they enter neutral ports. Thus it was that a motley collection of weaponry was installed, and much of it ancient First World War or pre-1914 pieces taken out of store. Three or four inch low-elevation guns to guard against surface attack were often installed, although one merchant seaman of the period remarked that they were sometimes more at danger from DEMS gunners on other ships than they ever were from the enemy. Hotchkiss guns were also a popular weapon of choice. Where they could be spared or found, Lewis machine guns to guard against air attack were installed and very often one or two Ross rifles would be carried aboard. However, the *pièce de resistance* in terms of anti-aircraft defence was the rather bizarre Holman Projector and some of the ships in the convoy that departed Southend-on-Sea on the morning of 7 August were fitted with this strange weapon.

The Holman Projector was, in effect, a steam-powered grenade launcher that would hurl grenades into the path of approaching enemy aircraft. A crudely constructed weapon that was merely a tube with a rudimentary sighting device, the Holman relied on the ship's own steam supply to launch its missiles and there were instances when insufficient steam pressure merely caused the primed grenade to plop out of the muzzle and explode on the deck – sometimes with fatal results for DEMS gunners and crew members alike. As for its effectiveness, there are no known instances where enemy aircraft were damaged, let alone downed, by Holman-launched grenades. Their range, of course, was limited and the problems of accurate sighting were just about impossible to overcome. That said, the black smoke from a barrage of Holman Projector grenades exploding above a convoy could possibly give an impression to attacking Luftwaffe crews that they were coming under heavy anti-aircraft fire. In reality, there was a wide gulf between the danger they were actually in and their perception of that danger.

One of a range of defensive measures put into place to combat air attacks on merchant vessels was the rather curious Holman Projector. Effectively it was a grenade launcher that hurled missiles towards incoming aircraft although sighting and ranging was problematical to say the least.

Of the Holman Projector, Prime Minister Winston Churchill was allegedly somewhat dismissive. Visiting a weapons demonstration where the prowess of the Holman was to be exhibited to him, the demonstrating team realised that no live grenades were available and resorted to using bottles of beer instead. As the bottles were flung from the launcher and smashed to the ground in a myriad of glass shards and foaming beer, Churchill is said to have turned away muttering "Oh my good God….well…I suppose it will save on explosives!" He was probably quite right in despairing of the Holman. Without doubt, it was a case of desperate measures for desperate times.

The Holman Projector, the DEMS gunners and the improbable arsenal of weaponry, some of which would most likely have been largely outdated long before the Boer War, were not the only make-shift defensive measures brought into play for the 7 August convoy sailing. Another master plan had been concocted to ensure the certain safety of the ships from attack by dive bomber – barrage balloons. On 31 July ship-borne barrage balloons would be towed for the first time by vessels stationed to the fore and aft of each of the convoy's two columns of ships and along its flanks. Flying at up to 3,000ft it was felt that the balloons would impede or discourage (or render impossible) attacks by dive bombers or low flying enemy aircraft. That, at least, was the plan – for although convoys had already been heavily attacked from the air these attacks had been unhindered by the cables of balloons.

Now, the Admiralty planners felt they had the answer. Certainly, as the convoy steamed east from Falmouth on 31 July, with balloons flying, it did not come under enemy air attack although reconnaissance flights by the Luftwaffe had certainly picked up the procession of its twenty-five vessels. In its own report on the convoy, the Admiralty soberly noted: "….there was no enemy attack and therefore the effectiveness of this form of defence could not be judged." However, some of those who had sailed in the convoy felt that the presence of the balloons had been their salvation. It hadn't. It was merely that the Luftwaffe had, for its own reasons, chosen not to attack this particular convoy. The presence of balloons was inconsequential. Indeed, we do not know if the Germans had even as yet noted the balloon protection.

It was a different story, though, on 2 August when off the east coast an aircraft of Fliegerkorps V reported that a convoy of merchant ships was seen 25 km from Great Yarmouth towing balloons. That the Germans were aware of this new defensive measure almost immediately became known to British Intelligence through an ULTRA intercept that same day which had commented on the balloon-protected convoy. So, the presence of balloons over convoys was certainly now known to the Germans. Considering how to deal with them and how to counter the hazard they might otherwise pose was not exactly difficult for the Luftwaffe.

Apart from the multifarious defensive measures on the merchant vessels themselves there was, of course, the additional protection of Royal Navy ships that guarded the convoy, and overhead an umbrella of patrolling RAF fighters. In respect of the latter, flights and squadrons regularly (but not always) put up standing patrols over the convoys passing through the English Channel, each RAF sector providing the patrolling aircraft as the convoy passed through its area of responsibility. Response times if a convoy was threatened by air attack (especially in the narrower parts of the Channel) would have been insufficient if early warning for

The Chain Home radar stations at Ventnor and Poling (seen here) picked up the incoming raids that threatened CW9 Peewit and relayed data that was ultimately fed through to the RAF controllers, allowing them to scramble fighter squadrons to deal with the threats.

such attacks was reliant upon the CH and CHL radar stations on the south coast. Quite simply, there would not have been enough time to scramble fighters, obtain altitude and get them into position to attack – although that situation should have been different once the convoys had reached the wider part of the Channel from, say, Brighton westwards.

Consequently, a naval liaison officer was allocated to the HQ of RAF fighter groups covering convoy areas to ensure that Fighter Command was kept apprised of shipping movements. Despite the best efforts of RAF Fighter Command though, it was not possible to provide a *permanent* daylight-period umbrella of fighters over the convoys. The fact of the matter was, quite simply, that the slowly plodding speed of the convoys along the Channel (never any more than about 8 knots maximum) and the length of the passage rendered it quite impossible to provide cover for every mile of the way. The navy itself, though, provided the close escort and almost 'rode shot-gun' with the coasters as they ran the gauntlet – but not always with the most suitable of ships.

As the RAF had its groups, so the Royal Navy had its various commands which divided the seas around the British Isles into individual command areas. In the context of this book, however, we are concerned only with Nore Command (southern North Sea, Dover Straits and eastern English Channel) and Portsmouth Command (Beachy Head to Bournemouth) which between them would oversee the passage of the 7 August convoy sailing. The various escort vessels were originally stationed at Portsmouth, Dover and Harwich and on 7 August the destroyer HMS *Bulldog* was the principal escort although it did not sail out to join CW9 (along with HMS *Fernie*) until the night of 7/8 August. This comprised three anti-submarine trawlers (increased to four at Dover) and six barrage balloon vessels. (However, the Dover-based destroyers had essentially been withdrawn to Portsmouth after a heavy air attack on 29 July 1940.) The escort ships were to pick up the convoy once it had left Southend-on-Sea, assembled itself into its allocated order of sailing and arrived off North Foreland. Here, the Royal Navy vessels would join the column of no less than twenty-four coasters as the entire procession, described by American journalist James M Minifie as "like a snake with a broken back", swung out around the foreland to commence what was considered likely to be the riskiest part of its run.

At 07.00 the convoy commodore aboard the SS *Empire Crusader* gave the order "Weigh

The SS *Empire Crusader* was the commodore ship for CW9 Peewit and was a German vessel that had been called *Leander* before she was captured as 'prize' by the Royal Navy in 1939 and re-named. With some irony she would eventually be sunk at German hands on 8 August 1940. Here she is ice-bound and flying the swastika flag at her stern before she became *Empire Crusader*.

anchor!" and all twenty-four vessels immediately got underway sailing on the morning tide down river and jostling in an orderly fashion for their position in the line; down through Sea Reach, The Warp, Oaze Deep and Knob Channel before swinging round in a southerly arc through North Edinburgh Channel and on towards North Foreland. On each bridge, respective captains tore open their sealed orders to acquaint themselves fully with the finer details of the trip: timings, routes, escorts, signals, station-keeping and any special instructions or points of interest. To the Royal Navy this was Convoy CW9; in other words, Convoy Westbound, number nine. (Using the same nomenclature, eastbound convoys became CE convoys, followed by a specific numeric identifier.) Away to the north-west of London, deep in the underground operations room at RAF Uxbridge, the naval liaison officer, signalled by HMS *Leigh*, notified the senior controller of 11 Group RAF Fighter Command of CW9's departure and of its status, course and speed. Using pre-selected RAF code words for such convoys the controller chose Peewit, and a WAAF plotter placed a white metal plaque with the word CONVOY in bold red letters onto the situation map just at the mouth of the Thames estuary. Whilst to the RAF this was only ever Peewit, it was only ever CW9 to the navy.

(Author's note: The code name Peewit was not exclusive to Convoy CW9 on 7/8 August 1940 and was adopted several times by the RAF for convoys passing through the English Channel during 1940. For example, Peewit was used for a convoy on 21 July and another again on 11 September. Other code names were also re-used, e.g. Booty (25 July, 30 July, 11 August, 8 November and 21 November) and Pilot (30 July and 4 August) Other code names used at various times during 1940 were Bacon, Bosom, Totem, Fruit, Table, Minor, Cat, Secure, Agent, Bread, Arena and Topaz – although this is not necessarily an exhaustively comprehensive list. Consequently, it would be inaccurate to label this convoy simply as Peewit, since there were also others by this same name. Convoy CW9 Peewit would be more accurate.)

As the convoy departed Southend-on-Sea and began its journey down the Thames estuary, RAF Fighter Command put into place its planned fighter cover over Peewit and it seems likely that at least part of its initial journey was covered by three Hurricanes of 85 Squadron who were on convoy patrol between 06.20 and 07.50. Later, other squadrons would cover the convoy at various stages in its journey around North Foreland, down into the English Channel and as far as Dungeness. Spread out over about two miles, CW9 Peewit inched forward on its dangerous passage through the Straits of Dover.

Initially, and at least until long after the convoy would reach a position quite some distance beyond Folkestone, its presence remained undetected by the Germans. Had they seen its assembly over the previous day, and observed the preparations to sail that morning, then the passage between Dover and Calais might have been rather more challenging. With advance notice to organise an attack, an air assault in the Straits might well have been planned. However, even if the Germans had had opportunity to plan such a raid the weather was against them. Despite a light SSE wind and a moderate sea, visibility was only moderate to poor – in other words, ranging from two to five nautical miles. Crucially, though, there was also what the navy described as "an overhead fog" down to 2,000ft and this might well have rendered difficult or impossible any dive-bombing attacks even if the aircraft had been able to locate the ships in the abysmal visibility. As the Admiralty diarist noted: "....it remains to be seen whether the same immunity will be enjoyed under conditions more favourable to the attacker." As it would turn out, it was a fairly prophetic observation and it seems likely that the diarist had a fair hunch that the rest of the voyage might not be such plain sailing. The forecast for the morrow, when the convoy would be much further westwards down the Channel and by then its presence probably well known to the Germans, was for rather better weather. In other words, it would be good for any attackers. For the present, however, the weather would be the convoy's immediate protection.

From Calais and its environs the passage of the ships would not be visible in the prevailing conditions. To further hide its presence the barrage balloons were close-hauled so as not to present a beacon above the white cliffs and thereby blatantly advertise the presence of the convoy. In any event, it was rightly adjudged that air attack in such unfavourable conditions was probably most unlikely and although there must have been considerable anxiety on board all the ships as they passed through the straits, no attack came. The dreaded Junkers 87 Stukas stayed away. Overhead, the groups of protective RAF fighter aircraft circled and patrolled intermittently. On the bridge of the commodore's ship, though, there was doubtless some frustration at the painfully slow progress of the convoy which was already way behind schedule.

The estimated time for the convoy to be off Dover had been 13.00, but it did not reach that position until at least 14.30 due, according to Admiralty reports, to "the tide and the constant precautionary zig-zagging of the vessels" in the long snake of a procession that was CW9. (Exactly why no account had apparently been taken of the tide and the convoy's zig-zag course in the planning of its timings is not explained in Admiralty records.)

During its passage around North Foreland, fighter cover had been provided by a section of three Hurricanes of 32 Squadron from 11.00 until 11.30, with more Hurricanes of 615 Squadron covering the dangerous stretch around Dover from 14.25 until 15.25 and 32 Squadron providing cover in two relays of six Hurricanes each between 17.55 and 19.15 and 19.00 and 20.25. These later escorts were for the passage past Dungeness and continued up until dusk when the risk of any concerted air attack on the ships had subsided and the operation of protective groups of day fighters was no longer viable. During its passage around North Foreland and through the Dover Straits, sections of 501 Squadron's Hurricanes were also involved in covering the convoy at various times between 14.00 and 17.25.

By 18.30, however, the convoy had finally been detected by the enemy in the improving visibility when the observer station at Wissant reported a large convoy five sea miles south of Dungeness and heading west. Although CW9 had slid through the straits unseen and escaped any form of interference, and although it was now far too late to organise and mount an immediate air assault, the trap had been sprung.

The Germans now knew the course of the convoy and its speed and were thus able to determine where it would later be and when it would be there. The information was immediately signalled to the operational HQ of the already 'blooded' 1. S-Flottille (1st S-Boat Flotilla) at Cherbourg under the command of Kptlt Heinz Birnbacher who ordered boats S20, S21, S25 and S27 ready for sea. (The S20, and her captain, had participated in the 4 July 1940 attack on OA 178.) Meanwhile, four naval motor torpedo boats (MTB 5 and

6 of the Royal Norwegian Navy and MTB 69 and 70 of the Royal Navy) of Dover Command were sent in the opposite direction at dusk on Operation MQ with orders to ascertain whether enemy motor vessels or other craft were moving along the French coast.

(Author's note: All previously published accounts of the passage of Convoy CW9 Peewit through the Straits of Dover have invariably stated that this passage was under cover of darkness and that the Germans were alerted to its presence by coastal FREYA radar at Cap Gris Nez. Further, most other published accounts state that the convoy departed Southend-on-Sea on the evening of 7 August 1940. None of these accounts are accurate and this error of detail has been perpetuated up to the present date in even the most respected accounts and histories of the Battle of Britain. Convoy CW9 certainly left Southend-on-Sea on the morning of 7 August at 07.00 and proceeded at an average speed of 6 knots. It passed through the Straits in broad daylight, and although the visibility initially precluded its observation it was eventually picked up, visually, by observers at Wissant. Whilst FREYA coastal radar was set up by the Germans around Cap Gris Nez it is by no means certain that it was operational on 7 August 1940.)

CHAPTER 4

Attack of the E-Boats

THE SS *Empire Crusader* had sailed at the head of the port column since leaving Southend-on-Sea. Aboard was 1,020 tons of coal bound for Devonport and twenty-one souls – including the master, commodore and six naval-ratings comprising the naval crew of DEMS gunners and commodore's signalling staff. As with all British merchant vessels that carried the prefix *Empire*, she was in fact a captured German ship that had been re-flagged and re-named. After being stopped off the coast of Vigo, Spain, by HMS *Isis* on 9 November 1939 when pretending to be a neutral Russian vessel, the ship had fallen into British hands. In fact, she was the *Leander*, of the Bremen Neptun Line. Captured, she was taken as prize to Plymouth where the ship was re-named *Empire Crusader*.

(Author's note: Although we know that *Empire Crusader* was the commodore ship for CW9 the surviving records unfortunately do not identify who the commodore actually was. At The National Archives, Kew, are to be found the 'convoy cruising orders' for the Channel convoys. Whilst just about all of the CE and CW orders may be found in these Admiralty archives, the documents for CW9 are missing. Frustratingly, the papers for CW8 and CW10 are extant, but there is no trace of those for CW9. Not only has this defied efforts to thus far identify the commodore by name but it has also caused some difficulty in assembling a definitive listing of the ships that comprised CW9.)

With sunset falling at 19.34 on Wednesday 7 August, and twilight ending at 20.13, it was already dark by the time the convoy had plodded on by Hastings, Bexhill-on-Sea and then slipped past Eastbourne. Way off to starboard, had the crews of CW9 been able to see it, the rusting creaking hulk of the beached SS *Barn Hill* at Langney Point stood as a ghostly reminder of the danger to which merchant shipping in a wartime English Channel were exposed. Thus far, and even through 'Hell-fire Corner' (as the Dover Straits had become known), it had been relatively event-free sailing for CW9. It seemed too much to hope that this would continue. Almost every convoy through the Channel since early July, both CE and CW convoys and others besides, had met with fierce attack. However, there continued to be optimism on board the commodore's vessel that this time they would get through unscathed. Doubtless the poor visibility through the Straits had helped build up that hope. After all, if they could not properly see the French coast then the enemy could not have seen them either. Not only that, but no snooping reconnaissance aircraft had been seen since they had set sail from Southend-on-Sea. Unknown to the convoy, however, the vigilant observers at Wissant had picked them out as they passed Dungeness just an hour and a half before sunset. Quite probably it was partly the smoke from some thirty-three funnels (which includes the escort vessels), silhouetted against the western sky as the sun began to sink, that had given the game away. The optimism that they would get away with it was misplaced. The first attack, when it happened, would be sudden and brutal. It would also come unseen and out of the terrifying darkness of a moonless night.

Shortly before 20.00, S27, under the command of Oblt.z.S. Hermann Büchting, S20 (Oblt.z.S. Götz Freiherr von Mirbach), S21 (Oblt.z.S. Bernd Klug) and S25 (Oblt.z.S. Siegfried Wuppermann) throbbed out of Cherbourg harbour and headed to a position south of Beachy Head and Newhaven. Sailing with them on board S27 was their highly respected commander, Kptlt Heinz Birnbacher, already a war hero with the Ritterkreuz (Knight's Cross of the Iron Cross) to his credit. En-route to a calculated position off Beachy Head it would appear they were seen by one of the Dover Command MTBs who "did not engage in view of the main objective of the operation". If Birnbacher had in fact seen the British vessels he might well have experienced a moment of concern, wondering if their plan of ambush had been rumbled. He need not have worried. Nevertheless, after the flotilla of German boats had waited for a while off Newhaven the convoy did not initially show up in the expected time and place. Perhaps the British MTBs had signalled the alarm after all? From being one and a half hours behind schedule off Dover the convoy had fallen yet further behind and according to the Royal Navy (Dover Command) war diary CW9 was already three hours astern of schedule when it had passed Beachy Head. This had been further compounded by a slight reduction in speed after dark.

One of the attacking E-Boats during the pre-dawn hours of 8 August 1940 was the S20 commanded by Oblt.z.S. Götz Freiherr von Mirbach.

A group of officers from 1.S-Flotille during the summer of 1940. Included in the photo are Oblt.z.S. v Mirbach (3rd from left), Oblt.z.S. Wupperman (4th from left) and Kptlt Birnbacher (6th from left) who all took part in the attacks on CW9 Peewit during the early hours of 8 August 1940.

The convoy had not been diverted, or dispersed, as Birnbacher might have at first feared and after a somewhat lengthy search it was finally located. The boats hove-to and waited the closer approach of the long procession of merchant ships. Quite possibly, and despite the blackout that was supposedly strictly in force for CW9, Birnbacher had spotted lights that gave the convoy away although it could just as easily have been sparks from a funnel – a problem already highlighted by the Admiralty as cause for concern on otherwise blacked-out ships. Later, however, Captain W H Dawson of the SS *John M* would report that he had seen two lights in the convoy moments before they were attacked, although these lights went out the moment the attack actually started.

If the convoy's fate that night had indeed been sealed by carelessly illuminated lights then the use of the familiar wartime slogan "Put that light out!" was never more apposite, although, in truth, Birnbacher's men would probably have found the convoy anyway – careless lights or not – since the reports relating to the next CW convoy (CW10) make an interesting observation in relation to the motor anti-submarine escort vessels that also formed part of the protective force around CW9:

"From the knowledge pooled in the last three Channel convoys it is the considered opinion of commanding officers that these motor anti-submarine vessels are a menace. Their perpetual booming roar, that was clearly audible 4 miles away, draws all enemy forces towards the sound and, incidentally, to the convoy. Additionally, and owing to their inability to go slow they leave a clear white wake which acts as a magnet to the enemy."

The coaster SS *John M* survived the night-time E-Boat attack although was damaged by gunfire during that assault and was further damaged by air attack later in the day. Put into Portland for repair she was further damaged in an air attack there on 11 August. One of her DEMS gunners blazed away with his Lewis gun at the enemy during the E-Boat attack as one of the German boats was held in the vivid glare of pyrotechnics.

The very vessels that were intended to protect the convoy had, most likely, drawn the enemy to it although, curiously, only anti-submarine *trawlers* are referred to as being part of CW9's escort in the various naval war diaries.

Inexorably, the plodding merchant ships continued to bear down on their lurking ambushers who were waiting like menacing sleek wolverines, unseen in the pitch darkness, and ready to pounce on what was an already doomed quarry. Birnbacher ordered his men to wait. Four sets of powerful marine engines quietly thrummed in unison as they ticked-over, their crews waiting, watching and listening. It was almost the nocturnal equivalent of a "wait until you see the whites of their eyes" order. When the order came it was as if the hounds of hell had been unleashed. So sudden was the impact of roaring engine noise on the convoy that most of the masters and crew were convinced they were about to come under attack from low flying aircraft.

Momentarily, there was just engine noise. Then came the explosions. Again, many of the seamen on CW9 were convinced they were being bombed. In fact, they were being torpedoed. First in was Büchting in S27 around 02.00, firing a single torpedo into what he thought was a 4,000-ton tanker. The weapon made a direct hit, and exploded with awful violence towards the ship's stern section. On board all the ships of the convoy, instant pandemonium had broken out. Gunners were called to the ready, those below decks resting

The German S-Boot (or E-Boat to the British) S27 was Oblt.z.S. Büchting's command on 8 August and also the vessel in which the Flotille commander Kptlt Birnbacher sailed. The S27 was responsible for sinking the SS *Holme Force*.

were ordered to their stations as masters and helmsmen swung wheels to port and to starboard as the convoy took on a collective but uncoordinated pattern of avoiding action. The first ship hit, Büchting's victim, was the SS *Holme Force*. Chief Officer William Pritchard related his dramatic account to the trade division's shipping casualties section:

"At about 2.15am I had just looked at my watch and when I glanced up I saw the wake of a torpedo about 20ft away from the vessel. It was too late to do anything as we hadn't sufficient weigh on the vessel at the time to avoid it. It struck us right on the water line amidships on the starboard side about 122ft from the bow. There was a blue flash, and thick black smoke smelling strongly of cordite. Water splashed over me, and the next thing I remember was finding myself outside the wheelhouse with part of my trousers blown away. I shouted loudly 'Anyone about?' but got no reply. The vessel had listed right over to starboard at an angle of 45 degrees. I went over to the port side hoping I could find someone, and then I went back through the wheelhouse to the starboard side but could still find no one. However, I heard a scramble aft and upon going back to the port side I saw the fireman coming along. I instructed him to get the boats ready as quickly as possible. I accompanied him aft and found the chief engineer already sitting in the port life boat waiting for it to float off when the ship went down.

"Just then, I saw the wake of the second torpedo on the port quarter. She came alongside and struck us in the after part of the No.1 hold about 100ft from the bow. It was well on the surface. There was a blast of flame, lots of smoke and sparks, but I saw no water. She immediately started to go down by the head so I went over to the starboard side and asked one of the naval ratings if everyone was in the boats. He said they were full and that I had better join them quickly so I jumped in and we managed to get away safely. The vessel went down immediately, having taken about ten or twelve minutes from the first torpedo."

Of the thirteen crew and four DEMS gunners on board, six were missing including the master and three of the gunners. The master, sixty-year-old William Cousins, had gone below for rest whilst Pritchard had taken over, and the gunners were asleep having been on duty all day. Acting-Able Seamen Richard Compton-Cook, Charles Gorman and Maurice Ironmonger stood no chance at all as the torpedoes slammed into the ship right by their sleeping accommodation. Cousins, in his cabin, died with them. For William Pritchard and the others, however, their ordeal was far from over. The E-Boats had not yet finished with them, or with CW9.

As for *Holme Force* herself, the bigger part of her cargo of 1,000 tons of coke – bound from the Tyne to Devonport – had spilled out as the second torpedo slammed into the No.1 hold and the coke floated out onto the surface of the sea forming a huge unseen black carpet while the ship slipped beneath the waves. Whilst this ten-minute snapshot of events was unfolding for the hapless crew of *Holme Force*, utter chaos was developing around them on board all the other ships in convoy. Suddenly, the sky was lit up by flashes and explosions and tracer bullets of different colours that zipped in every direction. Behind the *Holme Force*, and on board another ship further down the column, a startled and confused master gave the order "Stand by anchors!" and then "Full astern!" as he heard the sound

The coaster SS *Holme Force* was the first victim from CW9 Peewit, sent to the bottom of the English Channel off Beachy Head by the torpedo attack of 1.S-Flottille.

The SS *Fife Coast* succumbed to torpedoes minutes after *Holme Force* had gone to the bottom.

of what seemed to be crunching pebbles all along his hull. Convinced that he was running up onto a beach, the master hadn't realised he was in fact sailing into the floating raft of coke from the holds of *Holme Force*. He could make no sense of the sounds he heard, and his uncertainty and confused manoeuvring was typical of other vessels in the convoy.

Some had virtually stopped, dead in the water, whilst others had increased speed or turned about. Of those still sailing ahead, most had taken on a zig-zag course. The order of the convoy had broken down. In the pitch black darkness, the danger came now not only from the attackers who were still wreaking havoc, but from the danger of collision. One of those vessels whose master had become alarmed was the Norwegian vessel SS *Tres* whose captain ordered "Slow engines!" and, eventually, "Stop engines!" as the vessel with its 1,096 tons of coal bound for Plymouth drifted silently with the tide amidst the havoc going on around it. Mercifully, the *Tres* avoided collision or direct attack. Others were not so lucky, as events were to prove.

After the torpedoes had blasted the *Holme Force* to the bottom it was the turn of the SS *Fife Coast* (this time with a cargo of refined sugar rather than coal) to be singled out some twenty minutes later. Whilst the *Tres* was just about dead in the water the *Fife Coast* had taken the opposite approach and increased speed to 12 knots, maintaining its original heading but weaving a zig-zag course. Looking for the wounded or weaker prey, Birnbacher's flotilla was still amongst the now spread out convoy. Frequent bursts of gunfire were exchanged between the German boats and the DEMS gunners. Although the ships in convoy maintained complete darkness, the German attackers were not so shy and with the element of initial surprise now long gone they sought out further victims by firing flares that

HMS *Bulldog* was one of two Hunt Class destroyers that had gone out to join CW9 Peewit for escort duties on the night of 7/8 August 1940. The other was HMS *Fernie*. The pair of destroyers claimed to have "driven off" the raiders and to have probably sunk at least one of them. Neither claim is correct. The E-Boats had simply departed due to the approaching dawn and none of them were sunk or badly damaged.

briefly illuminated in a harsh glare the next intended target. On board the SS *John M*, Master William Dawson watched as an illuminated E-Boat sped in, close, as one of his DEMS gunners blasted away with a Lewis gun. It was pretty much a one-sided battle although the escort destroyer HMS *Bulldog* had also finally got herself into a position to engage the enemy.

It was not an easy task. For one thing, the fast German attackers were roaming at will, and at speed, in and out of the convoy. Getting a bead on the enemy was a problem and there was a very real danger that the very ships HMS *Bulldog* was supposed to be protecting would be at risk from unintentional 'friendly fire'.

As it was, the confused DEMS gunners on many of the ships were blazing away at whatever they could see move and there is little doubt that some of the damage to the ships of CW9 was self inflicted. It was no longer possible to make any sense out of the previously orderly two-column convoy when the scattered ships were briefly illuminated in gun flashes and flares. Every so often, a ship would loom menacingly, momentarily and unexpectedly in the ghostly artificial light before vanishing – but often not before a burst of Lewis gun fire was sent towards it by nervous and edgy gunners. Out of chaos and disorder was coming even more chaos and disorder, and before *Bulldog* could do anything of consequence to protect her charges the *Fife Coast* had gone. Captain H E Philpott gloomily described his ordeal:

"Twenty minutes later [after *Holme Force* had been sunk] I suddenly saw the wake of a torpedo loom out of the darkness to starboard and before I could give orders to the helmsman to alter course the vessel was hit. There was a dull explosion and a rending tearing sound. She was struck about 100ft from the bow on the starboard side. The stern was immediately submerged and she took on a heavy list of about 35 degrees to starboard. The freeboard of my vessel was about 33¾ ft, and when I looked over the side a minute or two later the belting of the degaussing [anti magnetic mine protection] was under water. I was on the starboard side of the bridge, and dropped down to avoid any possible splinters. We have concrete slab protection and it was difficult to see anything, but as far I know there was no flame, no water was thrown up and there was no smoke.

"The starboard lifeboat was completely destroyed and owing to the heavy list to starboard it was impossible to lower the port boat. I gave orders to throw the raft overboard together with other gear such as ladders and hatches for us to hang on to. I then gave the order to abandon ship. The men jumped overboard and I did likewise. The ship sank within five minutes of being hit."

With the unfortunate crew of *Fife Coast* thrashing wildly in the inky dark water, immediate salvation seemed at hand when, out of the darkness loomed the SS *Polly M* bearing down on them. Captain P Guy of the *Polly M* saw the ship "blown to pieces" in front of him and "steamed right through the wreckage". In the water he could see the survivors, but: ".....I dare not stop to pick them up but continued zig-zagging, together with an armed trawler, in an attempt to get away." Having survived the sinking, the men in the water were now lucky to survive being mown down by their own colleagues, who then sailed on into the night leaving them to their fate.

When Captain Philpott and his men were in the water they heard the sound of the *Polly M* passing, but knew that she would not stop. Stopping to pick up survivors when under attack like this simply meant that the would-be rescuer would quickly follow the other ship to the bottom. Although hard for the crews involved, sailing on past their stricken comrades was the only thing to do. It was tough….but necessary all the same. As it was, Philpott's crew would survive the night although their ordeal was far from over when *Polly M* passed them by. Philpott takes up the story again:

"The enemy remained in our vicinity for some time, being quite close to us at times. They opened fire and I saw the red tracers from their guns. The bullets were spattering the water all around us, sometimes dangerously close. A number of Very lights were sent up by the enemy. The convoy was very well blacked out and I saw no lights anywhere.

"We were in the water for about three hours before being picked up. The 2nd officer, along with a wounded naval gunner named Collins and I swam round the raft most of the time as we did not want to overcrowd it. As it was, this raft was continually capsizing as it was only small and the swell, combined with the wash of the E-Boats as they swung close, upset it very easily. Each time it capsized the three of us had to right it and put the injured men and a naval rating who couldn't swim, back onto it. The other men on the raft were less strong than we were and we thought it only fair to give them what chance we could. We all had our kapok lifejackets on and I personally could not have gone on without it.

"After about three hours we were picked up by HM Trawler *Talthema* and I am afraid we were in a completely exhausted condition owing to swimming for so long in such freezing cold water, and also through inhaling fumes from the fuel oil which covered the water. We were then transferred to an HM launch which finally landed us at Newhaven at about 8 am on 8 August."

Acting Able Seaman Thomas Wellspring, aged twenty-two, was lost with the SS *Fife Coast*.

(Author's note: Acting Able Seaman Thomas Wellspring, DEMS gunner, was lost when *Fife Coast* sank. It is not known if he was killed by the torpedo strike or whether he subsequently drowned when the crew jumped into the water. His body was never found.)

To an extent, Philpott's account is almost as unemotional as might be a relatively insignificant traffic accident report, and yet it belies the true horror, fear, exhaustion, stress and the absolute sheer misery of what had been endured. His account might well be one from a survivor of a torpedoed Atlantic convoy ship, very many hundreds of miles out into the freezing cold and lonely ocean. And yet it was an event that took place in home waters, just a few miles from the south coast, and at the height of summer. Whilst he and his crew struggled for their lives, the Shoreham lifeboat crew were readied and stood-to as gunfire was heard out to sea, and the flares fired by Birnbacher's men could be clearly seen. In the event, the lifeboat was not launched and it fell to the *Talthema* to rescue the crew of *Fife Coast*. The courage of Captain Philpott, 2nd Officer A Davis and of Collins the wounded naval gunner epitomised the stark fortitude that all of those involved in the unfolding saga of CW9 exhibited. Conveying adequately in words the full horror and the drama of what had happened that night must have been as challenging for those who were there as it now is for a third party to achieve some seventy years later.

Philpott's crew, though, were not the only ones struggling for survival in the English Channel as the battles raged on around them. When the survivors from the *Holme Force* pulled away from the swirling cauldron of foam that had briefly marked the death throes of their vessel they might have been forgiven for thinking that their ordeal, surely, would soon be over. However, like the men from *Fife Coast*, William Pritchard and his crew mates were about to endure yet more challenges:

"We had pulled away about two cables on the starboard side [from where she had sunk] when someone asked me if I wanted a compass, but as I knew the direction of the wind, which was NW, I just put the boat stern on and headed for the land. Just then I saw the dim outline of an E-Boat travelling at great speed in the same direction as myself. She had no mast. She started firing at us with tracer bullets. Some were green, and some were red but they looked very similar to our own. All the men lay flat in the boats and no one was hurt. This had given away her position and she was tackled by a merchant vessel that also fired tracer bullets which were white with a slight shading of red. The E-Boat started firing flares, and I saw flares going up from another E-Boat, too."

(See Appendix G – the commanding officer of HMS *Astral* intimates that the pyrotechnic illuminations were possibly fired by the defenders rather than the attackers!)

Although the survivors from *Holme Force* and *Fife Coast* all believed they had been under attack from the E-Boats when they were helpless in the water, it is probably the case that Birnbacher's men did not deliberately go out of their way to do so. There would have been no point, and they were also doubtless honourable men who followed the unwritten code of all mariners when it came to the treatment of ship-wrecked fellow sailors. In any case, such action would have been a waste of effort and ammunition and it is probably just that it was the survivor's *perception* that they were being machine-gunned. What was happening was that they were being caught in the furious crossfire that was going on around them, and they were probably just about invisible, anyway, to both the attackers and defenders – between whom the hapless mariners were now stranded. Certainly, machine-gun bullets were hitting the water around them but if the E-Boats *had* deliberately targeted the survivors then it seems inconceivable that nobody was hit and that there were no reported bullet strikes on either the lifeboat or raft.

Pritchard was luckier than his colleagues from the *Fife Coast* in being picked up, for they had been rowing long when they saw the SS *Rye* approaching them. Pritchard hailed her, and the ship slowed and picked up the shaken *Holme Force* survivors. In stopping to rescue them, Captain H W Abbott broke all the rules and exposed himself to even greater danger than he and his crew were already in. What happened next, however, is open to some

The SS *Rye* survived the nocturnal E-Boat attacks with her master placing himself in harm's way to rescue the survivors from *Holme Force*.

speculation and not a little confusion. Indeed, confusion is the key word that permeates all of the activities surrounding CW9 from the moment Büchting's first torpedo had struck until the last ships of the convoy limped into port much later that same day. Either way, Pritchard describes his rescue by the *Rye* but goes on to say: "Just after we had got on board, the *Ouse* was sunk and so the captain of the *Rye* rang 'Full Speed Ahead' and managed to save the survivors of the *Ouse*."

Yet again, we have Captain Abbott putting himself in harm's way to save fellow mariners although – in this case – the *Ouse* was *Rye's* sister ship, both of them colliers from the port of Goole. Both of them were named after geographical locations on the Sussex coast – a coastline off which they were now in so much trouble. Indeed, the *Ouse* went to the bottom just a few miles from the mouth of the river after which she had been named.

Unfortunately, the account of Pritchard in respect of the sinking of the *Ouse* fails to tally with other surviving shipping reports. According to the Board of Trade shipping records the *Ouse* was lost "….in collision with the SS *Rye* whilst evading a torpedo attack". Unfortunately, no survivors' reports for the crew of the *Ouse* have been traced and we are therefore left with the official reason for the loss of the *Ouse* as noted in shipping records being at odds with the account of a *Holme Force* survivor who was aboard the *Rye*. First impressions that there might possibly be some ambiguity or even some economy of the facts in Pritchard's statement that "…just after we had got on board, the *Ouse* was sunk" are dispelled further on in his report where he goes on to say: "The captain then returned to where the *Ouse* had been <u>attacked</u>…." So, no doubting what Pritchard was saying. In his view, the *Ouse* had been torpedoed and sunk. Official records say otherwise.

The SS *Polly M* with her cargo of coal was one of the vessels damaged in the night time E-Boat attack. Originally abandoned by her crew she was re-boarded and sailed into Newhaven for temporary repairs before going to Fowey for dry dock inspection on 23 August.

The E-Boat S25 was Oblt.z.S Wuppermann's command although failed to hit the SS *Polly M* with her torpedoes. Instead, the S25 raked the coaster with gunfire causing such damage that the crew abandoned ship.

Whatever the cause, *Ouse* had been sent to the bottom by the actions of Birnbacher's men – whether directly or indirectly. *Rye*, meanwhile, had attempted to enter the port of Newhaven to disembark the survivors but was unable to do so due to the prohibition on ships entering territorial waters during the hours of darkness. Laying offshore for a while, Abbott then decided instead to proceed westwards in the wake of a now widely dispersed convoy. He eventually put the survivors ashore at Cowes, on the Isle of Wight, which had in any event been the intended port of destination for both the *Rye* and the *Ouse*. (Author's note: Although the *Rye* survived this encounter with the S27 she was, in fact, sunk by that very same E-Boat off Cromer on 7 March 1941 with the loss of nineteen lives including Captain Abbott.)

Oblt.z.S. Wuppermann (S25) went in close to the SS *Polly M* and SS *John M* and engaged them both with machine-gun and cannon fire. On board the *Polly M*, Captain P Guy found himself under relentless and continuous attack for almost a full hour as his little ship was raked with gunfire. As soon as he came under attack, Guy turned the ship about and sailed on a course due north, putting two men on the port side of the bridge while he took up station to starboard, all of them straining their eyes in the darkness to look out for the tell-tale phosphorescent wake of torpedoes. Eventually, at about 03.15 Wuppermann got a bead on *Polly M* and Captain Guy heard the distinctive sound of a torpedo being discharged. He was able to watch its approach carefully, and put the helm hard over and increased his speed to 10 knots and with some skill and a good deal of luck he managed to avoid it. A few minutes later another torpedo was fired at them and passed astern, not more than 2ft from their rudder. It had been a close call.

On board S25, Wuppermann was not giving up. Out of torpedoes, he continued to pump shells and bullets into *Polly M*, causing damage to the hull, mast and superstructure. The bridge was liberally peppered with shots, and at least one round punched a two-inch hole in the thick plating of the starboard side of the ship. All of the glass, rigging and cables were shot away or hit, deck apparatus was holed, signalling equipment ruined and a mass of splintered woodwork made the deck take on the appearance of an accident in a matchstick factory. Incredibly, only one man – First Officer H Tredwell – was wounded. All the same, enough was enough and Captain Guy reasoned that discretion was the better part of valour and ordered the starboard lifeboat be readied (the port one was also riddled with holes) after he had "….decided that we should not be able to get away".

With engines stopped, all the men were seated into the one remaining good lifeboat and Captain Guy stood-off from his vessel as he and his crew watched *Polly M* being shot at for a further half an hour. Clearly, he had made the right decision because even if the S25 could not ultimately sink her, just being on board as the German navy used her for target practice would not have been a healthy place to be.

Adrift in their lifeboat, the men were left alone by Wuppermann and eventually the anti-submarine trawler *Righto* came on the scene to render assistance, transferring the injured Tredwell to a motor launch to be taken into Newhaven. In the light of dawn, Captain Guy and a few of his men ventured back on board the battered *Polly M* with some trepidation and, with assistance, managed to limp into Newhaven at around 10.30 am. Her sister ship, the *John M* (initially the fifth ship from the front in the port column) had fared rather better although had also been attacked relentlessly by gunfire for some one-and-three-quarter hours. Her DEMS gunners had returned fire when they could, and Captain Dawson recorded that: "As an E-Boat approached I told Thomas, who was at the gun, to open fire – and if he did not score a hit then it was his own fault because a Very light had fallen just to the southwards of the enemy, making it almost like day, and this had silhouetted the E-Boat in the glare."

If pandemonium had reigned for the crews of those vessels directly attacked and sunk, then it was chaotic, too, on board the other vessels in convoy. On board the commodore ship, SS *Empire Crusader*, Chief Engineer J E Cowper was able to get a good view of proceedings:

"At 2am on 8 August there was a violent explosion on our port side caused by a ship in our vicinity. About three minutes after this I saw a torpedo approaching the ship. It came towards us on the surface of the water and I could hear the swish of it through the water; it seemed to be a very small torpedo to me. This torpedo missed the vessel by about 6ft, passing by the stern. Approximately five minutes after this the ship following us blew up. We then realised that we had run into a nest of E-Boats. The commodore then gave orders to put on speed and zig-zag. Shortly after this there was another explosion which I both heard and saw myself: this was another ship which was much further astern. Then followed a series of engagements. Very lights were falling all around the ship continuously, but I do not know where they came from. In the light from these Verys I could see shots crossing and re-crossing. Our gunners were in action and we got shots back in return, but where the shots came from I could not say. After we had been in action for about an hour I definitely saw the wake of an E-Boat, going as quickly as it could away from the convoy and we fired at it. The E-Boat, I think, put out a smoke screen – or it may have been from its exhaust. Anyway, it was a whitish colour and then the E-

Boat disappeared. At daylight all the enemy craft had disappeared and the commodore returned to pick up the scattered convoy."

Apart from giving a feel for how it was to be on board one of the merchantmen under attack, Cowper's report is notable for three specific points. First, that it gives us an indication as to how long this engagement took. Cowper says "…after we had been in action about an hour" and then goes on to say that the enemy disappeared "at daylight". In fact, the attack commenced at around 02.00 and ended at around 04.15. This was not a quick in-

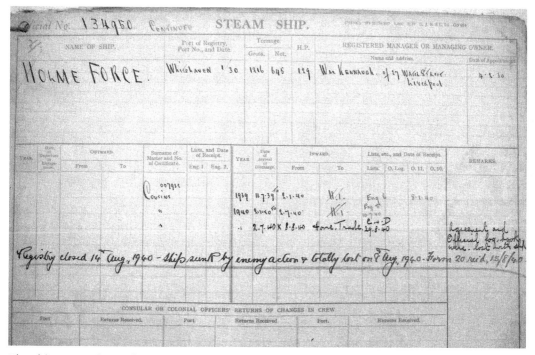

The ship's record card for the SS *Holme Force*.

Das Oberkommando der Wehrmacht gibt bekannt:

„In der Nacht zum 8. August 1940 griffen unsere Schnellboote einen stark gesicherten feindlichen Geleitzug an. Trotz heftiger Abwehr durch die begleitenden feindlichen Zerstörer, durch andere Bewachungsfahrzeuge und durch die stark bewaffneten Dampfer selbst wurden

1 Tanker von 8000 BRT.,
1 Dampfer von 5000 BRT. und
1 Dampfer von 4000 BRT.

versenkt. Ein kleiner Tanker wurde in Brand geschossen. Unsere Schnellboote kehrten unversehrt zurück."

German claims stated they had sunk tankers and steamers to the total tonnage of 17,000 BRT. In fact, the total tonnage lost that night stood at 2,587.

and-out, thrust and parry attack. It was a sustained onslaught lasting a good two hours, with the 1.S-Flotille harrying the convoy as it plodded along its route.

The four boats under Birnbacher's command roared in and out of the merchant ships and charged the full length of its two columns, port and starboard, back and forth, in and out, running at 20 knots or more. One crew member on-board a CW9 ship described the sound they made as being like "fast sports cars". Once their combined arsenal of sixteen torpedoes were all gone, however, the German craft continued to worry the convoy like a pack of dogs after a flock of sheep. Although their machine guns and cannons could have relatively little effect, now, on the steel hulls of the vessels – or at least were unlikely to cause sufficient damage to sink them – they did not give up, and their shells and bullets continually raked superstructures and decks, firing back at more than twenty DEMS gunners who were all blazing away into the night.

It was an audacious attack, and certainly not without risk to the German sailors who knew that the convoy would be escorted by at least one heavily armed destroyer and other surface vessels – quite apart from the defensive guns on board the merchant vessels. Even the tactic of roaring in and out of the scattering convoy in pitch darkness had its risks, especially that of collision. Despite their speed and agility they might not always be able to get out of the way of a merchant vessel bearing down on them as they cut across their bows. Being hit by a large iron tub laden with over 1,000 tons of coal was likely to spoil anyone's day. Certainly, they had the advantage of surprise and speed and they carried a formidable arsenal of torpedoes. But it was a courageous attack, all the same.

The second point in Cowper's report that is worthy of comment is his clarity about the number of explosions he heard; three. Without a doubt the first two were those that sunk the *Holme Force*, and the third must have been the one that struck the *Fife Coast*. That he does not mention any other explosions that might have been torpedo detonations is significant in that it perhaps indicates the *Ouse* was not, after all, sunk by a torpedo but have may well succumbed to collision. Other ships in the convoy also reported only three explosions, and had a torpedo exploded on the hull of the *Ouse* then it is certain that those in the convoy would have seen or heard it.

Lastly, Cowper speaks of a "nest" of E-Boats and ends his report by saying that "all" the enemy craft had disappeared as it got light. Both he and others on CW9 would probably have been greatly surprised to know that they had been attacked by only *four* E-Boats. The repeat attacks, and the craft roaring in and around the convoy for so long, doubtless gave the impression that there were many more than just four. Indeed, early on in the attack the master of the Norwegian vessel SS *Tres* reported that he had come to the conclusion that CW9 was "surrounded".

Sailing through the mayhem of the night time attack another little collier, the SS *Betswood*, got through without a scratch. Hers, ultimately, was to be a charmed life on the deadly Channel convoy runs. Time and again her name appears on the sailing orders of CE and CW routed convoys. In all, she completed no less than 120 passages of the English Channel during the war, all of them under the command of Captain J H Potts. But her adventures with CW9 were not yet over.

With the sun rising on 8 August 1940 at 04.34, and the final engagement from any of the E-Boats at around 04.15, it is likely that Birnbacher's marauders were driven off more by the brightening twilight and lack of ammunition, torpedoes and fuel than they were by the interventions of the Royal Navy escort. In the entirety of the engagement, the four anti-submarine trawlers had proved woefully ineffective in providing any meaningful form of defence and although the Hunt Class escort destroyers HMS *Bulldog* and HMS *Fernie* (the latter only joining the engagement later on, having been sent out to join the convoy en-route) engaged the E-Boats and claimed to have "driven them off", the reality is probably far removed from that. Indeed, *Bulldog* was also (mistakenly) of the opinion that she had sunk one. The Germans' departure southwards for Cherbourg was undoubtedly for the reasons already stated, and not because of the intervention of the Royal Navy.

In the chaos of the attack, and in the darkness illuminated only by sporadic gun flashes, explosions and a few flares it was a tough job for the naval gunnery officers on board the destroyers to get a bead on any of the attackers as they sped about their deadly business. And as if that was not tough enough, *Bulldog, Fernie* and the anti-submarine trawlers had to be very mindful indeed of the danger their charges might be placed in by anything more than the most careful shooting. As it was, there can be little doubt that at least some hits by shells, bullets and splinters to the ships of CW9 were caused not by the German attack but by defensive fire from on-board DEMS gunners or fire from naval vessels. It was, quite simply, unavoidable. In fact, the captain of one of the naval ships in convoy, HMS *Borealis*, later noted that "....some of the coasters appeared to be firing at each other".

Meanwhile, and just as the E-Boats were heading back to France, the first RAF involvement over CW9 Peewit on 8 August was underway. At RAF Thorney Island a Blenheim of 59 Squadron (TR-N) took off at 04.20 just as it was getting light. Detailed for convoy duties, Plt Off E Larcher with his crew of Sgts Walker and Vale found and recognised the convoy, although they were further detailed to search for damaged E-Boats between the convoy and the French coast. Clearly, they were looking for the craft claimed as damaged or destroyed during the night by the Royal Navy. Despite an extensive search almost to Cherbourg they could find absolutely nothing, and finally returned to Thorney Island at 07.20. Birnbacher's men were already well on their way home by the time Larcher and his crew had even started their hunt – if indeed they were not already in port!

As the exhausted E-Boat crews jubilantly returned to Cherbourg and a well-earned celebratory breakfast, they were able excitedly to exchange experiences and tally up the score. Büchting was sure that his hit had been on a 4,000-ton tanker, whilst Klug claimed he had also hit a tanker of 6-8,000 tons and von Mirbach claimed he struck a 5,000-ton steamer. In fact, two of the hits had been on the same vessel, the *Holme Force*. Not only that, but identification of the vessels as 'tankers' was incorrect – although, in the dark and the confusion of battle the captains can be excused that understandable error. So, too, was the estimate of shipping tonnage destroyed vastly over the top. Obviously, a 'double claim' had in effect been entered in error for two separate ships instead of two hits on the same ship. In addition, the total tonnage claim of 17,000 BRT was considerably more than the actual tonnage lost which stood at 2,587. Of the torpedoes they had fired, though, 50% had malfunctioned or missed their targets. Whatever the tonnage sent to the bottom however, the operation had been a resounding success for the German navy despite a hole having been shot through one boat's torpedo tube and at least one of the E-Boat's sailors wounded. Possibly, after all, Captain Dawson's exhortations had paid off; maybe this had been the result of hits from Able Seaman Thomas aboard the *John M*?

On the other side of the Channel, the four British MTBs were also returning home and had been able to report on the E-Boats they had seen but not engaged. Had they taken on the E-Boats it is tempting to speculate: might the devastating nocturnal attack on CW9 have perhaps been stopped or, at the very least, hampered? Meanwhile, as the sun came up, the remnants of CW9 were now scattered over a distance of more than ten miles of English Channel, and across a width of nearly five miles. It was no longer a convoy, except in name. As it got lighter, the ships tried to make sense of where they were and what had happened to the other ships in convoy. The captain of the *John M* found that from having been number five in line he was now almost at the head of his column, the leading four ships having vanished. Now, with only one ship ahead of him and the commodore's vessel some four miles inside them, it was clear that the convoy was widely spread out. The craft just ahead of the *John M*, by about four ship lengths, was a small Royal Navy vessel named HMS *Borealis*.

With the promise of a fine day came also the threat of further enemy attention and the early morning appearance overhead of a now familiar snooping Dornier 17 heralded what was to come. The aeroplane was a reconnaissance Dornier 17-P of 4(F)./14 which had been specifically tasked to observe the status of the convoy after the night-time E-Boat attack. The Luftwaffe crew duly reported seventeen ships fifteen miles SW of Selsey Bill at 06.20 hrs. In the wheelhouse of the *Empire Crusader* the helmsman narrowed his eyes as he peered up at the Dornier high above them in the bright morning sky and muttered through gritted teeth to Chief Engineer Cowper: "Look, the angel of death...."

(Author's note: The running battle with the E-Boats had continued for thirty-seven painful miles as CW9 Peewit made its night-time passage along the English Channel. The Royal Navy [Home Commands] war diary states that the action was initiated fifteen miles from Newhaven on a bearing of 190°.)

CHAPTER 5

Up Balloons…!

HMS *BOREALIS*, the ship which the *John M* had fallen in astern-of during the early morning light of 8 August, was a Royal Navy barrage balloon vessel and like many of the defensive measures put in place to protect the Channel convoys, *Borealis* was a make-shift craft born out of necessity. The need to provide vessels capable of towing barrage balloons that could sail with convoys and protect them from aerial attack had been identified as paramount long before the July bombings and the thinking was, quite simply, that if balloons could be stationed around the procession of ships and be towed along with them then it would be impossible for dive bombers to attack or for other low flying enemy aircraft in level flight to approach the vessels on bombing and strafing runs. That, at least, was the theory. As early as 17 April 1940 the plans for the establishment of a waterborne balloon unit were in hand, with a signal from the Air Ministry to the Admiralty setting out the initial arrangement for twelve units.

The mobile balloon barrage vessel HMS *Borealis* tows her balloon just a few days prior to 8 August 1940.

Of course, it first became necessary to assemble and convert a flotilla of suitable ships for the task and although it did not take the Admiralty very long to select a number of potentially usable vessels it took rather longer to put plans into effect. Initially, the craft were assembled at Grimsby but it took a further three months to move plans forward. Amongst the craft earmarked were a variety of tugs, including French vessels, a railway steamer and

Belgian pilot cutters. The French and Belgian ships that were later allocated had come across to assist with the Dunkirk evacuations and ended up being impressed into Admiralty service. Quite likely, it was the Channel attacks of July that accelerated arrangements to bring the waterborne barrage balloons into service.

Amongst the selection of converted vessels were His Majesty's ships *Rene De Besnerais, Gatinais, Elan II, Pingouin, Astral, Mamouth, Fratton, Pintade, Sioux* and, of course, *Borealis*. The *Borealis* was the command of Lt Arthur Hague RN, who fondly recalled the little ship that was his for just four days:

Lt Arthur Hague, captain of HMS *Borealis.*

"She had been an Antwerp pilot vessel, and was a beautiful little diesel-engined craft of 451 tons, built in 1930. When I first became acquainted with her at the very end of July she was being converted for her barrage balloon duties at Portsmouth where dockyard mateys were fitting the winch and towing gear with its protective wire cage. Of course, all the identification tallies and instructions were in French or Flemish. Her sister ship, another Antwerp pilot ship, was *Astral.* Mounted above the bridge were two Hotchkiss machine guns for anti-aircraft defence, although I should add that none of us had any idea at all how to use them! Of the crew, sixteen sailors from the Royal Navy Patrol Service made up the ships complement although, in addition, we had three RAF airmen to handle the balloons. Oh…and I shouldn't forget Malo the ship's dog. Malo was already on board when we all joined, and was a flea-ridden black and white terrier of indeterminate parentage. He had joined the ship with escaping British troops at Malo-les-Bains, a suburb of Dunkirk (hence Malo), and he had stayed on board ever since. This, then, was HMS *Borealis.*"

As we have seen, balloons were first employed in an eastbound Channel convoy (CE8) that sailed from Falmouth on 31 July, although Arthur Hague did not sail from Portsmouth with the barrage balloon flotilla (officially the mobile balloon barrage) to join the convoy until Sunday 4 August. That morning, the motley cavalcade of converted ships set out down Southampton Water to pick up the convoy off the Isle of Wight and thus provide the first waterborne barrage balloon cover for a Channel convoy. In the lead was the flotilla commander (Senior Officer Mobile Balloon Barrage – SOMBB) Lt Cdr G H F Owles, sailing in HMS *Astral* which was the other former Antwerp pilot ship. Lt Cdr Owles' men had

Prior to being pressed into Royal Navy service HMS *Borealis* had been a Belgian pilot ship. She came to Britain during the Dunkirk evacuations.

gleefully pointed out that his sobriquet SOMBB was an anagram of bombs, although doubtless they would be less inclined to find that so amusing by the end of the day. The other ships of the mobile balloon barrage that day were HMS *Elan II, Rene Le Besnerais, Pingouin, Sioux* and *Gatinais.*

Heading on eastwards, the convoy encountered no untoward incidents although *Sioux* fell out of line with engine problems off Dungeness and limped home much later when she was declared unserviceable. Meanwhile, Hague and his crew were able to get the 'feel' of their new ship without having to contend with any interference from the enemy. It was vitally important, too, for the RAF balloon handlers on board to get used to their new operating procedures and strange new environment. Whilst all of them were experienced balloon crews, flying a balloon from a ship instead of flying it tethered to a fixed spot on land was something entirely different. There had, of course, been no adequate training for the job in hand. There couldn't have been. This was going to be very much a case of on-the-job training. Some of the airmen had not even been to sea before let alone flown a barrage balloon from a moving ship.

The marine barrage balloon unit of the RAF was a Flight of 952 (Barrage Balloon) Squadron, commanded by Sqn Ldr R H Berryman and was, in turn, a component of No.1 Balloon Centre at Kidbrooke. 952 Squadron however, was based at Sheerness, Kent. Here, a total of forty balloons were held, thirty-two of them allocated as 'waterborne', although of that thirty-two there would be significantly fewer on the unit's inventory by the day's end.

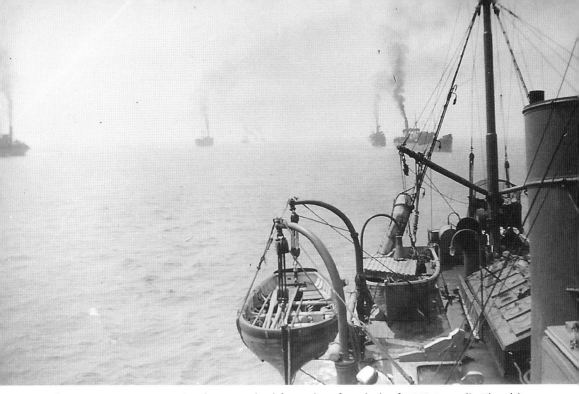

This is convoy CW9 Peewit, photographed from the after-deck of HMS *Borealis*. The ship immediately astern is the SS *Empire Crusader*, the convoy commodore's ship.

Sheerness, not far from the mouth of the Thames, was an advantageous location for 952 Squadron's balloons and, as a port, it could provide berthing facilities for its allocated barrage balloon ships. Situated as it was right at the beginning and end point of the CW and CE convoys respectively, and right opposite Southend-on-Sea, it was ideally placed for the purposes of the mobile balloon barrage.

In fact, it was to Sheerness that *Borealis* headed on 5 August after completing the CE8 escort in order to ready herself for the next assignment, two days later, with CW9. Early on the morning of 7 August *Borealis* and the rest of her flotilla slipped out of Sheerness and set sail down the Thames estuary on the morning tide to meet the convoy off North Foreland. Bobbing and nodding on the decks sat the squat silver balloons, close-hauled and secure, straining at their cables to be free. Around them, the RAF crews busied themselves with final preparations; checking and re-checking cables and ropes, checking the envelopes of the balloons and topping-up with hydrogen as necessary from the long cylinders mounted on the after deck. Despite the east-bound passage completed just over twenty-four hours earlier many of the airmen were still struggling to find their sea legs and trying to cope with the queasiness brought on by a mixture of sea-sickness and nervous apprehension.

On board the barrage balloon flotilla commander's ship, *Astral*, sailed the convoy balloon officer, Flt Lt A M Puckle, and as the small vessels finally joined the convoy by the Nore lightvessel at around 09.00 Puckle gave the order: "Balloon's up!" With *Borealis* at the head of the port column, and leading *Empire Crusader*, *Astral* sailing at the head of the starboard column and the other balloon vessels spread out down the flank and to the rear, the collection of balloons rose in unison as the convoy took on its shape.

On board *Borealis* Cpl William Will supervised his balloon crew, LAC Wardley and AC Warnes, their winch clattering as it paid out nearly 3,000ft of steel cable. The cable whistled and whined off its drum until the tethered silver monsters were at their operational convoy ceiling. At just below 3,000ft Cpl Will ordered "Stop winch!" and the cable drum was locked. The same procedure, repeated on board the other balloon vessels, gave a curtain of taught steel cable at strategic positions around the ships.

"That'll stop those bloody Stukas" commented the master of the *Rye* to his first officer as he eyed the barrage silently rise into position above them. Having been on the receiving end of recent and deadly Junkers 87 Stuka attacks, this to him seemed to be the answer. As the balloons rode above the ships, slightly head-down, the effect on the passage of the vessels could be felt. As the *Borealis* rode the crest of successive waves, the 'pull' of the balloon was discernible as the ship descended rather more gently into the trough of the wave than would otherwise be the case. The additional drag caused by the monsters

Cpl William Will was in charge of the barrage balloon on *Borealis* during the sailing of CW9 Peewit. He is photographed here with his bride, Phyllis, a WAAF balloon operator. Cpl Will received the British Empire Medal for the part he played in CW9 Peewit and other Channel convoys.

on these small ships also required careful adjustment of engine speed to compensate and maintain station. There was rather more to this operation than simply towing a balloon; the behaviour of the balloon having a direct impact upon the sailing of the ship and vice-versa.

Rounding North Foreland, the procession of ships was now very much into 'Stuka Alley' but there was an absence of any aerial activity save for the circling RAF fighters overhead on convoy patrol and there was no hint of any Luftwaffe interference. Then, as the convoy neared the narrower parts of the Dover Straits, Puckle ordered his balloons down and secured. It was a pre-arranged plan. The idea being that the visibility of the convoy would be increased from the French coast if the balloons could be seen above the white cliffs. No doubt to some of the convoy crews it was slightly disconcerting to see their reassuring new form of protection taken away from them just as they sailed into the most dangerous part of the passage. Wasn't this where attack by Stuka was usually most likely? However, and as we have already noted, the visibility was limited in any event and on board *Astral* Flt Lt Puckle discussed the tactic with Lt Cdr Owles. After all, if the Germans had seen the balloons on the previous convoy (CE8) they may well have decided that aerial attack was no longer an option.

There was reason enough, then, to suppose that was exactly why they hadn't been attacked at that time. And if they had seen the balloons flying above CW9 earlier in the day they may, again, have ruled out an air attack. Not only that, but even if the Germans had realised the balloons were down through the Straits it would have simply been impossible for them to organise an attack quickly enough to hit the convoy there, and by the time they had organised any such attack the balloons would be raised again once they had sailed past Folkestone. All in all, this barrage balloon idea seemed a resounding success. So far.

With the balloons raised past Folkestone, and as the convoy rounded Dungeness towards the descending sun, it may well have been that the balloons themselves rather than just the convoy's smoke had attracted the enemy's attention at Wissant. The six black blobs riding clearly and proudly 3,000ft above the flat beak of land that marked Dungeness and Romney Marsh provided a perfect silhouette against the bright evening sky through powerful German binoculars – just the form of advertisement that Flt Lt Puckle had tried to avoid above the white cliffs of Dover. Ironically, had the balloons flown when they sailed past Dover, then it is unlikely that the Germans would have been able to see them anyhow in the poor visibility that had then prevailed. Now, they had certainly helped to give the game away if not being entirely responsible for announcing the convoy's presence.

As dusk fell so did the balloons which now settled down onto their respective decks for the night and were made fast. On board *Borealis*, Cpl Will and his men now carried out their routine checks and completed daily maintenance and administrative chores. Thus far on CW9, and previously on CE8, the balloon crews had probably been lulled into a false sense of security but they were unwittingly sailing straight into a terrifying ordeal of many hours duration. Very soon they might well regret the sense of adventure that had led them to volunteer for the slightly more exciting and interesting-sounding seaborne barrage balloon unit. Certainly, in a few hours time 'dull and ordinary' might well have seemed infinitely preferable to exciting and interesting.

When the convoy had sailed into the E-Boat ambush during the early hours of 8 August, *Borealis* was at the very head of the port column and, as such, she was in one of the most dangerous places of all. As the first torpedoes hit, and the sky was lit up by gunfire and flares, Arthur Hague ordered "Hard to port!" and watched as the head of his ship swung oh-so-slowly around. His plan was simply to minimise the profile *Borealis* presented to her attackers who were clearly approaching from the beam, but as the ship swung around Hague watched astonished when the wake of a torpedo sped past from under his starboard counter and vanished to port. Had he maintained his original course then there was no doubting that the torpedo would have struck them squarely amidships. The resultant secondary explosion from the barrage balloon and its stored cylinders of hydrogen, along with the ship's fuel oil, would have been dramatic to say the very least. Most likely it would have literally blown Hague's ship out of the water. There would probably have been no survivors from such a blast, nothing left of the ship and in all probability little trace to be found of Hague or of his nineteen crew members either. Luck, for the moment at least, was on their side.

For a while, and as the convoy tried to sort itself out and reform, things were relatively uneventful. The barrage was raised again into the morning sunlight, the early rays of sun that pierced the broken cloud glinting off the silver-grey rubberised canvas of the balloons.

Meanwhile, *Empire Crusader* attempted to marshal the remaining ships back into some sort of order. Overnight, some of the ships had simply vanished. Others were trailing too far behind to be able to make enough headway to catch up, and at least one had limped into another port. However, the commodore was emphatic; the convoy must reform into its established pattern and the surviving ships should again take up their designated stations. With the journey's end almost in sight the worst was surely over, he thought.

Meanwhile, and unaware of the fraught situation his men had been in overnight, the CO of 952 (Barrage Balloon) Squadron, Sqn Ldr R H Berryman, settled down for the long train journey from Sheerness to Falmouth. He had departed at 06.00 that morning and would be in Falmouth by evening to welcome his men into port after the successful passage of CW9 Peewit.

CHAPTER 6 Unwitting Decoys

AT 04.30 on the morning of 8 August, and shortly after the vicious E-Boat attack on CW9 had ended some seventy-five or so miles further east, the Royal Navy examination vessel at Portsmouth signalled "Heave up" to the six merchant vessels laying at anchor in the eastern approaches of The Solent at St Helen's Road. They were to sail at once to a position just off St Catherine's Point where they would rendezvous at 07.00 with convoy CW9 and continue their passage westwards to Falmouth under convoy protection. The column of ships, led by the SS *Balmaha*, arrived off St Catherine's Point at 07.18, but of the convoy there was neither sight nor any trace to be seen. At first there was some concern that being nearly twenty minutes late the convoy had somehow been missed. However, that short passage of time would not have allowed the convoy to pass out of sight over the horizon. And yet there was simply nothing in sight. Looking back eastwards and down the English Channel they could see nothing there, either.

Unfortunately, convoy CW9 had already been some hours late when the E-Boats had fallen on them and that attack had caused yet further delay to its already hindered progress. Indeed, we also know that it was not until about 06.20 that the straggling remnants of the convoy were somewhere just past Selsey Bill and this position was getting on for some ten to fifteen miles distant of the little procession of six ships, led by *Balmaha*, as they had sailed down into Sandown Bay and past Shanklin en-route to the allocated rendezvous point. When he gave the order to sail, the master of the Portsmouth examination vessel evidently had no idea that CW9 was behind schedule, nor did he have any knowledge of the night-time attack off Beachy Head and Newhaven. If anyone at Portsmouth *did* know then it would appear they certainly hadn't relayed this information to the master. Consequently, the six merchant vessels were sent off to join a convoy that wasn't there. Meanwhile, by sheer bad luck, the snooping Dornier 17 that had observed the straggling CW9 off Selsey Bill at 06.20 had just been missed by the first RAF convoy patrol of the day.

Six Hurricanes of 601 Squadron from Tangmere, led by Flt Lt Archibald Hope, had patrolled over the convoy but had already left the vicinity and were landing back at Tangmere by 06.25 just as the snooping Dornier was arriving on the scene off the Sussex coast. Unhindered and uninterrupted in its work, the Dornier soon headed back with vital information on the course, speed and composition of the convoy.

Back on the ground in France the information on the convoy's passage from the

Flt Lt Archibald Hope (centre) led the Hurricanes of 601 Squadron over CW9 Peewit on an early morning patrol, but missed by minutes a snooping Dornier 17 reconnaissance aircraft. Coincidentally, the air attacks that day came at breakfast, lunch and dinner times. Hope and the pilots of 601 flew further operations over the convoy on 8 August but only met with limited success.

601 Squadron Hurricane.

Luftwaffe reconnaissance crew was flashed to operational planning staff. With the position and course of the convoy now known, and its timings quite accurately predicted, the notion of attack by the Stukas of FliegerKorps VIII had, presumably, already been given some advance planning anyway. The likelihood that all of the ships would have been annihilated by the E-Boats overnight was not high. There were surely likely to be at least some left for the Luftwaffe to finish off, and the report from the Dornier 17 crew confirmed so.

Consequently, by 08.00 fifty-seven Ju 87s of Stuka Geschwader1 were fuelled and bombed up and ready to go; their crews duly briefed and already preparing to board their aircraft for final preparations and checks.

Ten of I/St.G.1 Stukas carried a single 500kg bomb and four 50kgs apiece, whilst the other nineteen were loaded with a single 250kg weapon and four of the 50kg missiles each. As for the III/St.G.1 aeroplanes, nine of them carried a single 500kg bomb under the fuselage, with four wing-mounted 50kg bombs whilst another nineteen carried a single 250kg bomb and four of the wing-mounted 50kgs each. Overall, a formidable total of 285 high explosive bombs were scheduled for delivery on CW9. At 08.25 and 08.30 respectively, the Stukas of St.G.1 became airborne; the I Gruppe from Picauville led by

The first Stuka attack aimed at the ships of CW9 Peewit was carried out by phalanxes of Junkers 87s which struck at around 09.00 on 8 August although they had failed to find the main convoy. The formidable sight of the massed formations must have been terrifying for those on the little ships below.

Major Paul-Werner Hozzel and III Gruppe, led by Hauptmann Helmut Mahlke, from Théville. Over the Cherbourg peninsula the heavily laden dive bombers set course in the direction of the Isle of Wight. Covering them were large formations of Messerschmitt 109s of I and III JG 27.

Messerschmitt 109s of JG 27 participated in escort operations for the Junkers 87 Stukas during attacks against the shipping of CW9 Peewit.

On board the Dutch vessel the SS *Ajax*, Captain Jan Lits was following in the *Balmaha's* line when, at around 09.00, he was startled by the shout of his first officer from the bridge: "Fifty enemy aircraft attacking!!" In fact, there were seven more in total – although in the heat of the moment it was a pretty good count. What happened next for the crew of the *Ajax* was all over in little more than five minutes. Five minutes which saw the appearance of the dive bombers, being bombed and hit, getting in the lifeboat and seeing their ship slide beneath the waves. Lits takes up the story:

"I immediately ran to the bridge but could not actually see the planes which attacked us owing to the bridge protection, but I understand that three enemy aircraft approached on our port beam, two fighters and one bomber. They flew athwartships and the bomber dropped a salvo of three [*sic*] bombs. I saw the first bomb fall on the foredeck in the forecastle, the other two fell almost instantly on No.2 hatch, also forward. As the planes flew off they gave us a burst of machine-gun fire, but did not return for a second attack.

"The ship shuddered violently and listed 25 degrees to port. I think the whole of the port side forward was blown out. There were four men in the fo'castle, which had collapsed; two of the men went down through No.2 hold and managed to get out that way, but the other two were trapped and lost. There was no fire, but all the steam pipes broke, thus enveloping the ship in clouds of steam.

"Our naval gunner was at the gun on the bridge when the aircraft appeared and he let go at the enemy, immediately they attacked. He continued to fire after we were hit, in fact he continued to do so until the very last moment, and I consider he was very good indeed. He told me afterwards that he thought he had hit one of the planes as they flew over, but I cannot vouch for this.

"We lowered the port boat after we had been hit; the chief engineer, chief officer, a steward and a trimmer jumped overboard, the rest of the men got into the boat. I called out to the gunner, who even now was still manning his gun, and he jumped overboard as I stepped into the boat. The crew, including myself, numbered nineteen and we had on board one naval gunner. Of the crew, four men were killed and four injured. The confidential books went down with the ship."

Author's note: The position of the wreck of *Ajax* is 9.5 miles south of The Needles and 9.5 miles south-west of St Catherine's Point at 50° 30.540' north, 001° 32.640' west. Unlike the majority of ships sunk in the actions over 7/8 August 1940 that were carrying coal, the *Ajax* was carrying a cargo of wheat.

The attack on the six vessels in *Balmaha's* formation did not come entirely without surprise to RAF Fighter Command, as a formation of some thirty enemy aircraft had been detected off Cherbourg by the Ventnor CH radar station at around 08.40. Fifteen minutes later a formation of equal strength was located between the mouth of the Seine and Selsey Bill. Already, Fighter Command had a standing patrol over Convoy Peewit and again it was 601 Squadron and the same flight of six Hurricanes led by Flt Lt Hope. Having snatched some breakfast during a one-hour break, the Hurricane pilots were off the ground again by 07.20. But once again they had returned before there was any sniff of action – this time landing back at 08.50, just at the moment the Stukas were bearing down on the ships.

It was the same story, too, with twelve 609 Squadron Spitfires ordered off from Warmwell at 09.00 and arriving over the convoy just too late to engage the enemy. Also too late were the three Spitfires of 234 Squadron's Yellow Section who had been airborne from St Eval since 07.55. Vectored onto Peewit the three arrived over the convoy when the enemy had left, and by now the Spitfires were very low on fuel. Having flown at full throttle to reach the convoy, and having over-extended their operational endurance, the three Spitfires failed to make it back to base. Plt Off Hardy and Plt Off Parker managed to reach RAF Roborough instead in order to re-fuel, whilst Sgt Szlagowski crashed in making a forced-landing, out of fuel, at Pensilva in Cornwall. However, Hurricanes from 145 Squadron, up from Westhampnett, had just taken

Squadron Leader John Peel DFC who led the Hurricanes of his 145 Squadron into the attack against the raiding Stukas.

601's place. Squadron Leader J R A Peel led his Hurricanes off at 08.30, just in time to intercept the Stukas off St Catherine's Point – although not before the German aircraft had already bombed the ships. All at once the 145 Squadron Hurricanes found themselves embroiled in a hectic combat and facing a formidable armada of enemy aircraft. (Unfortunately, the 145 Squadron operations record book is slightly muddled in its recording of events and implies that only six Hurricanes took part in this engagement although it would appear that the whole squadron of about twelve aircraft were actually involved.)

Exactly what happened in the combat that unfolded, it is difficult to say with any certainty. However, we do know that Sqn Ldr Peel claimed one Me 109 and one Ju 87 destroyed and one Ju 87 damaged:

"I was leader of A Flight of 145 Squadron ordered to patrol convoy off St Catherine's Point. Received warning of enemy aircraft approaching from SW and climbed into sun at 16,000ft. Saw large formation of Ju 87s approaching from SW in vic formation with Me 109s stepped up to rear at 12,000ft. Approached unobserved from sea and went into attack on rear Ju 87s with Yellow Section before enemy fighters could intercept. Gave one Ju 87 a five second burst at 250 yards but did not observe results as I broke to engage two Me 109s. These fought by half rolling, diving and zooming in climbing turns. Got on tail of one Me 109 and gave him two five second bursts at 100 yards. Smoke came from starboard wing and he dived to south at sea level.

"Followed second Me 109 up in a zoom and caught him with a deflection shot at the stall. Enemy aircraft immediately dived to sea level and made off at 50ft. Gave chase for three minutes but unable to close up enough for effective shooting. Turned back towards engagement and found about twenty Ju 87s flying southwards at about 1,000ft in a vic on my beam. Attacked one straggler and shot him down into the sea. Me 109 then carried out a beam attack but didn't give enough deflection. Attacked another Ju 87 some distance behind with a beam attack but my guns stopped after a two second burst. Enemy aircraft dropped to sea level and flew off in a right hand turn very unsteadily and appeared badly damaged."

Other pilots, too, of 145 Squadron had engagements of varying success, with Plt Off P L Parrott shooting at a Messerschmitt 109 which flew across in front of him. He hit the German fighter, which then pulled up in a steep climb with smoke coming from its engine before it fell away in a spin. Parrott was unable either to see what happened next or to carry out any further attacks since his propeller shaft had suddenly thrown out oil which was now liberally coated across his windscreen, thus putting paid to him using his gun sight and engaging any other aircraft. Out of the battle, Peter Parrot beat a hasty retreat to base although it would not by far be the end of his action that day. For Plt Off Lionel Sears and Sgt Eric Baker, however, this skirmish would certainly be the end of their action with both young men failing to return from the battle. No trace of them was ever found.

Pilot Officer Peter Parrott of 145 Squadron was in action over CW9 Peewit three times on 8 August and shot down a Junkers 87 over the Isle of Wight during the last air engagements of the day.

Another of the 145 Squadron pilots involved in that action (flying Hurricane P3221) was Flt Lt A H Boyd DFC who had a closer than close brush with death when a bullet narrowly missed his head. He later broadcast his account of the action on the BBC Home Service:

"The other flight took off at half past eight in the morning to patrol the convoy sailing down-Channel south of the Isle of Wight. My flight took off shortly after that. We were lucky to find that the first two formations of dive bombers, Junkers 87s, were left to us. We went straight at them. Some turned back at once, but others went down on the convoy and attacked. We shot up a few of the bombers and then got mixed up with their escorting Messerschmitt 109s. I remember seeing two of them, about a quarter of a mile away, coming straight at me at 16,000ft.

"Suddenly, and for no reason at all, one of them did a half roll and went straight down. I followed, but although I had not fired at him – and as far as I could see no one else did either – he went straight into the sea. It just looked as though he committed suicide. I was so astonished that I could not believe my eyes, and while I was watching for others there was a crash behind my head. A bullet came through my hood, passed through the back of my helmet, tore through the back of my goggles and before I knew where I was the hood had flown back and my goggles had disappeared. After that all we could see were enemy bombers and fighters going like mad for home."

By a hair's breadth, and almost quite literally, Adrian Boyd had missed getting a German bullet in the back of his head. Escapes didn't come any closer or luckier than that.

Another 145 Squadron pilot engaged in that combat was Fg Off A N C 'Nigel' Weir. He had taken off in Boyd's B Flight (in Hurricane P2918) to join up with A Flight already over the convoy. As Boyd swept in to attack the formations of enemy aircraft they found everything happened so quickly that Weir was left behind in the turn. Diving in an attempt to catch up, three Me 109s crossed in front of him and one peeled off onto the tail of one of his colleagues' Hurricanes as Weir managed to get in a burst which sent the enemy fighter diving

Hurricane P3221 was flown by Flt Lt Adrian Boyd. Later, the bullet riddled-cockpit canopy was replaced by this one-off experimental bubble canopy with side blisters for extra visibility.

for the sea trailing black smoke. As he pulled up the sky seemed clear of all aircraft, but then a wave of Stukas passed him on the right. In the following few minutes Weir got in shots at no less than nine or ten of the Ju 87s, illustrating both the hectic nature of what was going on and just how many aeroplanes there were in the air at that moment. Weir saw white smoke curl away from one of his targets and another he fired at crashed into the sea. Still not satisfied he latched onto another of the Stukas and finished up all his ammunition on it without seeing any result. He landed back at base at 09.30.

As for the attacking German aircraft, two Junkers 87s of 9./St.G 1 had failed to return and their crews were lost, whilst another 9 Staffel machine and one from the 8 Staffel returned to France damaged after the engagement with 145 Squadron. Whilst some of the Me 109s flying as escort were also almost certainly shot down or damaged by the same squadron, surviving records do not make the specifics of the Messerschmitt losses during this action particularly clear. Neither is it possible, unfortunately, to identify Flt Lt Boyd's 'suicidal' Messerschmitt 109 pilot.

It seems very likely that the formation of Stukas that 145 Squadron engaged had in fact chanced upon the isolated group of six ships off St Catherine's Point, with the Germans quite expecting to find and attack a much larger formation of ships that comprised CW9. That, of course, had been the group of ships observed earlier that morning off Selsey Bill by the reconnaissance Dornier. Unwittingly, the *Balmaha* and the five other ships that had followed her had become decoys for Convoy CW9 and would pay a terrible price. Although

Hurricane pilot Fg Off A N C 'Nigel' Weir of 145 Squadron was another of the combatants. Here, he holds a Luftwaffe Mae-West lifejacket which was considered a useful trophy amongst RAF pilots who often wore them in preference to the Air Ministry issue jacket.

CW9 had made some headway since its 06.20 observation by the reconnaissance Dornier, it was still some miles astern of the six vessels now trying to find the convoy – and when these six were spotted through gaps in the 6/10 cloud cover they were presumably taken to be convoy CW9. On board the commodore ship of CW9, the *Empire Crusader*, still some miles astern of the *Balmaha*'s group, the explosions of the attack were heard and falling sea-spray could be observed in the far distance. However, it was too far away to see what was going on.

On board the *Coquetdale* it seemed to Captain William Harvey that the entirety of the German air force was trying to blow him out of the water, and his vessel was certainly blown to pieces around him in what would be repeat attacks as Stuka after Stuka dived down on him. The *Coquetdale*, like the other vessels in this small group, stood no chance. On 31 July she had left Falmouth in convoy CE8 and although the convoy was bound for Southend-on-Sea, she broke off at Portsmouth to deliver there her cargo of coal, intending to come out again and rejoin CW9 for the return to Falmouth on 8 August. Captain Harvey takes up the story of events that day in his account to the shipping casualties section:

"We were 15 miles to the SW of St Catherine's Point and travelling at about 8 knots, visibility was good, and the sea fine with a WNW wind. I had just given instructions to the engine room and as I glanced up I caught sight of a number of planes very high up on my starboard bow approaching from the WNW. I had three naval gunners on board, one of whom at that moment was at the wheel. I took over the wheel so that he could go and man one of the Lewis guns. The planes swooped down on us, almost vertically, and all three gunners opened fire immediately but I do not think they registered hits. The bombs, some of which made a whistling noise, were numerous and started dropping all around us, and many of them struck the ship.

"Not knowing what damage had been caused we stopped the ship. There was a few seconds lull in the bombing and we saw the *Ajax* sinking very quickly. I started up the engines again and put her hard to starboard, issuing instructions to lower two port

The SS *Coquetdale* was amongst the group of six ships that had sailed from St Helen's Road in the Solent on the morning of 8 August 1940 intending to join up with CW9 Peewit. She was sunk by Stukas south of the Isle of Wight at around 09.00 that day, along with the SS *Ajax*.

lifeboats to within 2 or 3 feet of the water, but before we could get her round there was another attack and the planes circled all around us. I tried to communicate with the engine room to stop engines, but we could not get in touch as it turned out the engine room was full of water. So I gave instructions to shut off steam.

"Bombs were still dropping and some of the splashes of water rose to a height of 50 or 60 feet. The water was very black. Some of the bombs hit us right amidships about 170ft from the bow and the whole port side was blown out. Three of the bombs dropped aft onto the gun and blew it to smithereens. The gunner was badly injured.

"When the planes pulled out of their dive they machine gunned us all along the decks. Unfortunately, during the second part of the attack the gunner on the port side had used up all his ammunition and the Lewis gun on the top deck had jammed. All three gunners behaved exceptionally well throughout the entire attack.

"I signalled to the *Balmaha* to come alongside and take off my crew but as she was in a sinking condition herself she did not think it advisable."

Author's note: The position of the wreck of *Coquetdale* is 15 miles south-south-west of The Needles at 50° 25.565' north, 001° 42.166' west.

Quite how many bombs actually hit *Coquetdale* is impossible to judge, although she certainly suffered multiple hits. That anyone on board actually survived is something of a miracle, but incredibly only two men were injured. While all this was going on, another 59

A merchant vessel comes under attack from Ju 87 Stukas in the English Channel during the summer of 1940. This vessel is too large to have been part of CW9 Peewit and may have been one of the Outbound Atlantic convoys, possibly OA178 on 4 July 1940. Near misses like these could still sink or cripple a ship, and black water like that described by the captain of the SS *Coquetdale* after the bombs had burst can be clearly seen in this photograph.

Squadron Blenheim (TR-P) had arrived from nearby Thorney Island for a further Channel patrol over the convoy. As TR-P approached the six ships off St Catherine's Point, Plt Off R A Ullman was surprised to see thirty Junkers 87s swoop in and dive-bomb the ships. With discretion being the better part of valour, Ullman retreated to a distance about four miles away as he and Sgts Thurkill and Lewis observed proceedings and radioed for help from RAF launches. These were the RAF high speed launches (HSL 116 and HSL 121) of the RAF Marine Craft Unit, Calshot. Both craft were despatched at around 09.10 to assist vessels in distress and to search for aircraft down south of the Isle of Wight. As for the *Balmaha*, her fortunes were slightly more favourable than those of the *Coquetdale* although after the attack the early indications were that she was certainly sinking. Again, it is the captain, one J M Forsyth, who takes up the survivors' story:

"At 09.15, and 15 miles west of St Catherine's Point, I observed a number of planes approaching from the starboard quarter. There were at least eight, and I think they were Junkers 87 bombers. I had just left the bridge and was standing on the lower bridge deck when, five minutes after I first sighted them, the first machine dived steeply, flew diagonally across the ship, and dropped a salvo of five bombs which fell very close to our port bow. As he pulled out of the dive he let go with his machine gun, wounding the gunner who was at the Lewis gun on the bridge. This man, Seaman H Antrobus, who was one of the naval gunners, had a bullet right through his leg but refused to leave his post at the gun. This salvo caused the whole ship to lift out of the water, perforated the plates,

71

Blenheims of 59 Squadron were airborne throughout the day on operational patrols and searches over CW9 Peewit, their crews looking for survivors from the sunken merchant vessels and downed aircraft. This photograph was taken just prior to the Battle of Britain.

and the water from the explosion splashed right up over the bridge to a height of about 40ft. This water was much discoloured, black and smoky, with a strong smell of cordite.

"The enemy aircraft were flying in single line; some dived over us one after the other to a height of about 200ft, while others attacked the *Coquetdale*. I ran up to the bridge, and as I did so a second salvo of five bombs fell almost in the same position as the first, very close to our port bow. The effect of each salvo was to lift the ship out of the water.

Every wooden bulkhead was blown out, the wooden structure was blown off the bridge, the fo'castle had perforated steel plates from the machine gunning, doors were blown off, beams fell off the hatches and No.2 tank started to leak. A number of bombs fell aft, but I do not know how many were dropped as I was not watching.

"I stopped the ship after the first salvo fell as I thought we had been hit, but finding this was not so I started the engines, swung the ship round and went full speed ahead again. She was not making any water as far as I could see.

"The attack lasted between five or ten minutes, during which time we had opened fire with the two guns aft and with one of the guns on the bridge. These all worked very well, and the gunners got off three or four drums each. One of the gunners reckoned he put a burst into the first plane, but without any apparent

High Speed Launch HSL 116. After being shelled by shore batteries which mistook the craft for E-Boats, HSL 116 had her propeller fouled on a drifting rope. Dead in the water she was then machine-gunned by German aircraft, killing one crew member and wounding another. Here she is shown later in the war with an RAF Lysander overhead.

damage. I did not see this, but I watched some of the tracers and they appeared to be going just ahead of the planes. There was no protection at all round the guns but everyone behaved very well, especially Antrobus, who still refused to leave his post although wounded.

"After about ten minutes our fighters came out to engage the enemy who very soon flew away. I turned my ship round then picked up the crew of the *Surte*, having to use the derrick to get the boat on board. Another ship, the *Scheldt*, had had her engines damaged so I put a rope across and was able to tow her into St Helen's Road where we anchored at about 13.00.

The sides of the ship were riddled with holes, some small round ones, and other fairly large jagged ones which I think were made by shrapnel. There were also a number of dents in the plating, but from the sound of it the enemy were only using machine guns."

(Author's note: In the Portsmouth war diary there is the following entry in relation to the SS *Balmaha*:

"At 10.35 on 8 August, St Catherine's wireless & signal station reported that SS *Balmaha* was passing east bound flying a signal for medical assistance and that a motor vessel was in company flying a signal: 'I have sprung a leak'. Shortly afterwards the SS *Balmaha* was sighted from Culver with a motor vessel in tow. The tow parted off Dunnose, but *Balmaha* went alongside and brought the MV *Scheldt* into harbour. It should be noted that *Balmaha* herself suffered damage consisting of splinter holes in the ship's side and miscellaneous defects to the upper deck fittings and rigging. The master of SS *Balmaha* acted in a creditable manner.")

Yet again, we have a dramatic account of the Stuka attack and the appalling carnage and damage that the onslaught had unleashed. The consistent use of machine-gunning following the dive bombing was simply the manifestation of an adopted tactic for rear gunners in the Junkers 87s of 'hosing down' the target area with their single 7.92mm calibre MG15 machine guns in order to suppress anti-aircraft fire. In other words, it had an intended purpose rather than being some kind of terror-tactic as is often suggested. The hit on the seaman, Antrobus, as he valiantly manned the anti-aircraft Lewis gun, was exactly what the German gunner had intended. Although the factual and contemporary reports of the survivors of CW9 and related ships are gripping accounts, the tale related by one un-named merchant seaman who came under the early morning Stuka attack on 8 August 1940 makes for an even more compelling read:

"We were six ships sailing to meet a westbound convoy off the Isle of Wight in the summer of 1940. We lost [sic] the convoy but were subjected to the most awful and frightening attack by Junkers dive bombers. I had served in the trenches for two and a half years during the Great War, but this was by far the worst experience of battle I had ever had. Nothing in the trenches even remotely compared to it. The attack came out of broken cloud and without warning when the German planes fell upon us. First, there was the screech of the first diving aeroplanes and a sound like sirens wailing over the roaring engines. Then, when the bombs dropped they made a shrieking whistle. I cannot be sure, but we must have had at least fifty dive down onto us in little over five or six minutes. One after the other they came. It was just a hell of noise. You cannot even begin to imagine it. Just the awful noise of roaring engines, banging guns and then huge great crashing explosions. It was just solid noise that went on and on and on. The shock waves hit you again and again and literally winded you, great plumes of water hit you, and the smell hit you, too.

"The whole side of our ship was blown out and when I glanced into the water as I made my way to the lifeboat I could see a mutilated body with great streaks of blood around it on the white foam of the wave crest. He was bobbing face down in the waves and surrounded by bits of smashed wood, clothes, bits of paper and charts, personal possessions, unused kapok lifejackets, several sodden but still floating loaves of bread and uncoiling pieces of rope. As if it wasn't enough that we were on fire and sinking and the whole bloody side of our ship was gone, they still came back time and time again to attack us.

"Then there was the smell. An awful acrid burning, of paint and wood and oil, and the terrible stench of cordite while great clouds of steam swirled all about, mixed in with thick black acrid choking smoke. All around you, empty shell cases clattered and clanged and pinged. Some of them hit you. You could feel great walls of tremendous heat hit you with each explosion and scorch your skin – and there were dozens and dozens of them. One after the other they came… CRUMP… BANG… CRUMP… BANG!! You could hear the shrapnel and bullets whizzing past you through the air, and you could hear shouts and cries through it all. But in the end you could hear nothing at all. I went temporarily deaf and could only see my ship-mates' mouths moving as they shouted at me. After a few minutes, although it seemed like hours, it just stopped. Just almost complete silence, it seemed, except for shouted orders and calls for help – but they were difficult if not impossible to hear as your ears were just ringing. Most people seemed dazed by it all, and were in a state of stupefied and speechless shock. It had been ten minutes of frightfulness when death seemed an absolute certainty at any second. Afterwards, I noticed the men in the lifeboat were shivering. It wasn't for cold. It was simply just fear and complete shock. Then I realised that I, too, was shaking uncontrollably. One lad of about sixteen or seventeen was crying like a baby. Mercifully, I couldn't hear his pathetic wails. He had also wet and soiled himself through the sheer terror of it all. We had gone into a living hell and somehow sailed out the other side alive."

The unknown sailor's vivid account of the ghastliness of that first Stuka attack is, perhaps, borne out by Captain W H Dawson of the *John M* whose ship had endured the E-Boat onslaught and then the dive-bomber attacks later on in the day. In his official report he stated: "The mate and one of the able bodied seamen have since cracked-up completely, and I do not think they will ever go to sea again."

Although the six ships caught by the Stukas of I/St.G 1 were not officially part of CW9 Peewit they were, nonetheless, caught up in the intended action against that convoy.

Adding to the mounting confusion and mayhem in the English Channel off the Isle of Wight that morning, the RAF high speed launches (HSL 116 and 121) had now arrived off

THE LITTLE SHIPS SAIL ON.

The artist A H Shepard, famous for his Winnie The Pooh illustrations, captured the spirit of the Channel convoys with this cartoon of the master of a coaster being encouraged by the ghostly figure of Sir Francis Drake. It was published in *Punch* on 4 September 1940.

The Needles to offer assistance to shipping in distress and to search for downed aircraft and aircrews. Onshore, at The Needles battery, observers had watched as they saw what they believed to be two German E-Boats moving in towards the shipping that had just been heavily bombed. Whilst they had been powerless to intervene during the Stuka attack, now was their moment. Consequently, at around 10.30 they opened up a heavy artillery barrage against the menacing 'E-Boats' – the barrage noted by various ships at sea.

In fact, what they had spotted – and were now busily shelling – were the two RAF launches. With their high speed and low profile, and with both vessels throwing up bow-waves, it is easy to see how the mis-identification arose. However, there were no German E-Boats anywhere in the Channel at this time, the last ones having left for home during the early hours of the morning after the attacks off Beachy Head and Newhaven. Whilst no hits were made and no damage was recorded we do not know how many shells were actually fired at the RAF marine craft, nor for how long the bombardment had lasted. Curiously, no mention is made of the shelling in the war diary of The Princess Beatrice's (Isle of Wight Rifles) Heavy Regiment, RA, who were then manning the battery, although the passage of convoy shipping and air attacks are logged. Possibly, another shore battery was involved although those at sea seemed satisfied as to where the shelling had come from. Suffice to say, the master of HSL 121, Plt Off J A Trayler, and his un-named compatriot on HSL 116 must have had some anxious moments as they tried to get out of range of the shells that were sending up columns of water all around them.

There might surely be considered some irony in the fact that Peewit is the common name given to the bird otherwise known by its proper name, Lapwing. The Lapwing is a bird so-called to describe its wavering passage of flight. Thus far, it is difficult to describe the passage of Convoy Peewit and her associated ships as anything other than 'wavering'.

(Author's note: Surviving Admiralty and merchant shipping records do not make it absolutely clear as to the identity of the five other ships with *Balmaha*. Whilst we can be certain about some of the names it seems likely, by a process of elimination, that the six vessels were the following:

Balmaha
Surte
Scheldt
Coquetdale
Ajax
Omlandia

The respective fates of *Balmaha, Coquetdale* and *Ajax* have been dealt with in the foregoing chapter. Of the others it would seem that the *Surte* was certainly damaged and disabled since we know that her crew were picked up by the *Balmaha*.

As for the *Omlandia* we know that she was hit by a blast, shrapnel or machine-gun bullets during the air attack. Her master was severely injured in the air attack "...by twelve enemy aircraft on 8 August 1940" and awarded the Dutch Military Willems-Orde, 4th Class. According to the naval officer in command, Portland, seven of her crew were badly wounded and one slightly. The same source also states that *Omlandia* was sunk, although it appears she was salvaged and actually survived until 1973.

The MV *Scheldt* of the Vianda Steamship Co. Ltd was disabled and taken in tow, with two of her nine crew wounded, one with a stomach wound from shrapnel and the other with a fractured leg. She had also taken two direct hits from 50kg calibre bombs and was further damaged by machine-gun fire and bomb shrapnel from near misses.)

CHAPTER 7

The Second Air Attack

A S THE battered *Balmaha* struggled back eastwards towards St Helen's Road during the morning of 8 August with the crippled *Scheldt* in tow, the two vessels passed Convoy CW9 steaming westwards. They doubtless wondered why it was that the convoy they should have joined was so far astern of schedule and what on earth had gone wrong. They could not have known anything of the night-time trauma the convoy had so recently endured. And neither could those aboard the ships of CW9 have had any knowledge of what those on the *Balmaha* and *Scheldt* had only just gone through, either.

However, if the six little ships in *Balmaha's* original grouping had indeed been the unintended decoys for the main part of CW9 then it wasn't going to throw the Luftwaffe off the scent for very long. Quite possibly, the escorting Messerschmitt 109 pilots in that first attack or maybe even the Stuka crews themselves had spotted the main assembly of ships way off to the west whilst the devastating assault on the six hapless merchantmen was in full swing. Possibly a single Messerschmitt 110 of 3(F)./121 that had carried out a reconnaissance of Bristol, Oxford, Weymouth and Portsmouth, and coincidentally just happened to be exiting over the Solent area at around 10.00 am, had spotted the convoy once again.

Either way, post operation de-briefing had doubtless established that the ships attacked certainly had nothing at all to do with the seventeen ships spotted during the early morning by the 4(F)./14 Dornier 17 P. For one thing, the convoy was eleven ships light. Not only that, they were surely not in the right position given the convoy's previously plotted location and speed. Almost certainly, the '*Balmaha* six' had just been exceedingly unlucky. The familiar story of being in the wrong place at the wrong time.

Back on the ground in France a great deal of feverish activity was again underway, this time to prepare yet more Stukas and their fighter escorts for another attack on the convoy. Such plans would not be being laid were the Luftwaffe anything other than absolutely positive that CW9 was still there. Certainly, effort of this kind would not be expended merely to eliminate the crippled survivors of the first air attack.

This time, it was the assembled might of the Junkers 87 Stukas of I. and III./St.G.2 which were called into action to finish the job. Again, a similar number of Ju 87s were assigned to the operation with forty-nine of them being loaded up with no less than 245 high-explosive bombs. At around 11.45 am the Stukas slowly climbed out of their airfields in the

On 16 August 1940 this Junkers 87 Stuka was shot down at Bowley Farm, South Mundham, near Chichester. The aircraft was serving with III St.G.2 and documents recovered by RAF Air Intelligence showed that this aeroplane (T6+KL, W.Nr 5618) had participated in the attacks against CW9 Peewit on 8 August.

Cherbourg peninsula for a rendezvous with their escort; the massed Messerschmitt 109s of I and III Gruppen of JG 27 and the Messerschmitt 110s of V./LG 1. At Ventnor chain home radar station on the Isle of Wight, almost overlooking the scene of the earlier action, operators had picked up the trace of a large enemy formation, at least 100 strong, and about twenty miles north of Cherbourg. It was headed on a course that would take it directly to CW9.

By now, CW9 was between St Catherine's Point and The Needles and was being patrolled by six Spitfires of 609 Squadron. As the information from the chain home station at Ventnor was filtered through to the 11 Group operations room at Uxbridge the WAAF plotters shuffled the 'hostile' markers on the map as the coloured counters marched steadily across the Channel. The threat was clear. With only the six aircraft of 609 Squadron over the convoy itself, and a force of 100 plus advancing, the controller ordered six aircraft of 601 Squadron up from Tangmere at 11.55 am.

Already airborne were the Hurricanes of 145 Squadron who were headed eastwards to intercept a threatening raid in the area of Beachy Head and Brighton, although when the new threat against Peewit became apparent, 145 Squadron were turned around and headed back towards the convoy. Unfortunately, valuable time was lost for 145 Squadron in what had turned out to be a futile pursuit and this delayed their arrival where they were needed most – over Peewit. Meanwhile, more Hurricanes were scrambled; 257 Squadron from Tangmere, 238 Squadron from Middle Wallop and 213 from far away Exeter. All of the three extra squadrons ordered up were airborne between 12.09 and 12.15 and vectored towards CW9.

Having survived the ordeal of the E-Boat attacks Lt Hague and his crew on board HMS *Borealis* were, at that moment, sailing at the head of the port column and watching Lt Cdr Owles's vessel, HMS *Astral*, off to their starboard. On board the *Astral*, Flt Lt Puckle had ordered down his balloon to engage in seaborne inflation trials when, at 12.19 exactly, Hague spotted enemy aircraft diving down on them. Almost at once, the Me 109s of 9/JG 27 shot up the balloon that was being towed at 3,500ft (just below a bank of cloud at 4,000ft) by *Borealis*. The balloon immediately erupted into flames and descended, burning, into the sea. Whilst its charred remains fell hissing into the water the Ju 87s of Stuka Geschwader 2 followed it down as they commenced their attack, diving down through the broken cloud directly above the convoy. At 12.20 precisely, one of the bombs scored a direct hit on *Borealis*.

Hptm Horst Liensberger was the enigmatic Austrian-born commander of V.(Z)/LG1.

The 50kg bomb struck the foremast, bringing it down over the starboard side of the bridge before the missile was deflected to the deck which it then pierced about half way between the bridge and the stern before it finally exploded below deck. Here, the blast blew a hole in the starboard bow just on the water line and immediately forward of the collision bulkhead, causing an immediate in-rush of water which flooded the forward compartment. The explosion from the bomb had caused havoc on the bridge, which it almost entirely wrecked, and had totally destroyed the gun positions on top of the wheelhouse. Of the

The gunner of a V.Z/LG1 Me 110 readies himself for ops.

chart table, charts and convoy orders there was no trace to be found and the principal steering position had been demolished along with the improvised concrete protection around the wheelhouse itself. On the bridge, all electrical switching gear was destroyed and every window had been broken. The thick glass of the portholes in the ship's hull had been holed by bullets or shrapnel. Behind the wheelhouse, the gravity diesel feed had ruptured and fuel oil was spewing out on the deck which was now liberally strewn with assorted bits of debris: wood, glass, metal splinters, bits of smouldering balloon fabric and wrecked equipment. Incredibly, there were only six casualties and only three of these were serious. That there were not more injuries, nor that there was not a single fatality, was nothing short of miraculous. Still intact on the after deck were the big hydrogen cylinders with not a mark or scratch on them, despite all else being liberally peppered with holes.

Trailing behind the *Borealis* for over 3,000ft was the now impotent steel balloon cable which was dragging on the sea bed like a kind of anchor before Cpl Will had managed to chop it free.

Leading Aircraftsman Puttick runs-up the Rolls-Royce Merlin engine of a 238 Squadron Hurricane during August 1940.

In a moment, Arthur Hague's tidy little ship had been reduced to a wreck, and he at once noticed that the ensign mast had been carried away by the falling balloon cable and, rather incongruously, he went off to the flag locker with the attack still in progress to find another White Ensign. Finding what he wanted, Hague managed to scramble over the mass of debris in order to lash the replacement to the after rigging. After all, naval tradition had to be upheld come what may. As she fell out of line, *Borealis* was at least still afloat. Just.

Overhead, the relentless Stukas dived one after the other onto the two columns of merchant ships. As with the previous attack, their *modus operandi* was to dive directly onto the target they had selected, release the bombs at no more than a few hundred feet and, as they pulled out of the dive, so allow the rear gunner to 'hose' the target area with suppressing fire as they departed. Apart from the *Borealis*, the Norwegian vessel SS *Tres*, with her cargo of 1,096 tons of coal, was hit by bombs in this attack; four bombs falling amidships at 12.25. All of them were 50kg weapons. She was lucky, since the single 250kg or 500kg bomb that would have been in that same salvo with the other four bombs had missed the ship by feet. Had it struck, then *Tres* would have been literally torn apart. As it was, the bombs had set her on fire and she was immediately in very serious difficulty.

Captain Vermund Kvilhaug, seconds after the four bombs had exploded, ran down from the bridge to the chart room to save the ship's papers but, on his way, he was struck by something that knocked him out. For a while, he was unconscious but managed to pull himself together enough to be able to head again for the chart room. When he got there, he found it a mass of flames and made his way instead to the boat deck where all hands were present except for the cook. Captain Kvilhaug, by this time, was in intense pain from burns to his face and hands – although he had no idea how he had been burned or what by.

This remarkable series of photographs was taken on board HMS *Borealis* on 8 August 1940 by its commander, Lt Arthur Hague, who nonchalantly reported that "….between raids there was not much else to do". They show general views of the debris-strewn *Borealis* and the wrecked wheelhouse with smashed windows and switchgear hanging from the bulkhead. In the view centre left *Borealis* is under tow from HMS *Elan II*.

The cook, Bjarne Arnsten, had been in the galley preparing lunch for the fifteen crew and three gunners on board the *Tres* and had finally managed to struggle up to the deck of the blazing vessel. When he got there, Arnsten found that his crew mates had given him up for dead and had already cast away from *Tres* in the lifeboat. Seeing the cook appear on the deck, they returned to rescue him. Painfully, the injured Bjarne Arnsten managed to lower himself down on the ship's derrick although unfortunately he lost his grip and fell into the sea. Willing hands hauled him into the lifeboat where the traumatised cook was gently covered

The Norwegian vessel SS *Tres* was towed into St Helen's Road. She sank later that day, although was later re-floated and repaired.

with jackets, sweaters and tarpaulin as the rest of the crew awaited rescue.

The *Tres*, a fortunate escapee from the night-time E-Boat attacks, had not been so fortunate now – although the crew were picked up surprisingly quickly by a Belgian tug, the *Ostende*, and taken ashore to Portsmouth later that day, but not before the men in the lifeboat had come under machine-gun fire. Ashore at Portsmouth, the captain was admitted to Haslar Royal Naval Hospital with perforated ear drums, severe burns and shock. Bjarne Arnsten sadly died of his injuries in the same hospital five days later.

With so many aircraft diving to attack the ships in convoy it was not just the *Borealis* and *Tres* which were having a hard time. Things were getting difficult for Captain W H Dawson and his men aboard the *John M*, too. His report to the shipping casualties section is worthy of repeating here, verbatim:

"At 12.15 when in a position 10 miles south of The Needles we were attacked by enemy aircraft. There were about fifty bombers of the Junkers 87 type flying at a height of 2,000ft. They dived out of the clouds at an angle of 45 degrees, to a height of about 400ft, when they released their bombs. Two of the bombers concentrated on our ship, diving over our stern to about 400ft when they released their bombs, then turned to port or starboard, but mostly to port, climbed out of the dive, circled and again dived over our stern. They did not machine-gun us at all, but I could see bullets spattering on the water ahead of us, and when the crew of the *Tres* took to their lifeboat the bullets spattered all around them.

About fifty bombs fell very near us, within a few feet, in eight salvoes with each salvo containing from four to seven bombs [Author's note: In fact, if there were eight 'salvoes' falling near the ship then she must have been targeted by eight individual Ju 87s rather than the two which Dawson mistakenly thought had repeatedly concentrated on them. With five bombs per Stuka, then we can conclude that forty bombs fell immediately around the *John M* in total. Given the stressful conditions under which Captain Dawson made his observations it is understandable that his accuracy might have been somewhat compromised!]. The effect of each salvo was to lift the ship completely out of the water.

The first salvo fell on the starboard bow. Two of these exploded on impact and two rebounded from the water, almost struck the ship, then fell back and exploded. The next salvo fell right ahead. The third salvo fell on our starboard quarter, two bombs exploded immediately, but the other two had a few seconds delay, then exploded and threw out about ten incendiary bombs to a height of about nine feet which then fell into the water. The fourth salvo fell right aft, the fifth salvo alongside the port quarter and the sixth almost amidships on the port side. The water thrown up by the explosions was a brownish colour."

Dawson's observations about the bombs, and their behaviour, are interesting. First, he talks of bombs exploding some seconds after impact with the water and this was something observed, too, by others on CW9 who noted the delayed-action of the detonation. The answer to this is provided by Hptm Plewig, a Stuka pilot who participated in the attacks on CW9 that day. Although Plewig, gruppen kommandeur of II/St.G.77, had participated in a later attack that day there is no reason to suppose anything other than that the bombs in use during all the attacks against CW9 on 8 August would have been similarly fused. Plewig explains:

"It did not matter much about scoring direct hits on the ships themselves because all our bombs were fitted with delayed fuses so that they didn't actually explode on hitting the sea but after penetrating the water. This caused a strong pressure wave which could badly damage a ship's hull."

Hptm Waldemar Plewig who led one of the Stuka raids directed against CW9 Peewit that day with his II/St.G.77.

On board the *John M*, Dawson and his crew knew all about the pressure waves described by Plewig, and as it would turn out those blasts had indeed buckled the plates of the hull sufficient for her to take on water. Without any doubt, the consequences of forty near misses had been dramatic to say the very least:

"The vessel had stopped and everything breakable on board was smashed. The only thing left intact was the main engine. The auxiliary pipes, pumps and even the fresh water service pump were all useless. The only drink we had was the brackish water out of the lifeboats."

With the situation on board so dire it was fortunate that none of the incendiary bombs ejected from the explosions had landed on the ship. Quite apart from the threat this would pose to the cargo of 650 tons of coal, anything else flammable on the vessel might have ignited, too. From Dawson's description, it would appear that at least some of the bombs used in that attack were *Phosphorbrandbomben* – literally phosphor fire bombs. These weapons contained glass ampoules of phosphorous that were flung out on detonation, the bomb casing either being of 50kg or 250kg size. Had any of these cascading burning projectiles hit the ship and caused a fire there would have been precious little that Dawson's men could have done to extinguish it, given the virtual incapacity of all the main on-board pumps. For the duration of the attack, though, some of his men were manning the guns rather than the pumps:

"The gunners had taken their stations during the attack and they did remarkably well. However, all three (Lewis) guns jammed. The cause of stoppage being the same in every case, was when one bullet was in the chamber the one in the barrel had failed to eject itself. There may have been a misfire, but there was no mark on the cartridge. Our own gun worked very well."

Once more we find the Royal Navy DEMS gunners working with extraordinary courage and efficiency in difficult and trying circumstances. The reference by Dawson to "our own gun" relates to the *John M's* own designated defensive weapon, another single Lewis, as opposed to the three RN weapons on board. Apart from the four Lewis guns, however, the *John M* was one of the Merchant Navy ships equipped with the singularly ineffective Holman Projector. Again, Dawson tells the story:

"The first salvo of bombs threw a column of water right over the ship and down into the engine room. At the same time I heard an inrush of water and thought the ship had split open. I found afterwards that this sound was in fact the air bottles of the Holman Projector. The blast had disconnected the pipes. The second salvo threw all the bombs out of the stowage tray and onto the deck at the side of the projector. The seaman-gunner, Thomas, threw all the bombs over the side. He was a very brave man."

In all of the attacks we find, time and again, examples of the bravery of the DEMS gunners shining through. It is impossible to conclude anything other than that they were very much the heroes of the day. They certainly fought overwhelming and impossible odds with woefully inadequate weaponry. The courage, though, of Dawson and his other stalwart crewmen cannot be doubted:

"At the third salvo I noticed that the ship seemed to be listing and labouring somewhat, probably owing to the shock of the explosions taking a certain amount of weight off her. She seemed to me to be making water. All the after hatches were lifted out of their beams, and at that time I was under the impression she had broken her back. Each time the water splashed up I thought we would be swamped, and as she appeared to be settling I ordered away the starboard lifeboat – not knowing, of course, that she had been damaged. Immediately we put her in the water she sank, as the whole of one side had been blown away, probably during the E-Boat attack. There was so much gear in the boat that we could not see the damage until she was lowered.

"About this time the chief engineer reported that she was making water in the engine room. I asked him if he thought they could stick it down below and he said they would try. I told him to keep her going full, and then let me know how things were going. We have a gadget fitted whereby we can shut off the fuel. I pulled on this and it just carried away. Then I noticed that its flywheel was just throwing up water.

"We had by this time received about eight salvoes near us, then our fighters came into action and the attack was over as far as we were concerned."

Whilst the attack may have been over, the drama for Dawson and his men certainly was not:

"I put up a signal 'D.Q.' indicating that I was in danger of sinking and one of the balloon barrage boats came alongside and offered to tow us. The chief engineer came up and reported that they were able to keep the water down but could only manage to keep the pump on the engine room and would be unable to keep it on the hold as well. I therefore asked the tug to stand by for about half an hour to see how we got on. I made straight in for the land, intending to beach her if possible. He advised me to make for The Needles which I did, although the compass had become unshipped. After about half an hour I signalled by semaphore that I was all right and not in need of assistance and that I was proceeding to Poole.

When we got to Amble Point I decided to carry on to Weymouth, after consulting the chief engineer. I took it that we had the tide with us until three o'clock and thought the ship would last that time. We arrived at Weymouth at 6.30pm when I signalled to the salvage tug and left the rest to him."

Exhausted but physically unharmed, the crew finally got ashore later that evening not having had anything to eat or drink since breakfast. They thankfully left their battered *John M* riding at anchor in Weymouth Bay. Later that evening, however, it was decided unsafe to leave her off Weymouth and she was towed into the adjacent Royal Navy Dockyard at Portland. According to the Portland war diary at the National Archives, Kew, it is recorded that:

"Five ships from Convoy CW9 which had been heavily attacked by aircraft off the Isle of Wight came into Weymouth in the evening. The Dutch SS *Veenenburgh* had slight damage and the SS *Paul M* [sic: should be the *John M*] more serious. The latter was brought into Portland due to the possibility of E-Boat attacks along with the other merchant vessels in Weymouth Bay."

Despite all that the convoy and its associated shipping had endured, CW9 continued to sail on westwards with the commodore ship *Empire Crusader* still in control of her charges,

Royal Academy artist Norman Wilkinson's painting of an air battle over a Channel convoy off Beachy Head is thought to be based loosely on CW9 Peewit although a degree of artistic licence has been applied by Wilkinson since the action off Beachy Head was at night when the E-Boats struck. The air attacks depicted here did not take place until CW9 Peewit had reached the Isle of Wight. The original of this painting hangs in the National Maritime Museum.

although she too would be hit by the Stukas of St.G.2. Chief Engineer J E Cowper was able to continue his tale of high drama, following on from his earlier account of the E-Boat attacks:

"At 12.15 we were ordered to action stations again. I was having lunch in the saloon at the time with the 2nd mate and a naval rating when there was a terrific explosion forward as a bomb struck the fore deck. Both the men immediately left the saloon and went towards the bridge. I made for the engine room. Just as I got to the engine room there was another violent explosion, approximately two or three feet from the ship on the port side which lifted the ship into the air. A huge column of black water was thrown up about 60ft in the air and completely deluged the ship. The engine room skylights were broken and the steam pipes burst. The whistle control was shot away and this added to the general pandemonium. Bombs were falling astern of us in all directions.

"I got hold of the 2nd engineer and asked him if he was all right and then he went aft to see about lowering the raft and I went forward to see the damage. The main mast had gone, the paravanes had gone, all the hatches had been stripped off and there was a crater in the coal which was now on fire. The front of the bridge had been completely blown in. I went alongside the starboard lifeboat which was hanging by the falls, where I found the 2nd mate who had had his hand shot off and he had a very bad wound.

"I looked over the side and realised that the engines were still going full speed ahead, although I thought they had been put out of action. I stopped them by the engine control on the deck. I then went to see what I could do for the 2nd mate and noticed an attempt being made to get out a boat, although the 2nd engineer and 3rd mate succeeded in getting a raft out.

"I then got a naval rating to assist me in getting the wounded 2nd mate across the skylights to the boat. While he was assisting me he was hit by a machine-gun bullet, and although wounded he did not complain until we had got the 2nd mate onto a raft. Until the naval rating was hit I did not even realise that we were being machine-gunned – I could not hear anything because the noise from the aircraft and the bombs falling round us was so terrific.

"By this time a boat had been partly lowered and the commodore went down the rope into it and we managed to get the 2nd mate into the boat. The commodore said that the captain had last been seen on the bridge and had said that he was going to the chart room. I went to the chart room but could not see anybody there. The whole front of the chart room had caved in and there were papers, books and drawers all lying in a heap. As I came out of the chart room I found two naval ratings. One of them was dead, and the other was so seriously injured that I knew I could do nothing for him.

[Author's note: Only one naval rating is shown as having been lost on *Empire Crusader* and that was Ordinary Signalman Peter J Turner and so it is likely that the second body Cowper saw was, in fact, the captain for whom he had actually been vainly searching.]

"In the meantime, the fire was travelling to the front of the ship. The bridge had also caught fire and the ship seemed to be going down by the head. There were about eight or nine of us who were not injured and we managed to get away in the boat, together with the injured we had taken from the ship. We rowed to the escort trawler which was coming towards us. The wounded were taken on board the trawler and first aid was immediately administered to them. The 2nd mate died as a result of his wounds.

"We proceeded on board the escort trawler and on the way 'Action Stations' were sounded again, but there were no further attacks. We landed in Portsmouth, where there were ambulances waiting, at about four o'clock in the afternoon of 8 August.

"I should like to recommend the naval rating [Able Seaman William Robson] who was afterwards wounded. If it had not been for him we should never have been able to get the 2nd mate into the boat."

The helmsman on duty aboard *Empire Crusader* earlier that morning had been prophetically accurate when he remarked upon the high-flying Dornier 17 reconnaissance aircraft, dubbing it the 'angel of death'. Last seen, *Empire Crusader* had capsized after her visitation from the grim reaper. She was bottom-up, well ablaze and drifting many miles to the south of The Needles.

Author's note: The wreck of *Empire Crusader* is 14 miles south east of The Needles and 9.5 miles south south west of St Catherine's Point at 50° 27.025' north, 001° 27.108' west.

From land, and as far away as Portland, huge pillars of thick oily black smoke which were the funeral pyres left by the Stukas could be seen coiling upwards into the summer sky. At Portland, the naval officer in command was able to report: "12.20 hours. Four columns of smoke observed 15 to 20 miles from shore at 124°, 125° and 133° and rising 2,000ft into the air."

Overhead, and regularly throughout the day, the Blenheim aircraft and crews of 59 Squadron, based at RAF Thorney Island, had carried out patrols over the convoy. In all, some twelve sorties were flown by them over the Channel that day (with one aircraft and its crew being lost during the late afternoon) including two sorties at around the time of the second Stuka attack when one of the crews noted of the flight: "photographs taken". Unfortunately, no trace has yet emerged of what would be truly historic photos.

Amongst the ships that they circled, observed and doubtless photographed was the SS *Pattersonian* which had

When divers located a wreck south-east of The Needles and south-west of St Catherine's Point it was originally thought to be unrelated to CW9 Peewit although the discovery of this pedestal and the brass plates inscribed with German text finally unlocked the mystery – this was *Empire Crusader*, formerly the German ship *Neptun*.

suffered some near hits that had caused damage to the ship's engines and badly disabled her. She eventually limped into Poole later that evening for repairs. As for the *Tres*, although she was badly damaged she was towed into St Helen's Road where she sank later that day. However, she was eventually re-floated and repaired and sailed the rest of the war with Captain Kvilhaug remaining in command.

When the Stuka pilots of St.G.2 had centred the black and buff hull of *Empire Crusader* with its bright pillar-box red funnel in their Revi sights they could not have imagined that the ship they were about to send to the bottom had, only nine months earlier, been sailing under the German flag. However, it was now the Stuka pilots themselves who were coming into the sights of the defending RAF fighters.

CHAPTER 8

Fighting the Stukas

R ACING BACK westwards from their unsuccessful attempt to find and intercept a raid of thirty-six Messerschmitt 110s that were last seen fleeing southwards between Beachy Head and Brighton, the twelve Hurricanes of 145 Squadron were straining every last ounce of power to get quickly back to Convoy Peewit. Below, broken cloud left dappled dark patterns flecking across the blue-green sea whilst the summer sun blazed above them at its zenith. The apparently tranquil sea and sky belied the deadly intent of the Hurricanes and of the fierce battle that was about to be joined. One of the pilots was Flt Lt Adrian Boyd:

"I myself led the three machines in my section to a point well south of the Isle of Wight. There we saw two separate squadrons of Messerschmitt 110s. Something went wrong with my radio set. I could hear the squadron leader calling: 'Where are they?' He knew that I had spotted some, but he could not receive my message. So there were the three of us, circling high above the Messerschmitts, which were now flying in an uncompleted circle at about 4,000ft. We were at 16,000ft.

"I was curious to know why they were circling around like that, and we decided to have a crack. We went down on them. The Messerschmitt which was at the end of the circling line of fighters was shot down into the sea immediately. The lad on my left shot down one Messerschmitt 109 which I think was intended to be a decoy. It was probably supposed to lead us down to the circle, but our pilot shot him down first before we started our dive.

"Well, we broke up the happy little circle quite effectively. All three of us got at least one, and I think we must have taken them by surprise. We started climbing again, but after about a minute I thought I would like to go back and find out what was happening. I flew over another circle of enemy fighters for about five minutes before they had all cleared off. Then I went down and saw one of their pilots in the water. He was easy to spot, for all around him was a big patch of bright green dye – a special method used by the Germans when they get in the water. It shows their friends where they are. I have come across it before. You can see the green colour five miles away. [See pages 158 – 164.]

"While I was investigating this I was attacked by a Messerschmitt 110 which I suppose

I had overlooked. I skidded round and climbed for him, but he broke away to the left. I was still turning and at about 1,000ft when I stalled. He was right in my gun sight. I just gave him a quick burst, he heeled over, and went straight into the sea and broke up. He really was a sitting bird. Then we went home."

If Adrian Boyd's account seems somewhat gung-ho then that is understandable since this is a verbatim transcription of a BBC broadcast made by Boyd not long after the action he describes. It was clearly aired as a morale-boosting piece with public consumption in mind. As a first-hand account it is an invaluable impression of what the air fighting was like on 8 August 1940 and of 145 Squadron's encounter with the Messerschmitt 110s. These, in fact, had been the aircraft of V./(Z)LG 1 who were led into battle that day by their Austrian commander, Hptm Horst Liensberger. As a counterpoint to Boyd's testimony we also have Liensberger's account of the action written the next day:

Lt Beck (left) with his radio operator Uffz Busch with their 13 V./(Z)LG 1 Messerschmitt 110. Their aircraft was hit during an escort mission flown in support of attacks against CW9 Peewit and Busch was seriously injured with a bullet wound in his thigh and a splinter in one eye.

"9 August 1940 – yesterday. Twenty ships below us in the water. And so it began. Although we only had sixteen machines it was sufficient. The Stukas attacked the ships, just at the door of England. We swept between the opposing RAF fighters, once above and once below. Suddenly there was hell to pay. They came at us in force, from above and below, about fifty [sic] at a time. They were all around us, brown and camouflaged. Then there were the phosphorus stripes of the bullets going by. That was really a dogfight! I hit two of them, but what happened to them I don't know. There were still enough others to attack! Below us the ships exploded and from above fell an enemy aircraft near to the English coast. Unfortunately, I lost one too. We gave quarter to those who circled around the scene of the accident."

Liensberger's lost crew were Feldwebels Alfred Sturm and Helmut Brunner of 14V./(Z) LG 1 who were shot down in what became a massive dogfight involving dozens of RAF Spitfires and Hurricanes. In the confused nature of the fighting it is difficult to ascertain who shot down who and it is very clear that there were multiple claims being made by different pilots for the destruction of the same aeroplanes. Such over-claiming was quite normal in air fighting, and especially so in such a big and confused melee as this one. In the case of Sturm and Brunner, however, it seems likely that they fell to the guns of 145 Squadron's Flt Lt Adrian Boyd who spoke of their Messerschmitt being a "sitting bird". Interestingly, Boyd also talks about going down to see a German airman floating in the water with his green marker dye. Flt Lt Boyd must therefore have been one of the RAF pilots to whom Liensberger and his pilots chivalrously "gave quarter" as he circled the scene of downed aircraft and airmen. However, it was not just the Messerschmitt 110s of (V)LG 1 and the Hurricanes of 145 Squadron that were in this particular fray.

Aside from the Stukas there were the Hurricanes of 257 and 601 Squadron and Spitfires of 609 Squadron. In total, well over 160 aircraft were milling around in a furious aerial battle in quite a small space of sky. Little wonder that the claims and counter-claims were confused and confusing. That said, there seem to have been two distinct seats of combat; one involving the Stukas and escorting Me 109s directly above the ships and the other involving circling escort fighters a couple of miles or so distant. The dive bombers exploited the conditions of broken cloud above the convoy to dive through into attack, the cloud at least partly hiding where they were coming from to the ships' gunners below and partly shielding them the view of attacking RAF fighters above.

Meanwhile, the main formations of escort fighters circled in two areas of fairly cloudless sky to the south and to the east of the convoy. It was an apparently well thought out tactic that resulted in both these groups of German fighters standing between the attacking Stukas and the RAF aircraft that were approaching from the west and the direction of Tangmere and Westhampnett. It was only the Spitfires of B Flight 609 Squadron, approaching the convoy from the north after flying down from Middle Wallop and across the Isle of Wight, which actually engaged the dive bombers.

As 609 Squadron approached the convoy, led by their CO Sqn Ldr H S Darley, they saw the Messerschmitt 109s of JG 27 diving to shoot down the remaining barrage balloons – at least one of them falling to the guns of Oblt Max Dobislav of 9/JG 27. One of the attacking Spitfire pilots of 609 Squadron was Flt Lt J H G 'Butch' McArthur, leader of Green Section:

"I only had my No.3 with me and took off behind Blue Section and stayed behind them until over the convoy. I then heard the controller tell Blue Leader (Sqn Ldr H S Darley) to come down below clouds. In trying to follow him down I lost Blue Section. At the same time my No.3 became separated from me. Below the clouds I saw

Squadron Leader H S Darley led the Spitfires of 609 Squadron into action during the second air attack directed at CW9 Peewit.

a balloon in flames and many aircraft of all types in a general scrimmage. Owing to my inexperience I could not pick out a suitable target with any certainty so I climbed into the sun and headed out to sea. On reaching 6,000ft, where there was just about 4/10 cloud, and after having cruised about for around five minutes I saw one Me 110 down at sea level."

McArthur had flown off and away southwards from the attacking Stukas and had headed out towards the circling and waiting fighters, although by now the Stukas that had been the first into attack were already headed home:

"I dived down and on the way I found that the Me 110 was following a squadron of Ju 87s in vic formation heading for home. I dived on the outside Ju 87 from about 3,000ft and fired a seven second burst. I saw him turn over on his back and go into the sea. The formation then split up and I regained 4,000ft very quickly. The height of the Ju 87s was about 100ft. I then dived and gave another long burst of ten seconds on another Ju 87 which started to emit black smoke and dived into the sea. I then found the Me 110. I climbed up a bit and was coming in at him from the port side and slightly above him. I turned quickly away from him and after a turn or two found myself quickly on his tail. I then found that I had no more ammunition so pulled the over-ride tit and hurried home."

Apart from McArthur's claims, Darley claimed a Messerschmitt 110 as having being shot into the sea and he also took 'pot shots' at a number of Ju 87s. Plt Off Curchin also claimed to have accounted for a Me 110 and the squadron operations record book noted:

"Though a good day for 609 Squadron this was a bad day for the navy. The convoy advertised its presence by flying silver barrage balloons and made it difficult to bring prompt aid by sailing 15 miles out to sea."

Plt Off Michael Appleby, who got home with his Spitfire badly peppered with holes also noted: "Perhaps if the balloons were camouflaged they would not stand out so well or perhaps they could have been flown in the cloud instead of below it."

When they were finally back, the six Spitfire pilots had missed lunch. Whilst it might seem trivial in the overall picture of the fighting it was clearly an important issue and a sore point. After all, it is said that an army marches on its stomach and the same was surely true for fliers as well. Certainly the compiler of the squadron's operations record book felt moved to note that if pilots on operations missed the station's fixed meal times then they went hungry. It was as simple as that. The station commander, Wing Commander GV Howard stated his case imperiously: "I commanded a fighter squadron myself some years ago and we always had our meals at regular times."

He, of course, quite overlooked the point that this had been during the ordered days of peacetime, and not with fighter pilots facing the exigencies of real combat flying. With more than a hint of tongue-in-cheek sarcasm the 609 Squadron diarist went on to say: "All our efforts to get the Luftwaffe to respect meal times have failed."

Instead, it noted that Sgt Fitzgerald and Cpl Walker did a magnificent job of bacon and

Plt Off John Curchin was one of the 609 Squadron Spitfire pilots who engaged escorting Messerschmitt 109s on 8 August 1940, and claimed to have hit at least one of them. The twenty-two-year-old Australian is seen here (centre) larking around with fellow 609 Squadron personnel. A squadron Spitfire can be seen in the background. Curchin was killed in an engagement with Me 109s over the English Channel on 4 June 1941.

eggs on a Primus stove. Incredible that during the heat of wartime activity, and amongst all the reports of derring-do, considerable time should have to be expended over discussion regarding the feeding arrangements for hungry pilots – and all due to the intransigence of an inflexible station commander. On 8 August 1940 the Luftwaffe just happened to make a nuisance of themselves at breakfast, lunch *and* tea times. At this rate, noted one pilot, death by starvation seemed more likely than death through combat!

Apart from 145 and 609 Squadrons, 601 Squadron and 257 both threw their Hurricanes into the fray, with six Hurricanes of 601 Squadron leaving Tangmere at 11.55 and the twelve Hurricanes of 257 Squadron (flying from RAF Tangmere as their forward operating base and away from their home station of RAF Northolt) getting off at 12.10. With the attack literally closing on the ships of CW9 Peewit, and despite the short flying distance from Tangmere, there was precious little time to get the fighters into position. Quite likely the controller had been wrong-footed after he had sent 145 Squadron haring off towards the feint attack to the east. Now it was a case of getting 145 Squadron back as quickly as possible and plugging the potential hole in defences with 601 and 257 Squadrons – although he still had 43 Squadron's Hurricanes in reserve and on the ground at Tangmere.

Although it is hard to understand why, 601 Squadron were ordered to orbit Tangmere at 20,000ft instead of making directly for Peewit, and this was notwithstanding the clear indications that were already coming in from the chain home radar station at Ventnor that

A group shot of the Spitfire pilots of 609 Squadron during August 1940. Many of these men were engaged in the actions associated with CW9 Peewit on 8 August 1940. They are from left: Tobin, Ostaszewski, Goodwin, Edge, Appleby, Howell, Darley, McArthur, Feary, Nowierski and Overton. Front, from left: Staples, Crook and Miller.

showed a big German force bearing down on the convoy and just minutes away. Possibly, and until the Germans' intentions were absolutely clear, the controller had preferred to keep 601 Squadron covering the airfield, and at least until 257 Squadron were up. Either way, 145, 257 and 601 Squadrons were still some minutes from the convoy and 609 some minutes away to the north. Also racing up the Channel from far-away Exeter were six Hurricanes of 213 Squadron but their departure at 12.15 did not put them over the convoy until long after the Luftwaffe had left for home.

From the north, too, came yet more Hurricanes – this time twelve aircraft of 238 Squadron operating out of Middle Wallop who got off the ground at 12.09, hot on the heels of the just recently departed 609 Squadron. To an extent, the convoy – already badly mauled – was still dangerously exposed. And yet, given the advance warning, it would have been possible to have had all three Hurricane squadrons from Tangmere and Westhampnett up and over the convoy long before the Stukas arrived. With the advantage of height (the squadrons would have had sufficient time to climb to altitude) and the mid-day sun at their backs, the impact those three squadrons might have had on the attackers can only be guessed at. Such, though, is the luxury of hindsight and the comfortable lot of armchair strategists. The reality was that the four squadrons had to make the best of the situation they encountered.

It was not until 12.30 that the Hurricanes of 601 Squadron finally had contact with the enemy; the Me 109s of JG 27. Led by Flt Lt Archibald Hope (the squadron CO, Sqn Ldr The Hon. Edward Ward, did not fly operationally that day as he was about to go away on apparently urgent business to RAF Northolt), the six fighters bore into the enemy some ten miles south of St Catherine's Point. In a hectic combat, Plt Off J K U B McGrath accounted for two Me 109s claimed as destroyed. Breaking away from his section on sighting the enemy, McGrath did a stall turn onto the tail of an Me 109 that was, in turn, on the tail of a Hurricane and did a head-on attack. Stall turning again as the enemy aircraft passed dangerously close underneath him, he caught sight of the Messerschmitt as it rolled onto its back and spun into the sea. Now though a Messerschmitt was on McGrath's tail. Diving at full throttle he then zoomed up vertically and fell off the top of a loop, flattened out and did another stall turn only to find that despite his aerobatic gyrations the Messerschmitt was still on his tail. Truly, this was dogfighting. Sweat poured from under his flying helmet and trickled down his face as he twisted and turned and, after some minutes, finally got onto his opponent's tail. A two second burst did the trick. The Messerschmitt wobbled and dived into the sea with McGrath following him down. Later he noted: "Presumably the pilot was killed immediately." Plt Off H C Mayers also claimed a Messerschmitt 109, although his combat seemed somewhat less dramatic. He noted: "One Me 109 turned across my sights. I turned on his tail and gave him a

Pilot Officer John McGrath. The particulars of his recommendation for the award of DFC cited amongst others his action on 8 August 1940, with Air Chief Marshal H C T Dowding signing-off the award on 14 August beneath the following text: "This gallant young pilot has shot down five enemy aircraft confirmed and seven unconfirmed. He has shown great courage and determination which, coupled with his fine spirit, has contributed to the very high morale of his Squadron. I, therefore, very strongly recommend him for the immediate award of the Distinguished Flying Cross."

five second burst. I saw black smoke coming from the engine. The enemy aircraft turned over and dived into the sea." For no loss, 601 Squadron had claimed three Me 109s destroyed but had failed to get at the dive bombers.

As they landed back at Tangmere at 13.08 the CO, Sqn Ldr Ward, was preparing to fly off to Northolt and he departed at 14.25. He didn't return until the following day when he participated in a forty-minute squadron formation practice, but by 19 August had been relieved of his command. Part of Ward's business at Northolt had been to meet the CO of 257 Squadron, Sqn Ldr Hill Harkness. Harkness's 257 Squadron was at that moment at Tangmere, where it would be led into action by Flt Lt Noel Hall.

Harkness himself was later much criticised for his unwillingness to fly operationally with his squadron during the Battle of Britain, and by 12 September 1940 he had been posted away leaving Sqn Ldr Stanford Tuck to sort out a demoralised and shambolic squadron. Whilst Noel Hall was much admired and respected, his leadership on 8 August had unfortunately led to his death and with Flt Lt H R A Beresford and Flt Lt L R G Mitchell both being lost one month later (again, this was when Harkness was not flying) the rot had finally set in for 257 Squadron. It was a rot that had started on 8 August.

Flt Lt Noel Hall led all twelve Hurricanes of 257 Squadron into the engagement with fighters south of the Isle of Wight in which 601 Squadron and 145 Squadron had been embroiled. Here, in the frantic fighting, Plt Off A C Cochrane and Plt Off K C Gundry each claimed a Messerschmitt 109 destroyed, with Gundry also claiming another as damaged. Sgt R V Forward, meanwhile, claimed a Dornier 17 as damaged but since no such aircraft were involved in the action he must have mistaken the identifiable twin tails of a Me 110 for those of a Do 17. On the debit side, things were not good. Flt Lt Hall, Fg Off D'Arcy Irvine and Sgt K B Smith had failed to return and nothing had been heard or seen of them by the rest of the squadron. An attrition rate of 25% per operation would be impossible for any squadron to sustain if it became a pattern, and morale on 257 Squadron was already rock-bottom.

Meanwhile, Sgt R H B Fraser in Hurricane P3775 had either experienced some technical difficulty or combat damage that had resulted in him beating a retreat to RNAS Lee-on-Solent, from where he did not return to Tangmere until 18.40 that evening. Despondently, Plt Off Gundry went off again from Tangmere in Hurricane P3708 at 13.50 to search the sea area where the combat had taken place to look for Hall, D'Arcy Irvine and Smith. Despite a search of one hour and fifteen minutes he found only the depressing detritus of war drifting about on the tide.

238 Squadron had also lost pilots, and according to the operations record book:

"When our aircraft arrived the enemy aircraft were dive bombing the convoy. Flt Lt D E Turner and Fg Off D C McCaw have been missing since this engagement although at least one of them is believed to have baled out and landed by parachute. Fg Off McCaw came to the RAF through the University of Cambridge and had been with an army co-op squadron before coming to 238 Squadron, of which he was an original pilot. Of Celtic colouring, blue eyes and black hair, which was already tinged with grey, and his slightly dreamy dignified personality he is greatly missed. He was clearly material from which the best type of officer is made.

"Flt Lt Turner's keenness, energy and good humour made him very popular with everyone and his strong reliable character made him an excellent second-in-command. He has been greatly missed."

The claim by 238 Squadron for two Messerschmitt 109s and two Messerschmitt 110s destroyed and a further two of each unconfirmed and a Dornier 215 [sic – must have been an Me 110] also unconfirmed did very little to soften the blow of losing two popular and experienced pilots.

When the headcount had finally been completed for all the returning RAF squadrons, and a reasonable time had passed to allow for any stragglers to get back, it was clearly apparent that the two pilots of 238 Squadron were not coming back to RAF Middle Wallop. Unsettled by their disappearance, the CO, Squadron Leader Harold Fenton (who had not participated in the action) decided to go off at 13.20 to carry out a search of the sea area

IN PROUD AND LOVING MEMORY
OF
FLIGHT LIEUTENANT
DONALD ERIC TURNER
R. A. F. V. R.
KILLED IN ACTION IN THE
BATTLE OF BRITAIN AUGUST 8TH 1940.
AGED 30 YEARS.
"AT THE GOING DOWN OF THE SUN
AND IN THE MORNING, WE WILL REMEMBER HIM."

Flight Lieutenant Donald Eric Turner of 238 Squadron was a native of the Falkland Islands and a memorial plaque to him is situated in the cathedral at Port Stanley.

where the combats had taken place in Hurricane P2947. Like Plt Off Gundry of 257 Squadron who was searching the same area at the same time, Fenton would find no trace of his pilots. Arriving over a sea littered with debris, floating coke, oil slicks and with burning ships on the distant horizon his anxious search for the unfortunate Turner and McCaw was suddenly interrupted by the appearance on the scene of a Heinkel He 59 seaplane low over the water – itself intent upon searching for downed Luftwaffe airmen.

Approaching the seaplane and going in to attack, Fenton was surprised by a brief burst of fire from the aircraft and before he could even think of any retaliation it quickly became apparent that an unlucky round had severed an oil feed pipe in his Rolls-Royce Merlin engine. Acting quickly, and as oil pressure began to drop and the temperature ran higher, he started to climb. If he could gain some altitude it may allow him to glide back to land or, if needs be, to bale out. However, as he reached 3,000ft his engine promptly seized and the propeller jerked alarmingly to a halt. One way or another, this was journey's end; it was just a question of whether he now baled out or rode his Hurricane down and ditched in the sea.

The first option did not seem very attractive. After all, at least one of the two pilots he had just been searching for had been seen to bale out and was now missing. If Fenton jumped he might end up missing as well. Alternatively, he might be fished out of the sea by prowling He 59s. Captivity wasn't attractive, either. By good fortune, and as his altitude began to fall away, Fenton spotted a distant naval trawler of some sorts about five miles south of St Catherine's Point and decided that it would be best to attempt a landing as near to it as possible. To make his water landing safer, Fenton undid his parachute and the Sutton seat harness. When the impact came he would need to get out, and mightily quick! As it was, the big radiator scoop of the Hurricane dug into the sea resulting in the nose going under and the tail shooting high into the air. The result was that the unsecured Fenton was catapulted forward on impact with the sea – his torso striking the instrument panel, control column, and gun sight causing injuries to

Squadron Leader Harold Fenton, the CO of 238 Squadron.

his face and chest. As he was thrown upwards and outwards he hit his head hard on the canopy frame causing severe cuts and abrasions. Additionally, he had badly injured his leg on something lower down in the cockpit.

Fenton had put down at about 14.00 hrs, approximately one mile from HM Trawler *Basset* whose captain, Lt Nigel Herriot, at once altered course and proceeded under full speed to the stricken pilot's assistance although it took Herriot a full half-hour to reach him. Arriving on the scene, *Basset* found Fenton struggling in the water and if it were not for the courageous and prompt actions of Second Engineman J Alexander the outcome may have been rather different. The crew of *Basset* were not easily able to get the injured squadron leader aboard, and so Alexander unhesitatingly jumped into the water with a line and secured the rope around the battered and dazed pilot, thereby allowing him to be hauled up onto *Basset's* deck. Once again, we have another instance that day of selfless valour from a Royal Navy sailor.

On board the *Basset*, Fenton was given first aid treatment before he was taken below to warm up and dry out in the boiler room. What happened next is best described by the writer of 238 Squadron's operations record book:

"Later, the trawler picked up a German officer of Flt Lt rank whose total luggage, a special Very pistol with cartridges, and a large packet of twelve contraceptives, gave the crew an amusing interlude. The pistol and its cartridges are used to draw attention if a pilot comes down in the sea. Whilst Sqn Ldr Fenton and the Bosche were drying out they had toast and tea but were much interrupted by bombs which were falling with insistent regularity. After a time they got used to it and they were in a somnolent state when the boat hove to. On enquiry they discovered that port had

HMS *Basset* which rescued two pilots that day.

not yet been reached but that they had hove-to in mid Channel to pick up a Dutch skipper from a raft. Closer examination showed that he was dead as a result of accidental strangulation by a line which had caught around his neck. He was left, and the trawler headed for port where it arrived at around 1am, putting ashore Sqn Ldr Fenton and the Bosche who were both transferred to the Haslar hospital."

The German airman who became Fenton's reluctant travelling companion on board HMS *Basset* was, in fact, Stuka pilot Oblt Martin Müller the adjutant of Stab I./St.G.3 who had been shot down off the Isle of Wight during the attack by the Hurricanes of 145 Squadron. His bordfunker, Uffz Josef Krampfl, was killed and his body later washed ashore on the French coast. Müller would endure over five years of captivity, whilst Fenton went on to serve out the war in the RAF and to retire as a group captain in 1945. The ordeal of 8 August 1940, though, had had a lasting effect on Harold Fenton as it was later discovered that the blow to his head when the Hurricane hit the sea had caused damage to his auditory nerve and by the 1960s he had become almost totally deaf. As to the He 59 he had encountered that day, Fenton claimed to have possibly shot this down before he too ended up in the water. (See footnote to Luftwaffe Aircraft Losses in Appendix B.)

Before Lt Herriot bade farewell to Harold Fenton as the injured squadron leader was taken off to Haslar hospital, he was glowing in his praise of Fighter Command. According to the 238 Squadron operations record book he and his officers "....made inspiring remarks

Sgt L G Batt of 238 Squadron and his Hurricane with its bat emblem and two victory tallies.

about our fighter aircraft". However, the adulation was not necessarily mutual and one of Harold Fenton's 238 Squadron's pilots who had taken part in that day's actions, Sgt Leslie Batt, would later make his feelings plainly known: "I absolutely hated convoy work. We were trying to protect them....and what did we get? Well, I can tell what we got; getting anywhere near a convoy or a Royal Navy ship was asking to be shot at. They really didn't mind much whether you were friend or foe. You got shot at either way!"

Batt's view was one that was echoed by the majority of RAF fighter pilots tasked with convoy protection duties. Sqn Ldr P W Townsend, CO of 85 Squadron was a veteran of dozens of convoy escorts:

"The convoys were distinctly trigger-happy and sometimes fired on us. We forgave them. Recognition was difficult and sailors were never masters of it. One day my brother Michael, captain of HMS *Viscount* wrote me: 'My guns are so old I do not think I could ever deal with a Hun plane. But a Dornier flew over us the other day and I let her have it – but not for long, because she was an Anson.' "

Whilst the rescue of Fenton and Müller was going on, preparations were already underway in France for yet *another* attack by Stukas on the battered remnants of Convoy CW9. This time, it would be the turn of various elements of Stuka Geschwaders 3 and 77 and it had been their bombs that had so rudely interrupted the tea and toast of the two drying-out pilots.

CHAPTER 9

Final Assault

A FTER THE mid-day attack that had crippled Hague's little ship, HMS *Borealis* had bravely limped on with the intention of at least reaching port. No longer effective for her intended purpose and now barely afloat, her master was determined to save her if he possibly could. Unfortunately, the Luftwaffe had other ideas. Hague takes up the story from the point when he had stopped his engine and fallen out of line after *Borealis* had been hit:

"With my chief engineman I inspected the collision bulkhead which was holding well and then put the ship into hand steering from aft – the bridge steering gear being no longer effective. The chief engineman, J Taylor, with great difficulty had caulked the fuel supply tank sufficiently to keep the main engine supplied and it was found that the ship would still work.

'Malo' was the ship's dog on board HMS *Borealis* and is seen here getting a survivor's bath after his fur-raising escapades with CW9 Peewit.

"At this time HMS *Astral* came to my assistance and ordered HMS *Elan II* to take me in tow and for me to send all hands not required to work the ship to HMS *Astral*. I had already transferred my three serious casualties to HMS *Greenfly* and I retained my two officers and seven ratings.

"HMS *Elan II* took me in tow with three hawsers stern first because of the pressure on the collision bulkhead. It was found impossible to steer *Borealis* however, so *Elan II* cast off and came alongside with her bow to my stern and was secured. Owing to the rising westerly wind and sea this method was also found to be impracticable and likely to cause too much damage to *Elan II*. In the meantime, HMS *Renee* had arrived to stand by and an attempt was made to tow *Borealis* stern first by *Elan II* while *Renee* made fast forwards and steered her. This method proved highly satisfactory and the three vessels proceeded towards Portsmouth. At about 17.00 [*sic. This was, in fact, nearer to 16.15-16.30 hrs*] however a further enemy dive-bomber attack was made, and with the ship being unmanageable and it being impossible to make any effective defence, I abandoned her with my remaining hands in the only boat that was left and lay off until the bombers had been driven off by our fighters. We then pulled back to the ship with the intention of securing her again as bomb splinters had severed the tow ropes. Unfortunately, we found her listing heavily to port apparently having suffered a further direct hit or near miss which had started her bulkhead. There was the sound of escaping gas which suggested that the hydrogen bottles on her after deck had been hit. I therefore considered it unwise to board the vessel again and we were picked up by the *Renee*."

The final raid of 8 August 1940, and the one that had finished off *Borealis*, was first picked up by radar as an estimated eighteen-plus force of aircraft detected at 15.34 off Le Havre and it was headed, once again, directly towards CW9. However, the slightly deteriorating weather in the English Channel during the mid to late afternoon period had earlier caused a question mark to hang over any further Stuka operations that day. Indeed, at around 14.25 Major Paul-Werner Hozzel had again led his I./St.G 1 off towards CW9 for another attack, this time with twenty-two aircraft, although he aborted the mission when it was found that cloud cover in the target area was too low to press home an attack. Although the day had remained dry and with moderately good visibility, the broken cloud had gathered somewhat to the extent that by 15.00 the Germans were reporting 9/10 cloud cover and with a cloud base down to somewhere between 3,000 to 4,500ft. Hardly optimum conditions in which to conduct dive-bombing operations against a

The pilot and gunner of a St.G.77 Stuka supervise the loading of a 250kg bomb onto the under-fuselage bomb rack.

convoy. In fact, the broken cloud during the first attack of the day had most likely already caused some difficulty in properly identifying the correct target.

That the continuation of the late afternoon operations (which were to be flown by no less than three Stuka Gruppen) had been in some doubt was certainly borne out by Hptm Waldemar Plewig, the gruppen kommandeur of II./St.G 77. Frustrated by the refusal of the Oberbefehlhaber der Luftwaffe to give the green light for the late afternoon attack because of weather conditions encountered during Hozzel's aborted mission, Plewig took up the gruppe's Dornier 17P to have a look for himself over the target area. As an experienced Junkers 87 combat pilot, Plewig was able to make an objective assessment and satisfied himself that even if these were not optimum operating conditions then they were currently quite within operational limits. Not only that, but he could see the convoy and felt that the target – or targets – were clearly recognisable. Returning, he made his report. By early afternoon his attack was given the green light.

As was the case with countless military operations of World War Two, or of any other war for that matter, and including every service of every combatant nation, things did not always go entirely to plan. It only needed one small delay, a simple equipment failure, breakdown of communications or a glitch with the weather to foul things up. And so it was with the final assault against CW9 that day. Already the uncertainty over whether the attack was on or was off had not helped. Doubtless the waiting pilots and aircrew were getting edgy and restless – and for the waiting crews of III./St.G 1 this, for some of them at least, may have been the second operation of the day. Tiredness and nervous exhaustion was an ever present and aggravating factor for combat fliers, and uncertainty just made matters worse.

Waiting with the twenty-two Junkers 87s of III./St. G. 1 for the word to go before Plewig's confirmatory reconnaissance were twenty-eight others from I./St.G. 3 and another thirty-two from both the Stab. and the II Gruppe of St.G. 77 – eighty-two aeroplanes and 164 aircrew in total. And another 328 high explosive bombs destined for CW9. When the word to go finally came, the aircraft of I./St.G. 3 departed from Barly between 15.30 and 15.45 with Major Walter Sigel leading the formation to rendezvous with their escort, the Messerschmitt 110s of II/ZG. 2. The aeroplanes of St.G. 1 and St.G. 77 departed a little later at between 16.08 and 16.20. Plewig of II./St.G. 77 takes up the story:

A formation of Junkers 87s over the French coast.

"Besides the gruppen commanded by Sigel, and another commanded by Hozzel [*sic: Hozzel had in fact led the aborted raid earlier in the afternoon and did not participate in this action*] my gruppe was to assemble over Cherbourg and carry out a large scale attack. My gruppe started as ordered, but noticed that one of the other gruppen was not ready for take-off. Climbing up steadily, we proceeded to the gathering point. As we approached the coast, I realised that the third gruppe was already hanging over the Channel above us, and long before the stated time. Our own fighters must have split up as only a few 109s and 110s were to be seen. The majority of the fighter escort must have already flown to the target area with the gruppe of early starters. Only this could explain why my gruppe, when later approaching the convoy, flew right into the arms of the RAF fighters which had been lured up by the first gruppe; our escort then split up, the first gruppe returning with the escort whilst my far weaker escort had to fight against overwhelming odds."

As we can see, the carefully planned massed-group attack with its fighter umbrella had lost its cohesion long before any ships were sighted. The groups of dive bombers, with their fighter escorts, were now strung out over many miles of the English Channel sky. Almost a full hour had separated the departure of the first and the last Junkers 87s from their French bases. Additionally, the escorting Messerschmitt 109Es had a limited operational endurance, especially over the distance of sea (around sixty miles) that separated the Cherbourg peninsula from the Isle of Wight area. Given that distance of travel, the Messerschmitt 109s' available time to 'loiter' over the target area and protect the dive bombers was severely restricted and there was certainly no margin that would allow them to hang around waiting for straggling groups of their charges to catch up. As it was, and even if things were going to plan, their low-fuel warning lights would already be winking on during their return flights. The Messerschmitt 110s, of course, had a greater range and endurance but their effectiveness against their more agile Spitfire and Hurricane opponents did not always best suit them to this kind of escort operation.

Whether it was the weather, the disorganised start of this particular Stuka operation or the appearance on the scene of considerable numbers of defending RAF fighters it is difficult to say, but the fact of the matter is that the Stuka attacks that day had experienced diminishing returns for the effort expended since the first attack. In addition, by the time the bombers were over the target area during the late afternoon, convoy CW9 had begun to disperse. This, the last attack, was by far the least successful and it also saw the greatest number of Luftwaffe casualties. Moreover, in view of the massed formations of Stukas once again ranged against them, the actual ships of Convoy CW9 and its various survivors and stragglers would this time get off more than lightly. Again, other ships would take the brunt.

As the Stukas approached the Isle of Wight it seems that at least some of the gruppen, if not all of them, were initially attracted by the columns of smoke from the burning ships of the earlier attacks, and especially the blazing hulks of *Empire Crusader*. By now, the rest of the convoy was sailing on and was well past the Isle of Wight and getting towards Weymouth Bay, although some of the vessels had already split away and were going in to Yarmouth Roads at the western end of The Solent. Other ships, though, were in the vicinity of the burning and sinking hulks and were trying to give assistance. HMS *Basset* was already on station, as were other sundry smaller craft including the RAF launches HSL 116 and 121 – still very much afloat and for the moment undamaged, notwithstanding the best efforts earlier in the day of The Needles gun battery. Present too were at least a couple of tugs along with other naval vessels ordered out from Yarmouth Roads to assist. These included HMT *Cape Palliser*, HMS *Wilna* and HMS *Rion*. Adding to this varied collection of shipping, HMS *Borealis* was still just afloat and limping along in the general vicinity with the *Elan II* and *Renee* still in close attendance.

It was this group of shipping that the Stukas chose to attack and, in so doing, they had struck the final blow to *Borealis*. Again, we return to Arthur Hague's much harassed crew who were all now aboard the *Renee* – including the little dog, Malo. To say that they were safely aboard might be overstating the case given the ongoing attentions of the Luftwaffe, but as they stood on the deck of *Renee* the crew of *Borealis* watched as her list to port steadily worsened and she gradually sank lower into the water. Finally, the end came at about 17.20 as she slid beneath the waves, bow first. As she went, the White Ensign lashed up by Hague still flew proudly from the rigging. Suddenly, as the *Borealis* slipped under the water, the master of *Renee* bellowed loudly from the bridge to one of his crew: "Sailor! Take off your hat, man.

After the first attack Lt Arthur Hague had disembarked all non-essential men from HMS *Borealis* leaving just a skeleton crew on board. They are pictured here just prior to abandoning *Borealis* before she sank.

Show a mark of respect for one of His Majesty's ships." Corporal Will, erstwhile NCO in charge of *Borealis's* balloon, was less concerned about His Majesty's ship than he was about his uniform tunic still hanging in his quarters on board her. In its breast pocket sat thirty shillings and his wrist watch. Will reasoned that His Majesty had many more ships....whereas he had only thirty shillings and one watch.

Author's note: HMS *Borealis* had sunk at a position 15 miles south east of The Needles, and 5.5 miles south of St Catherine's Point at 50° 29.050' north, 001° 42.166' west.

Of the *Borealis* crew, Arthur Hague and two of his men would be recognised for their meritorious service that day. In addition to Hague, Second Hand Cyril White and Engineman Joseph Dell Taylor (both of the Royal Naval Patrol Service) were rewarded with Mention in Dispatches.

Five minutes before *Borealis* had finally gone to her watery grave, the crew of the Bembridge lifeboat, *Jesse Lumb*, were called out at 17.15 to go to the aid of an aircraft down "10 miles SSW from Bembridge Point". Quite which aircraft this might have been it

No.

9ᵗʰ December 1940

This is to Certify that _Arthur HAGUE_
has served as _Lieutenant R.N.R._ in
H.M.S. BOREALIS under my command, from the 1ˢᵗ day
of _August_ 1940, to the 8ᵗʰ day of _August_ 1940, during which
period he has conducted himself* _Entirely to my satisfaction._
He was in Command of H.M.S. Borealis which
was sunk by enemy action on its second voyage.
During these actions and the attempted salvage
of the vessel he conducted himself most
creditably and was Mentioned in Despatches.

arth M Dukes.   Commander.
                              (Captain) Senior Officer
                              (H.M.S.
                    * Here the Captain is to insert in his own handwriting the conduct of the Officer   **S. 450**
                    Channel mobile Balloon Barrage.

The message from Lt Hague's commanding officer with notification to C-in-C Portsmouth of Hague's valiant performance.

is impossible to say. There were certainly plenty to choose from. However, *Jesse Lumb* was finally launched at 17.45 and went to the position given. Here, an RAF Blackburn Roc aeroplane circled over the lifeboat, went off, returned and repeated the operation to show the direction she should take. There was no sign of any aeroplane in the water, but *Jesse Lumb* found instead the RAF's HSL 116, disabled and flying a distress signal. During the last of the Stuka attacks she had been raked with machine-gun fire, her relatively flimsy construction offering little or no protection to the men on board. Sadly, one had been killed and another badly wounded although she was unable to make her way ashore for aid as a rope amongst the floating debris and wreckage of Peewit had fouled her propeller.

Consequently, the lifeboat towed HSL 116 to port, putting the wounded man, Sgt Wilfred Vosper, ashore for admission to Haslar hospital. They also took ashore the body of the seventeen-year-old wireless telegraphist, AC1 Raymond Wheeler. A local boy from Southampton, Wheeler's praises were later sung in the *Southampton Daily Echo* of 12 August 1940.

The newspaper described how Raymond, suffering terribly from seasickness, had remained at his post in the small wireless cabin of HSL 116 sending messages as the launch sped to the aid of a downed German airman. So ill did Wheeler become that another crew member had to sit beside him to support the wireless operator as he tapped away at his signalling key. As they made towards the reported position of the enemy flier the RAF craft was machine-gunned, killing the young signaller instantly while he sat at his post.

Despite the dive-bombing attacks on the disparate grouping of ships that the Luftwaffe had again mistaken for CW9, and the alarming and deadly experiences still being lived through by those on board the various vessels, the Stukas and their escorts were far from having it their own way. Plewig again takes up the story:

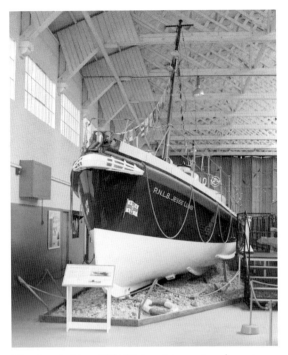

The Bembridge RNLI lifeboat *Jesse Lumb* was launched during the late afternoon to go to the assistance of an aircraft down off the Isle of Wight. Today, she is preserved at the Imperial War Museum, Duxford.

"Despite our predicament with the fighter escort, there was no turning back and I ordered the three staffeln of II Gruppe to attack. I, along with the reinforced Stabs Kette, waited until the end. As we could see more and more enemy fighters appearing above us, I decided not to climb up to the usual altitude and started the attack instead from about 12,000ft. After the three staffeln had attacked their targets, I chose mine and went into a dive and released my bombs from about 1,800ft. The Spitfires and Hurricanes dived with us but we were able to observe some near misses on the ships.

"Now, I attempted to throw off my adversaries by irregular flying at sea level – we always flew that way as it gave fighters less of a chance to hit us. However, during the descent, I was repeatedly shot at. My gunner, Fw Schauer, fired back until he was hit. I think he was hit in the neck and the thigh, because I noticed a jet of blood. In the meantime, I was hit in the right arm and right calf and had to fly with my left hand. At the same time, the oxygen supply was hit and a box of ammunition was struck by tracer bullets. When the plane started to show signs of burning on the right side, I decided to bale out. My gunner did not reply over the intercom, and I could see him hanging lifelessly in his harness. As he did not react to my orders to throw off the canopy, and I had levelled off above the water and the plane was well alight, I decided to jump at the last moment. I had failed in my efforts to throw out the gunner – he was certainly dead and I just hoped that his body might be washed up somewhere. So, I said goodbye to my companion and friend, Kurt Schauer."

At 16.15 hours, and at the same time that *Borealis* was on the receiving end of her further unwelcome attention, HMS *Wilna* was also coming under Stuka attack. In fact, it is clear that *Wilna*, along with HMS *Rion*, (both anti-submarine yachts) and the anti-submarine trawlers HMS *Cape Palliser, Kingston Chrysoberyl, Kingston Olivine* and *Stella Capella* – in company with the *Borealis, Elan II* and *Astral* – were the group of ships that the attacking Stukas had found and targeted. The ships of CW9, meanwhile, steamed safely off to the west and far out of harms way, whilst six little Royal Navy ships that had sailed out to help them became the second group of unwitting decoys on 8 August. From HMS *Wilna*, Commander A D W Sumpter reported the events of that day to the commander-in-chief, Portsmouth:

AC1 Raymond Wheeler, the wireless operator aboard HSL 116.

"At 16.15 on 8 August 1940 *Wilna* was in approx position 160° St Catherine's Point, steering 045° at 14 knots. At this moment a large number of aircraft, estimated at sixty to eighty, were observed southward at a great height, perhaps 15,000ft. In a diesel ship at full speed it is impossible to hear aircraft at a distance. The alarm was at once sounded and I stepped into the chart house for my telescope. Before I could use it, however, I saw three dive bombers attacking from vertically overhead, and at too great an elevation for my Lewis gun to bear. No R/T signal was made as the first salvo put the wireless out of action. Before the enemy released their bombs I ordered 'Lie Down' and did so immediately before each attack. Six attacks were made in ten or twelve minutes, each being made by three Ju 87s and each machine dropping a cluster of five bombs. These burst on the surface of the water. Some of these machines, but not all, fired on *Wilna* with machine guns. All of the salvoes of bombs were very close, I should describe them all as 'inners' but fortunately there were no 'bulls'.

"The groups of three all dived vertically from a great height and appeared to flatten-out at about 500ft; fire was opened on each group after they had flattened out with the Lewis gun, *Wilna's* sole anti-aircraft armament, and it is possible that a couple were hit. One round of four-inch shrapnel was also fired.

"It was not possible to take avoiding action beyond going at full speed as the electric steering gear was deranged by the first salvo and the hand gear was rather difficult to engage. The course therefore remained at approximately 045°.

"After about ten minutes British Hurricanes were seen to be engaging the

HMS *Kingston Chrysoberyl* was one of the group of Royal Navy vessels damaged in the final Stuka assault of the day.

enemy and the bombing ceased. Three of my men were killed, one of them inside a half-inch thick steel shelter on the bridge that was penetrated by splinters. The other two were on the port side, aft, below the promenade deck. I cannot say whether these two were lying down or not. Eleven were wounded in varying degrees. Fortunately, just before being ordered to sea I had landed liberty men at Seaview, so that the 1st lieut, chief engineer and seven of the ship's company were out of the ship, leaving a total of thirty on board. A greater number on board would have made no difference, except that there would have been more casualties. It was also a comfort, on our return to St Helen's, to have some fresh and unshaken hands to secure ropes etc.

"Two lessons were firmly impressed on me:

1) At the moment bombs are falling to lie as flat as possible near the midship line.

2) To reduce glass to a minimum. This ship was one mass of broken glass everywhere.

It is hard to speak highly enough of the conduct of my ship's company; nearly all of them fishermen or yachting hands. Though we were quite helpless to ward off these alarming attacks, and this ship being by no means constructed to withstand such treatment, there was not the slightest sign of any 'wind up' and some might have thought they had been used to that kind of thing all their lives. None of the wounded made any complaint and all were most patient. Leading Seaman Stuttle, though wounded early in the attack, was very smart each time in jumping up and firing the Lewis gun after the bombers had straightened out. Lieuts Behennah and Dimmick RNVR, and the boatswain, Little, all of them wounded slightly, were indefatigable in doing all in their power for the badly wounded men on our way back, with no thought for themselves. A fire in the wood store, forward, caused me some anxiety as it was at no great distance from the depth charge for the demolition of ASDIC if necessary. No pump would work and the fire extinguishers had all been deranged by shock and the smoke was too thick for men to remain below for more than a minute or so. However, the pistol of the depth charge was finally removed and our fire was extinguished by hoses from an examination vessel at St Helen's.

"Damage to the ship cannot at present be stated, she is riddled with splinter holes above the water line but appears to have suffered no structural defects.

I have the honour to be, Sir,
Your obedient servant,
A D W Sumpter (Commander)"

(Author's note: Although *Wilna* survived this ordeal she was lost at Portsmouth on 24 March 1941, when she finally succumbed to another air attack.)

As she limped back to St Helen's Road, the *Wilna* passed the floating wreckage from earlier attacks, including an empty lifeboat with its sides bullet-holed and splintered and the complete wheelhouse of a Dutch vessel with its ship's bell still hanging inside. The muffled sound of its occasional ring while it floated by was like some ghostly tolling for the ships and lives already lost that day.

In all, *Wilna* had evidently been singled out by virtually one fifth of the entire attacking force of Stukas. The ship had not, in any way, been part of CW9 and her significance (or that of the others with her) as a naval vessel hardly warranted such comprehensive attention from the dive bombers. It was attention that had cost the lives of Quartermaster Edgar Brown, Able Seaman Alfred Fullick and carpenter, Samuel Keat. In addition, eleven more wounded men were admitted to Haslar hospital which was now rapidly filling up with casualties from the day's action; RAF and German aircrew, an RAF marine craftsman, merchant seamen of various nationalities and an increasing number of British sailors.

Again, in this action, we have shining examples of Royal Navy seamen displaying exemplary courage in the execution of their duties. And again, we have wounded men staying at their stations to fight, or assisting others perhaps more badly wounded than they. In respect of *Wilna*, however, we also have formal recognition of that gallantry and the devotion to duty of the Lewis anti-aircraft gunner, Leading Seaman George Alexander Stuttle, P/JX 129588, who received a Mention in Dispatches for his bravery in sticking at his post and defending the ship despite his grievous wounds. The story on board *Rion*, *Kingston Chrysoberyl*, *Kingston Olivine*, *Stella Capella* and *Cape Palliser* was much the same.

The captain of HMT *Cape Palliser*, Lieut Dennis C Hayes, also compiled a comprehensive report in which he described how "three formations" of Stukas dived on the little group of ships, with the attack on *Cape Palliser* coming from the third formation. Quite likely this had been the group of Stukas led by Waldemar Plewig. However, and like all of the vessels in this group, *Cape Palliser* was not well equipped to defend herself against air attack with her single four inch gun and two Lewis guns. Once again, the gunners of the latter gave a good account of themselves – although this time with fatal results for both:

"Lieut McEwan was in charge of the Lewis guns and continued to keep them firing until two of the Lewis gunners were killed and one badly wounded. We were only able to get off one round of four-inch when all of the gun's crew, except one, were badly wounded. Everyone stuck to their guns magnificently and continued to fight until they were killed or wounded."

In all, around fifteen salvoes were aimed at *Cape Palliser*. Of these fifteen or so attacks some of the bombs fell within fifteen yards of the ship but the majority dropped between twenty-five to thirty yards away. Hayes also talks of some bombs being dropped "....as far as half a mile away once British fighter aircraft had appeared on the scene", thereby implying that the attackers had ditched their bombs and fled. Whilst this is entirely possible it might also have been because so many aircraft were attempting to dive on so few targets. With the sky so crowded, and Stukas almost literally queuing up to attack, it may have become clear to some of the dive-bomber pilots that the limited target opportunities presented by the little group of ships, and the increasing menace of defending RAF fighters, meant that the only real option was to dump their bombs and head for home. After all, trying to avoid Spitfires or Hurricanes with the weight of a full bomb load was not the best option for survival. At the end of the attack the *Cape Palliser* was badly damaged, the onslaught leaving Seaman Isaac C Bowles and Engineman Fred Pile killed. Of the seven crew members left wounded, Seaman (Cook) Jeffery W Hinton died in Haslar hospital the next day. The officer in charge of *Cape Palliser's* Lewis gun crews, Temporary Lieut Ronald McEwan, was Mentioned in Dispatches for his gallant action.

On the *Rion*, the crew found they were entirely defenceless when the sole Lewis gun jammed before even a single round could be fired. Drawing back the cocking handle the gunner discovered that the full withdrawal could not be made and he also found that he was gazing impotently up at a Stuka which drew closer and got bigger by the second. Losing his battle with the recalcitrant cocking lever, the seaman flung himself to the deck as five bombs crashed into the sea around him while the departing Junkers raked the ship from stem to stern with machine-gun fire. Two ratings were injured by gunfire, but during that first attack the captain, Commander J K B Birch, was also seriously wounded as he stood on his bridge. Unfortunately he succumbed to his injuries in Haslar hospital on 14 August 1940. Birch, aged fifty-nine, was no stranger to war at sea and had served on board HMS *Duke of Edinburgh* at the Battle of Jutland in 1916.

The *Rion*, meanwhile, was a mess. All her windows were gone, the anti-submarine recorder and wireless were wrecked, the dinghy was lost and both launches were badly shot-up and holed. Bullets had punctured the funnel, split open a water tank and severed air lines. More seriously, bomb shrapnel had split open the casing of a depth charge and damaged one of the others. The consequences had the explosive fillings detonated would have been disastrous; the small ship would have simply been blown to smithereens. There could have been no survivors from such a blast. It was just one of many lucky escapes that day.

In the aftermath of the attack, it fell to Flag Officer Humber, under whose command *Cape Palliser* fell, to write a report on the inadequacies of that ship's anti-aircraft defences. The rear admiral stated, *inter alia*, that:

> "It appears from information received from the skipper of HM anti-submarine trawler *Cape Palliser* that the casualties which occurred among the gun crew on 8 August 1940 were caused by a lack of proper understanding of the correct action to take with regard to the L/A guns in the case of a vessel being attacked by aircraft....

> "....It does not appear that firing at an aircraft serves any useful purpose from these guns, [*four-inch guns*] and to have the gun crews closed up around the gun instead of lying flat under the gun platform exposes the men needlessly to danger."

The crew around *Cape Palliser's* four-inch gun certainly had no surrounding protection and both the guns and the men were entirely exposed. Furthermore, firing their low-elevation gun against the attacking Stukas was utterly futile in any case. The ammunition in use was a shrapnel shell and had only been fitted with impact as opposed to proximity fuses. It would have needed a direct hit on one of the low-flying and departing Stukas to have had even the remotest hope of being effective, and that had to be more than a million-to-one chance. When it came, the reply from the director of training & staff (duties division) was hardly helpful and certainly rather unsympathetic to the rear admiral's case:

"The correct policy is for L/A gun crews to lie down in the event of <u>high-level</u> bombing attacks, against which their guns are useless, but to fight with all their guns to the best of their ability against aircraft carrying out any form of <u>low-flying</u> attacks.
By Command of Their Lordships."

Flag Officer Humber could have been excused if he found the reply slightly ambiguous if not a little insulting. Was this dive-bombing attack a "high-level bombing attack"? Even if it was, then surely the strafing attacks came into the category of "low-flying attacks"? Either way, and whether he found it ambiguous or not, the exhortation that the gun crews of *Cape Palliser* should "fight to the best of their ability" was both insensitive and patronising given what they had so recently endured and how magnificently they had all performed.

Whilst the absence of any form of armour plating for the gunners on *Cape Palliser* and other RN ships was cause for concern, so was the perceived existence of under-belly armour plating to Spitfires to one gunner of I/St.G 3 after this particular attack. In the ULTRA intercepts for 19 August is to be found the following: "On 8 August, in a battle with Spitfires five kilometres south of the Isle of Wight, he noticed his machine-gun bursts glancing off the underneath of the Spitfire's cockpits. It was to be presumed that the Spitfires had recently been armoured in that part."

Of course, the unknown Luftwaffe airman's perception was a little like his shooting and rather wide of the mark. No such armour had been or ever was fitted, and what he had observed must have been either just a fluke or a trick of the light. On the other hand, one gunner from Stab.II/St.G 77 on that operation (Uffz Karl Witton) had claimed a 'confirmed' Hurricane destroyed over the English Channel. Maybe our frustrated gunner from St.G 3 had heard about his comrade's success and was anxious to explain why *his* hits had not met with the same success?

The late afternoon attack by the Stukas that had been directed against the ships of Convoy CW9 had been an abject failure. Not a single ship of the convoy had been hit, nor had the attackers come anywhere near them. Further, the collection of Royal Navy vessels and the RAF launch that were attacked were somewhat insignificant in the grand scheme of things. Whilst all were damaged, and fatalities and casualties had been sustained, none were sunk with the exception of the already crippled *Borealis*. The vessels targeted were hardly ships of the line, and really not desperately important within the Royal Navy's Home Fleet. When set against the losses sustained by the attacking force, and even taking into account the losses to the RAF's defending fighters, the effort was certainly disproportionate to the results obtained.

Well over 100 Stukas (in three raids) and scores of escort fighters had been pitched into this last battle of the day. The cost to the Luftwaffe in aircraft and crews during that attack was very heavy with twenty-three of their airmen killed. In hindsight, the decision by Paul-Werner Hozzel to abort his earlier attack, and the subsequent refusal of high command initially to sanction any others, had been the right calls.

Early that evening, Plt Off Puckle finally got ashore at Portsmouth after his gruelling stint along the English Channel in charge of the mobile balloon barrage and at 19.16 he telephoned his parent unit at Sheerness asking to speak to his CO. Informed that Sqn Ldr

Berryman was waiting for him at Falmouth, Puckle finally got through to Berryman at the King's Hotel, to give him the news; all the balloons had been shot down and only two of the barrage ships were serviceable. At once, Berryman set off to collect his survivors. It must have been a depressing train journey for him as he travelled back to Portsmouth where he found the night sky flecked with anti-aircraft bursts and stabbing searchlights.

Puma versus Peewit

B Y LATE afternoon the Hurricane pilots of 43 Squadron must have been frustrated by the lack of any call to action. Since early that morning they had seen their colleagues on 145 and 601 Squadron come and go to do battle with the Luftwaffe. Worse, an 'imported' Hurricane unit from RAF Northolt, 257 Squadron, had had *their* share of the action also! The famous fighting cock's squadron was having to live by its motto *'Gloria Finis'*….. glory in the end. And in the end, that day, they would surely have their glory.

When an incoming raid was again plotted off Le Havre at 15.34 it was clear that, once more, the Luftwaffe's intentions were directed towards CW9 Peewit. Since the various RAF fighter squadrons had departed home after the lunch time engagement the convoy had been unprotected by air cover and the 11 Group controllers sought immediately to rectify that by sending off at 15.40 the Hurricanes of 43 Squadron from Tangmere and Spitfires of 152 Squadron from Warmwell with orders for 43 to proceed at once to Convoy Peewit with 152 headed for St Alban's Head and Weymouth Bay. As the threat grew more immediate, so the controller bolstered his forces over Peewit by sending off 145 Squadron for its third operational sortie that day at 16.00 and with 238 Squadron again being called on at 16.20 – the former being sent to their by now familiar battleground off the Isle of Wight and 238 Squadron following 152 Squadron down into Weymouth Bay. Doubtless the controller didn't want to be caught out again, being so tardy in getting his defences in place over the convoy and on this occasion he was a little more timely. This time, the Stukas were actually caught over the ships – even though they were not actually the ships of CW9 Peewit!

In Waldemar Plewig's account of the dive onto his target he speaks of the RAF fighters diving with him, and that is indeed what the Hurricanes of 43 and 145 Squadron succeeded in doing. Not quite early enough on the scene to prevent at least the majority of Stukas diving to attack, the massed Hurricanes certainly managed to wreak some havoc as they got in amongst the enemy aircraft. Plt Off Peter Parrott was again in action, and this time he managed to get a positively confirmed victory over one of the Junkers 87s:

"The best strategy was to hit them in the dive or as they pulled out. I got one from the beam as it recovered from dropping its bombs. I followed it as it flew on towards the Isle of Wight after pulling out of its attack. We were very close to the sea, about 100ft or so, and its only evasive action apart from flying low was to make a series of gentle turns each way."

This was the Junkers 87 Stuka of 4./StG 77 shot down by Plt Off Peter Parrot during the last air attack of the day that had been directed at CW9 Peewit. It became the first Ju 87 captured relatively intact in the British Isles. Its pilot, Uffz Pittroff, was captured unhurt but its gunner, Uffz Schubert, had been shot dead although investigators found only about eight bullet strikes in the aircraft. One of those had severed a petrol lead and thus disabled the Stuka's engine.

Parrott managed to get in a short burst of fire which severed the aircraft's fuel lines and killed outright its rear gunner, Uffz Schubert. With the damage he had sustained to his aeroplane there was no chance that Uffz Pittroff would be able to make the return flight across sixty miles of English Channel and he had no choice but to put down on land. Wobbling on past the St Lawrence hospital the Stuka pitched down in a field by Orchard Bay, bounced across a small depression and careered into the next field where it finally rolled to a halt in the far hedge. Of all the enemy aircraft shot down in operations against CW9 Peewit that day this was the only one to fall on land and before it had finished its final approach, local lad, Alan Twigg decided he would lend Plt Off Parrott a helping hand. Grabbing his 'Daisy' air rifle he took a pot-shot at the Stuka as it went overhead, only to be admonished for his apparently extreme foolhardiness: "What if you'd hit one of its bombs?" shouted one of his elders and betters "…you'd have blown us all to kingdom come!" In fact, the Stuka had no bombs by this stage and even in the somewhat unlikely event that one of Alan's low-velocity .22 lead pellets had 'pinged' off a bomb, if it had had one, then the most dramatic effect it would have had would have been to assuage young master Twigg's hostility for the German raider. Such was the impetuosity of youth!

(Author's note: Despite Parrott's belief that he had attacked Junkers 87 after it had dropped its bombs, the pilot was still carrying a single 250kg bomb and four 50kg bombs when he crashed. These are mentioned in the RAF air intelligence report concerning the aircraft.)

Gradually, the targets became fewer for 145 Squadron as the fighting spread out like the ripples on a pond and then dissipated as the enemy aircraft finally withdrew southwards and the defending RAF fighters returned home out of ammunition. One of the pilots with 145 Squadron that day was Fg Off A Ostowicz, a twenty-nine-year-old Pole. He reported:

"I attacked an Me 109 and gave him a burst at a long range of 300 yards. I had hardly started firing when black smoke belched out and he shot straight into the sea. My very first bullets must have got him for I hardly pressed the button for even a full second. Later I returned to the convoy but the fight had moved on and I was not able to find any more aircraft so, after searching, I returned to base at about 16.30 hours."

Nineteen-year-old Schubert was buried at Ventnor on the Isle of Wight on 13 August 1940 as another battle raged overhead. His body has since been moved to the German Military Cemetery at Cannock Chase in Staffordshire.

From the sky being full, Antoni Ostowicz found he was all but alone in the space of just one or two minutes. Sadly, he was to lose his life in another big battle over this same patch of sea just three days later. No trace of his body was ever found.

Whilst we have already dealt with Waldemar Plewig's experiences that day, we also have a contemporary account given in a German radio broadcast from one of the participating Stuka crewmen who flew in this attack with II./St.G 77. Clearly, it was made with the German public and propaganda in mind but it provides an interesting insight and some 'balance' to Flt Lt Boyd's radio broadcast for the BBC:

"At the briefing we were told that our target was a British convoy trying to force the Channel route. We were given a code name for our attack; 'Puma'. We had no proper location and so we had to fly our mission most accurately by compass. Our wing leader had to give each squadron commander short and accurate instructions from what he knew, then everyone got dressed. The most important piece of clothing is the life jacket. Then, shortly before 16.00 [sic] the whole group is ready, the first formation to take off being our commander's formation. A small signal lamp flashes and like a flock of large birds the squadrons rose up one after another into the sky. We all circle our base and collect information, then head off towards the Channel battleground. After only a few minutes we are at the coast. Below us, as far as the eye can see, is the Channel. Once it was the busiest shipping lane in the world. Now it is the largest ships' graveyard.

"Water – nothing but water below us. We cannot see the coast or the enemy ships. Our thoughts are with our engines, those reliable humming helpers in our operation. Our eyes go from instrument to instrument, checking; water cooling, tachometer, pressure gauge – all of them are regularly checked. If our engine gives up there is only one thing for us and that is 'the ditch'. The Channel is large and wide and on the other side is the enemy island.

There, carefully, one would like to say shyly, there is a light strip emerging from the blue-green water. At first you can hardly make it out. The English south coast, and the white cliffs of the steep shore. A few hundred metres above us fly some squadrons of fighters – Me 109s and the long-range destroyer Me 110s as protection for us. Half-right in front of us at about 3,000 to 4,000 metres the first air battle has already begun. You can hardly tell friend from enemy. We can only see small silver specks circling. Now we must be especially alert. The coast is getting nearer, to the left, below us, the Isle of Wight and we already see ten or twelve ships. They, as they in turn spot us, try somehow to avoid our attacks by zig-zagging. We fly steadily eastwards towards them. Suddenly we hear through our R/T: 'Number four aircraft has crash-landed!' One of our 4th Staffel machines has had to go down into the water. His engine must have failed. We hope everything goes well for them as we press on.

"'Puma one – to all Pumas – Puma attack!' We are above the convoy, it all seems to be small ships, coasters. Our 1 Staffel has already started to attack. Now the formations pull apart. Each one of them chooses a ship that has not yet been hit by one of the other squadrons. Our Staffelkapitän's formation starts its attack dives near to the coast. But what is this? I cannot believe my eyes. There is a third formation which attacks with us in a dive from the left. At the same instant I hear 'Puma – alert. Enemy fighters diving from above!' When we are diving and banking vertically the English fighters have virtually no chance to shoot our Stukas so they always try to intercept us earlier or catch us later on when we have pulled out of our dives. On account of them being so much faster than us we always form up for mutual protection.

"That's for later. Right now I select my formation's target which is the most southerly ship of the convoy. Before I commence my dive I make sure by asking my radio operator if everything is clear behind us. I receive the reply 'All clear!' Then we dive down without braking [i.e. they did not deploy their dive brakes] as in our perilous position we need speed to get back into our unit formation again. My bombs land close alongside the ship, my left-hand *Kettenhund* aircraft also scores a near miss by a very near margin, but the third aircraft of the formation hits the ship square amidships with his bombs. Within seconds a huge flame shoots up from the ship and a large cloud of smoke bellows out of her insides. As we fly away, we can see her listing badly and on fire.

"Now the English defenders are right on top of us! Spitfires and Hurricanes. From a distance you cannot distinguish these from our own Me 109s. Above the Isle of Wight it makes for a terrible battle. About sixty aircraft of all makes, German and English, all fighting for their very lives. Some of the English draw back towards the coast of England, on the left of me an Me 109 drops into the sea. The pilot is able to get out and slowly he guides his parachute towards the water. Another aircraft, the make I cannot see clearly, circles in flames like a bonfire above us. Then it explodes and falls in many small pieces. You can only recognise the engine compartment.

"When we all collect towards the south the English take us on. Only weaving helps you if you want to escape the eight machine guns of the English fighters. Our radio operators shoot whenever they can get their guns to bear. Again and again the English attack from astern. Again and again I feel the bullets striking my aircraft but I don't think the engine has been hit. The motor is quiet and smooth. The closer we get to the centre of the English Channel the fewer English aircraft attack us. Our squadrons find each other bit by bit and we form up. To the left of us flies our 4th Staffel. One of the planes has a smoke trail behind it. The pilot gives the message: 'Aircraft damaged, going into the water!' At that moment a Spitfire [sic] comes from ahead, shoots, and down into the water the damaged Stuka goes. But the Englishman does not live long to enjoy his cheap victory and glory, as he veers away after his attack he gets hit by an Me 109 and dives vertically into the sea.

"After thirty minutes flying, we at last see the coast of Normandy. We all sigh with relief. My formation comrades approach to the side of the aircraft, nod and smile. Everything in our squadron seems to be all right. We land at our base. Unbelievably all of the aircraft from our staffel have returned. Some have up to forty bullet holes in their fuselages and wings, but all land safely despite this. Later, we heard that our commander, Major Plewig, is missing. Also, a hauptmannn and unteroffizier as well. We cannot believe it. Nobody saw the CO ditch."

In its content, this broadcast was surprisingly frank and informative and of particular interest is the comment that the formation had "no proper location" for the target ships. As we now know, this lack of clarity evidently caused the actual convoy to be missed. As for the code name 'Puma', we cannot be certain that this was actually a code name used during that operation or if it was simply made up for the purposes of the broadcast.

Apart from 145 Squadron, others were obviously also mixed up in the fierce battle

Squadron Leader John Badger led 43 Squadron and their Hurricanes into battle off the Isle of Wight during the late afternoon action. Here, he is pictured as an officer cadet having just been awarded the Cranwell Sword of Honour. Badger was shot down and grievously wounded on 30 August 1940 but did not succumb to his injuries for ten months when he died in the RAF Hospital at Halton on 30 June 1941.

that the squadron had fought with the Junkers 87s and their escorts. For 43 Squadron this was the first time they had gone into action that day and its pilots had an exhausting and eventful time. The squadron had been led by its CO, Sqn Ldr J V C 'Tubby' Badger. As he took his men in to attack a formation of Me 109s, four of them detached themselves from the main group and came towards the Hurricanes as Badger turned to attack. As he did so, he saw Sgt H J L 'Jim' Hallowes send one of the

Sgt Jim Hallowes was another of the Hurricane pilots of 43 Squadron in the same action off the Isle of Wight.

Messerschmitts down in flames but then immediately Badger suffered a serious problem as the oxygen regulator controls suddenly broke away from his instrument panel. As the regulator fell away so a blast of oxygen caused dirt, dust and sand to fill the air around him – blown up from the floor and every nook and cranny of the cockpit. Despite this, he managed to put in a claim for one Me 109 definitely destroyed before heading back to Tangmere.

His other pilots had mixed fortunes too and Sgt Hallowes also watched a Hurricane going down in a spin – its pilot baling out just before the aircraft hit the sea. This was not before Hallowes had climbed up to re-join what he took to be the rest of his squadron, and only after he had tagged along did he spot the distinctive tail plane struts and twin radiators of Messerschmitt 109s!

The Hurricane pilot Hallowes had seen baling out was most likely either Plt Off J R S Oelofse or Plt Off J Cruttenden, both of 43 Squadron, and both of whom had failed to

Plt Off John Cruttenden who was shot down into the sea south of the Isle of Wight.

return from this combat sortie. South African Johannes Oelofse's body was eventually recovered from the sea and he was laid to rest in St Andrew's churchyard close by RAF Tangmere by his fellow officers. The sea, however, did not deliver up the body of twenty-year-old John Cruttenden and along with the other RAF pilots who simply vanished that day, his name was recorded on the RAF memorial at Runnymede for those of the commonwealth air forces who have no known grave.

Although many of the other 43 Squadron pilots had got caught up amongst the Me 109 escort, Flt Lt T F D 'Tom' Morgan, leading Blue Section, found himself immediately into the Ju 87 dive bombers. With him was Sgt C A L Hurry (Blue 2) and Plt Off H C Upton (Blue 3). Engaging the rearmost Stuka in an echelon formation of five he fired short bursts of between two to five seconds whereupon the enemy machine immediately caught fire and dived into the sea. Morgan then tackled the next Ju 87 which turned over emitting black smoke after a short burst before he then turned his attention on the remaining three Stukas. With Blue 2 and Blue 3 he moved in to attack, but the escorting force of JG 27's Me 109s had different ideas.

Suddenly, each pilot in Blue Section was fighting the Messerschmitts, with Morgan claiming to have sent one of the enemy fighters into the water. During the dogfight, however, Morgan was attacked by a Hurricane although he could not identify whose it was. Plt Off

Another casualty of the 'Fighting Cocks' squadron was South African Plt Off Johannes Oelofse shot down over the sea. His body was washed ashore at Worthing in September.

Upton, after claiming to have shot two Junkers 87s in the sea, and with another probably downed, found that his engine had been hit by either return fire from the Stukas or by the intervening Messerschmitts and was obliged to make a forced landing, unhurt, at Ford Farm, Whitwell, on the Isle of Wight in Hurricane P3267. Sgt Hurry, too, had his Hurricane hit and damaged and beat a retreat back to Tangmere with hits in P3466. In all probability his attacker could well have been Lt Helmut Strobl of 5./JG 27 who was certainly involved in that same combat with 43 Squadron and who claimed hits on at least three Hurricanes.

In an odd twist of fate it would be Alex Hurry who would shoot Strobl down over Appledore in Kent, on 5 September 1940 – the young Luftwaffe pilot remaining missing until his discovery, entombed in his Messerschmitt, far beneath Romney Marsh exactly forty-six years later. Writing to his family on 10 August about the action on 8 August, Strobl told how he had added to his score of aircraft downed and went on to add: "…we only fly when there are ships on the water!"

It hadn't only been Morgan, either, who had been attacked by a mystery Hurricane, because when the pilots were able to compare experiences back home at Tangmere that evening, Sgt Hallowes revealed that he too had been set upon by a Hurricane. Not only that,

Flt Lt Tom Morgan of 43 Squadron.

Plt Off Hamilton Upton, another 43 Squadron pilot.

but Sgt F R Carey had made the same error as Hallowes by mistakenly trying to join up with a formation of Me 109s quite believing them to be his own squadron. It all went to illustrate just how easy it was to make mistakes in the highly confused and stressful game that was air fighting. Those mistakes could sometimes be fatal. Frank Carey, however, like all of the others on 43 Squadron, had had some other worrisome moments in that particular battle:

"When we were over the convoy off the Isle of Wight we came across a most formidable and orderly array of enemy aircraft that had arrived to interfere with things. First of all, at the top level (around 15-20,000ft) came formations of Me 110s executing roughly oval patrol flights and eventually stretching from the French coast to the Isle of Wight. About 5,000ft below them, squadrons of Me 109s came out taking up station at intervals and also stretching right across the Channel. Then underneath this 'umbrella' came a sizeable force of Ju 87s. We did nothing about the fighters to start with, except that with my section of three above the rest of the convoy patrol I climbed up to gain height. When the 87s appeared on the scene, those in the squadron lower down went into attack them while I was trying to keep the 109s from interfering. This I only managed with partial success, but in the fight that followed I lost contact with my other two aircraft.

"On my own, I then spotted a vic formation which I took at first to be our squadron and went off to join them but found that they were Me 109s. On discovering my mistake I was happy to note that I had not been seen by them and I continued until I had got

behind one of the outside members of the Me 109 formation. I had just settled down to fire at this aircraft, with some success as bits started to fly off it, when a very large explosion nearly blew me upside down. A Messerschmitt 110 had seen what was happening and had come down and was sitting about thirty yards behind my tail and his explosive 20mm shots had blown up all the ammunition in my port wing leaving a hole big enough for a man to crawl through. By the time I had righted the aircraft, all of the 109s had disappeared, and so I laboriously climbed back up to get back over the convoy again when I was once more jumped by some Me 110s. This time they blew off one elevator and the rudder and the Hurricane did a half 'bunt' before I had collected my senses. I had also been hit in the arm on the first

Sgt Frank Carey (right) was wounded and had his Hurricane badly damaged in the combat but made it back to Tangmere where he was promptly shot at by the anti-aircraft defences! On the left, playing his guitar, is Plt Off Tony Woods-Scawen who was also hit and wounded in the same engagement. He also made it back home to Tangmere.

occasion and what with that and only having about three quarters of an aircraft to control, I thought discretion to be the better part of valour and slowly brought the remains back to Tangmere. As if I hadn't had enough, the Tangmere ack-ack guns opened up on me as I entered the circuit – I suppose my silhouette must have looked a bit odd. Fortunately they didn't hit me."

Despite the battering Carey and his Hurricane (P3202) had taken, it was within the capabilities of Flt Lt Bill Sharman, 43 Squadron's engineering officer, to have the machine repaired on the unit. By 12 August it was back flying on an air test. Carey himself was also sufficiently repaired by that date to be back in action.

As with all squadrons involved that day, over claiming was clearly a feature of the battle. However, with over 100 German aircraft mixing it with so many Hurricanes it is hardly surprising. Very often, more than one pilot was shooting at the same aircraft – even if not always at the same time. If an aircraft was hit and going down it only needed the attacking pilot to take his eye off it for seconds, and by the time he looked back he could have been then seeing a completely different aircraft dive into the sea. In the confusion, too, it was often difficult to make out exactly what was going on and the pilots claiming victories doubtless were all convinced that 'their' aircraft had gone down. Very often it had. But very often also, another pilot had shot at it and claimed it as well.

Fg Off James Storrar, a 145 Squadron Hurricane pilot.

However, 43 Squadron had one unusual confirmation of a claim in that action and this came from one of the squadron ground crew, Aircraftsman De Haag. This particular squadron 'erk' was on leave on the Isle of Wight and stood watching his own squadron in action. Later, he was able to confirm that the aircraft claimed by Plt Off H C Upton in his second attack had crashed into the sea in flames and this was duly recorded on Upton's combat report. Even from the safety of land, De Haag was overwhelmed by the scale of the battle he had witnessed. It was a battle that led Frank Carey to describe it as "…a raid so terrible and inexorable it was like trying to stop a steam roller". His CO, Sqn Ldr Badger, remarked on the swarms of aircraft steeped up in serried tiers: "It was like looking up an escalator on the Piccadilly underground."

Apart from the adventures of Badger, Hurry, Morgan, Carey and Upton and the loss of Oelofse and Cruttenden, one of the squadron stalwarts Plt Off C A Woods-Scawen had also been in the thick of the fighting and claimed "One Me 110 confirmed and three Ju 87s probable" on his personal combat report. Despite having been hit and wounded, Tony Woods-Scawen carried on with his attacks and only flew back to Tangmere when the enemy had dispersed. Rushed off to see the medical officer on his return it was found that he had multiple foreign bodies in both legs. Hardly surprising that his combat report had been written in a rather unsteady hand!

Aside from the claim by Peter Parrott for the Ju 87 downed at St Lawrence, the rest of 145 Squadron had also put in multiple claims for aircraft destroyed. The total squadron 'bag' for the late afternoon shoot was six Junkers 87s and two Messerschmitt 110s destroyed. One of the pilots who added to this claim was Plt Off J E Storrar who attacked a Ju 87 Stuka:

"As I finished my ammunition with little obvious effect I suddenly became aware that there was a flame around his right undercarriage leg. I came up alongside. There was no sign of the rear gunner but the pilot was looking at me and I was no more than twenty or thirty yards away. I could see his face clearly and could virtually see his hand on the stick. The flame suddenly burst over the top of the wing. We both looked at it for what seemed like seconds when the Stuka's wing suddenly buckled – the aircraft turned over, smashed into the sea and exploded.

Sub Lt Francis Smith was a Fleet Air Arm pilot attached to RAF Fighter Command and flying with 145 Squadron. No trace of him was ever found.

"I circled the smoke a couple of times, and was then joined by another Hurricane from 145 Squadron which headed back with me towards the Sussex coast. I could see as we pulled back our hoods he was giving me the thumbs-up and that it was Sub Lt F A Smith, a pilot who had joined our squadron from the Fleet Air Arm. I then had a sudden urge to look back over my other shoulder and saw two Messerschmitt 109s pulling in behind us. I yelled 'Break!' over the R/T and turned in hard towards them. As I got round to engage I pressed the button and it just hissed – of course, no ammunition. So I kept turning to avoid them and they eventually disappeared. Sub Lt Smith didn't come back and was never found. I was the last person to see him alive."

On the credit side, 43 and 145 Squadrons had certainly downed a number of aircraft, albeit that the final 'score' was over inflated. However, Oblt Werner Andres of Stab.II/JG 27 was one of their victims:

"I was hit in the instrument panel and the engine, thick white steam and plumes of black oil rushed past the canopy of my aircraft and much of it managed to enter the cockpit, maybe my controls had been shattered as well because I had no control over the now fast descending aircraft. The waters of the Channel were fast coming towards me; I knew that the situation was hopeless. I managed to throw off the cockpit hood and took all the necessary precautions for a crash landing in the water. It was my good fortune that I was approaching the water at an angle so as to make a belly landing. Had I been diving straight down it would not have been possible to survive. I prepared myself for the impact, then suddenly I was pushed forwards and my arms cushioned the impact as a wall of white water engulfed my Me 109 and the icy waters seemed to cut me in half. I jumped from the aircraft almost before it had come to a standstill, and within one minute the tail of the aircraft rose dramatically and the Me 109 slid headfirst to the bottom."

For Andres, it was the start of a long and lonely ordeal in the cold water – wondering if rescue would ever come. (See chapter 12.)

Flt Lt Roy Dutton, leader of 145 Squadron's A Flight was also in the thick of it. As he went into action, and to his absolute horror, Dutton's engine suddenly stopped. To be over the sea with a dead engine was bad enough, but to be over the sea and surrounded by enemy aircraft was a very bad situation to be in. As he fell away from the engagement and down to what he thought must surely be a ditching in the English Channel, a Junkers 87 appeared in front of him. Firing off a burst, the enemy aircraft caught fire, just as his own engine coughed back into life. Attacking and then claiming another Stuka, Dutton's engine finally packed up although by this time he had sufficient altitude to glide back over the

This group of flying personnel from II Gruppe JG 27 was taken in February 1940 but includes Me 109 pilots from that unit who took part in actions against CW9 Peewit on 8 August 1940. From the left, Hptm Werner Andres, Oblt Mithalek (addressing the group), Lt Troha, Lt Fludel, Lt Daig and Lt Strobl. The remaining NCO pilots are not identified. Andres was shot down into the sea during the late afternoon action on 8 August but rescued by a He 59 seaplane.

coast and get into Westhampnett on a dead-stick landing. It was a creditable piece of airmanship with the inherent danger of a fatal result if the glide was extended for too long and flying speed fell to the point of stall. Luckily for Dutton, he had got back home.

Sub Lt F A Smith and Plt Off E C Wakeham would not be coming home. Missing, too, was Fg Off Lord Richard Kay-Shuttleworth – a member of the British aristocracy. Lord Kay-Shuttleworth's father had been killed in action in France during the First World War, and in 1939 Richard became Lord Shuttleworth upon the death of his grandfather, the First Baron Shuttleworth of Gawthorpe. What happened with him on 8 August 1940 and exactly how Lord Richard died is unknown. He simply didn't come back and nobody saw the going of him. Last sight of him was probably had by the Flt Sgt 'chiefy' in charge of the fitters who looked after Shuttleworth's Hurricane. It was Flt Sgt Ted Bowen who strapped him in and waved him off that afternoon:

"I led two teams of fitters and riggers who looked after the Hurricanes regularly flown by the CO, Sqn Ldr John Peel, and by Lord Shuttleworth – although he was known to us as 'Peter'. He was a smashing fellow and I fondly recall that he always had his pockets full of sweets and would dish them out generously to everyone. Anyway, he had returned from an earlier sortie that day at around lunchtime with a bullet hole in his windscreen about the size of your little finger nail. [This was presumably through one of the Perspex side panels rather than the armoured glass] Our job was to re-fuel and re-arm the Hurricanes as quickly as possible before the next sortie. We also repaired any minor damage that we could easily deal with. Whilst my crew frantically dealt with the fuel and ammo, I climbed up to the windscreen and fixed the hole with Bostik. It was like that

124

when it went off on its next and last sortie, and it was a sortie for which I strapped 'Peter' in. He was regarded as a great character by all who had the pleasure of knowing him."

It had been a hard and bloody day, all told, for 145 Squadron who had had five of their pilots killed. In fact, and taking into account the losses sustained by 43 Squadron, the last engagement of the day had resulted in the loss of almost a quarter of the defending force involved in the battle off the Isle of Wight that afternoon. The pilots who had survived must have felt a curious sense of mixed emotions; gratitude that they were still alive, sadness for those of their friends who had not come back and a kind of elation over the victories claimed. All told, it was a time of keyed-up high drama for the fighter pilots and those of 145 Squadron might not have been much in the mood for a royal visit at Westhampnett later that afternoon when they found HRH The Duke of Gloucester waiting to greet and congratulate them on returning from their last sortie. The platitudes that were no doubt duly delivered, and the deference the weary pilots had to appropriately show, was probably not what they wanted right then.

Flt Lt Roy Dutton, another of the 145 Squadron pilots caught up in the hectic actions of 8 August.

Roy Dutton's log book entries for 8 August 1940.

125

Whilst 43 and 145 Squadron had been ploughing into the massed formations to the south of the Isle of Wight, some of 152 Squadron's Spitfires had been headed down towards the Weymouth Bay area and there is little doubt that the controller had thought this was where the incoming attack was headed. After all, the remnants of CW9 Peewit were already in the bay, or else dispersing from there, and the small collection of ships that were still off the Isle of Wight were not of any significance at all to the RAF controller – even if he knew about them. It made sense to him that the incoming raid was headed for the main concentration of CW9 Peewit ships and the expectation was no doubt that 152 and 238 Squadrons would engage the enemy above the convoy.

In the event, 238 Squadron did not even see the enemy on the operations that they flew between 16.20 and 18.05. All of the action was going on some miles off to the east, although it was all but over, anyway, by the time that 238 Squadron had reached the Swanage area. The operations record

Fg Off Richard Shuttleworth was in fact Lord Shuttleworth and a pilot with 145 Squadron. No trace of this twenty-seven-year-old Hurricane pilot was found and he is commemorated on the Runnymede Memorial.

book merely states: "Twelve aircraft patrolled a convoy entering Weymouth Bay, which was done by sections at 2,000ft intervals. No enemy were seen."

Similarly, the nine Hurricanes of 213 Squadron haring down the English Channel from Exeter also failed to make it in time to see any action over the convoy, having taken off at 16.05. However, on the way home Red Section of 213 Squadron (Flt Lt J E J Sing, Sgt P P Norris and Plt Off M S H C Buchin) encountered two Me 109s "15 miles north of Guernsey" at 17.35 and went into attack. Flt Lt Sing reported as follows:

"No.2 of Red Section sighted two Me 109s. Having identified them Red 2 attacked one while I was trying to find the second who had climbed into the sun. I saw Sgt Norris (No.2) open fire and hit the auxiliary tank on the Me 109. He then broke away. The machine had apparently suffered no other damage so I attacked and shot it down in flames. I then saw the second Me 109. This I caught up and gave it a second burst before running out of ammunition. No apparent damage done to second Me 109."

Whilst credit for the destruction of this Me 109 went solely to Flt Lt Sing, it perhaps ought to have been more properly awarded as a half-share between Sing and Norris since the latter clearly is reported as having put hits into the Me 109's fuel tank. Unfortunately, it has

Fg Off Edward Hogg, a Spitfire pilot with 152 Squadron, also engaged the Messerschmitt 109s of JG53 over Weymouth Bay on 8 August 1940.

not been possible to identify the Me 109 involved. As for Sgt Norris, he was shot down and killed in action over the English Channel just five days later, his body subsequently being washed ashore on the French coast and later buried in Etaples military cemetery.

Things were slightly different than they had been for 238 Squadron for the Spitfires of B Flight, 152 Squadron, who ran into the Messerschmitt 109s of JG 53 – having arrived over the sea some twelve miles south of Swanage shortly after 16.00. Plt Off D G Shepley was one pilot to make a claim:

"B Flight of 152 Squadron were ordered to patrol convoy at 16.00 (approx) and on reaching the convoy the flight was attacked by numerous Me 109s. We were in sections of two and I was Black 1. I did a steep turn to the right and found nothing on my tail so climbed to 16,000ft where there were approximately ten Me 109s. I had just opened fire when an Me 109, which had evidently been on my tail, overshot on my port about 20ft away. I immediately opened fire on him at about 50 yards range. By this time the range had increased to about 250 yards. Black smoke was pouring from the machine and bits were coming from it. His tail unit was apparently very seriously damaged. I then returned to Warmwell."

Quite why these Messerschmitts were over the *real* convoy but with no escorted bombers might be due to one of two reasons: either they had correctly flown to the appointed location but missed the main formation that had already been misled by the ships found off to the east, or their purpose was to intercept any fighters that might be flying down from the west to attack the Stuka formations.

Alternatively, they may have been intended as a rear-cover escort to ward off any interference when the Stukas and the other escorting Me 109s of JG 27 (which would by now be low on fuel) had retired and were turning for home. If the latter scenario is correct then they would clearly have flown to meet the returning formations where they had expected them to be – i.e. south of Weymouth Bay. Finding nothing there above the ships except the Spitfires of 152 Squadron, the Me 109s entered into a brief engagement with them before themselves turning for home. It was an engagement in which Hptm Günther von Maltzahn (the geschwader kommodore), Oblt Richard Vogel and Hptm Richard Bretnütz each claimed an RAF fighter destroyed. In fact, only two of 152 Squadron's

Spitfires were downed. One of them was flown by Sgt Denis Robinson. He was one of the last RAF Fighter Command casualties that day and was returning in Spitfire K9894 from the action over Weymouth Bay. Robinson takes up the story of his escapade that afternoon:

"There were three of us flying in vic formation with Beaumont on the left of the flight leader and myself on the right. We were flying in very tight formation, probably about a foot from the leader's wingtips. Therefore Beaumont and I had our eyes and concentration firmly fixed on the leader's aircraft. This was the way we flew in close formation early in the battle – until we learnt better later. Unfortunately, a group of Me 109s spotted us and carried out an attack on our unprotected rear, which we had offered them on a plate. We ought to have known better. We knew that it was vital to keep a good lookout at all times, but were lulled into a false sense of security and had relaxed our vigilance briefly. After all, we had had our scrap, were nearly safely home and, anyway, we had no ammo.

Plt Off D G Shepley (right), a Spitfire pilot with 152 Squadron.

"The first thing I felt was the thud of bullets hitting my aircraft and a long line of tracer bullets streaming out ahead of my Spitfire. In a reflex action I slammed the stick forward as far as it would go. For a brief second my Spitfire stood on its nose and I was looking straight down at Mother Earth, thousands of feet below. Thank God my Sutton harness was good and tight. I could feel the straps biting into my flesh as I entered the vertical with airspeed building up alarmingly. I felt fear mounting. Sweating, dry mouth and near panic. No ammo and an attacker right on my tail.

"All this happened in seconds, but now the airspeed was nearly off the clock. I simply had to pull out and start looking for the enemy. That's what I did, turning and climbing at the same time. As I opened the throttle fully, with emergency boost selected to assist the climb, I noticed wisps of white smoke coming from the nose of my fighter. Oh God, no! Fire!

"Suddenly the engine stopped. Apparently a bullet in the glycol tank had dispersed all the coolant and even the faithful Merlin could not stand that for long at full power. So that explained the white smoke. Blessed relief. The fuel tanks of high octane fuel are situated very close to the pilot in a Spitfire. The dread of being burnt to death was one of the worst fears. It drew heavily on any reserves of courage one had. You can imagine

Messerschmitt 109 pilots Hptm Günther von Maltzahn (centre) and Hptm Heinz Bretnütz (far right) of II/JG 53 both claimed a Spitfire shot down south of Swanage during the engagement with 152 Squadron.

by now, my eyes are searching wildly, frantically looking for my adversary – but, as often happens in air combat, not a single plane was to be seen in the sky around me. The release of tension as I realised my good fortune is something that cannot be described. You only know what it is like to be given back your life if you have been through that experience.

"The problems that still confronted me, sitting in the cockpit of a battle-damaged Spitfire, seemed almost trivial in comparison with my situation of a few seconds before. I experienced this feeling several times during the Battle and it had a profound effect on me, which remains with me to this day. It somehow changed my value system, so that things that had seemed important before never had the same degree of importance again. Maybe

Sgt Denis Robinson of 152 Squadron who had a very lucky escape.

this is what generated the anti-authority behaviour amongst us. It was no good telling us not to do a victory roll over the airfield when we returned from a scrap, because our aircraft may be damaged and we might end up like strawberry jam in the middle of the field. This seemed a trivial risk compared to our experiences of combat in battle.

"The end of the episode was something of an anti climax. I still had plenty of altitude and time to think. I prepared to bale out and began going through the procedure in my mind. Release the Sutton harness, make sure all connections to flying helmet are free, slide the canopy back, roll the aircraft until inverted, push the stick forward and out you go. Then start counting before pulling the D-ring. How many? My memory went blank. Was it three or ten? God! There's a vast difference between the two, I thought. Well, as long as the interval is sufficient to get clear of the aircraft before pulling the D-ring it should all be OK.

"During this soliloquy I'd got the Spit into a steady glide. It was gliding rather like a brick, but handling reasonably well and responding to the controls almost normally. I surveyed what I could see of the damage from the cockpit. Not much, apart from a few bullet holes here and there, particularly in the starboard wing. It worried me to abandon the old bus to certain destruction on to heaven knows what, perhaps a school full of children.

"Besides, I was by no means convinced that the baleout procedure I had rehearsed was not without considerable risk. I could get caught up in the cockpit paraphernalia... I might be struck by the tail plane... or what if the parachute didn't open? No. I convinced myself that was bloody dangerous. I would stay with her and force land in a suitable field.

"By now most of the fields looked pretty small, so I decided it would be with the wheels up. I picked a field near Wareham that looked suitable, slid back the canopy and commenced an approach. At about 200ft the boundary loomed up. Full flap and a flare out near the ground achieved a creditable touchdown. So far so good, I thought. I was quite pleased with myself as the Spit slithered across the grass.

"Then suddenly, I felt her going up onto her nose and, I thought, onto her back. With an almighty crash the canopy slammed shut over my head and the cockpit filled with dirt, completely blinding me. The aircraft seemed to me to be upside down and I was trapped. That awful fear of burning returned at full strength. I grabbed the canopy with all my might and threw it backwards. To my utter amazement it shot back easily, and the excessive adrenaline-boosted force I had used nearly tore my arms from their sockets. Now I could see that the aircraft had finished up vertically on its nose and in a ditch I hadn't seen from the air.

"My actions now became somewhat comic. It was obvious that I could easily jump clear and I commenced to do so without much hesitation. To my utter horror I couldn't move. Suddenly, I realised I was struggling against the Sutton harness, still buckled firmly in place. An instant pull released the pin. I was free. As I stood up to jump my head was jerked violently backwards. This time it was my flying helmet, still attached to the radio and oxygen sockets in the cockpit. Removing this final impediment I jumped to the ground, leaving my helmet in the cockpit.

"To my surprise the Spitfire didn't burn. I stood back and took in the scene as locals arrived to convey me off to a pub in nearby Wareham and fill me with whisky. I had a slight bullet graze on my leg, but was otherwise unhurt and felt strangely elated. Next day I was back on ops again.

"Later my thoughts turned to my actions at the time and to my survival. Firstly, I must have sensed without fully realising it that the tracer from the enemy fire was coming from left to right direction. Since I was on the right of the section leader I could not turn left and collide with him. The only way to go was a right turn, which would enable the attacker to tighten his turn and would have made me an easy target.

"The instant reaction of stick hard forward causing the Merlin engine to belch smoke from the exhausts may have convinced the Me 109 pilot that he had been successful in his attack, or perhaps the sudden change in attitude of my aircraft caused the attacker to overshoot his target. Also, the Me 109s operating over the Dorset coast were very far from their French bases and were short of fuel therefore couldn't hang around at length in a dogfight or chase situation. It would have been nice for us if we had known this fuel problem at the time, but we did not. I only found this out years later, after the

Managing to nurse his bullet-riddled Spitfire back to land, Robinson made a crash landing near Wareham where his Spitfire nosed-up in a ditch and tore off its port wing. A line of bullet holes can be clearly seen in the starboard wing.

war. To this day I still do not know what gave me that sixth sense and instant reaction to jam the stick hard forward, but I think it saved my life.

"Telling this story helps me to deal with my survival syndrome. In a difficult-to-describe way, it is as though I am speaking for the other chaps who did not make it. Their final story would have been infinitely more readable than mine. One constantly asks: Why did I survive... and why did others not?"

Certainly, Robinson had been lucky. He had flown straight and level in a combat area and without keeping a proper lookout – cardinal sins for any fighter pilot. He had been more intent, instead, on maintaining formation.His survivor's guilt was probably not unique amongst those who lived through the fighting of this August day – whether at sea or in the air. Of the others who did not survive, and to whom Robinson so poignantly refers, twenty-three RAF aircrew were lost in air fighting over the south of England on 8 August 1940 and in actions associated with CW9 Peewit. In addition, no less than twenty-four mariners from the Royal Navy, Merchant Navy and RAF Marine Craft Unit also lost their lives that day.

In summarising the air fighting over Convoy CW9 Peewit, RAF Fighter Command was singularly up-beat in its assessment:

> "Three engagements took place and considered as a whole may be reckoned from the point of Fighter Command the most successful battle of the war. Altogether eighty-four enemy machines were destroyed or severely damaged, at least sixty of these being confirmed, as against the loss of eighteen of our aircraft and fifteen pilots. The German High Command reverse the ratio and claim the score as forty-nine to twelve in their favour."

It was hardly an accurate or objective appraisal of events that day. In Chapter 11 we are able to take a closer look at the realities of the fighting and the claims and the losses made and suffered by both sides.

By 16.45 the English Channel was clear of any further significant enemy air activity.

CHAPTER 11 Elsewhere that Day

WHILST THE main thrust of this book has been concerned with the passage of convoy CW9 Peewit through the English Channel and in following the air actions associated with that convoy, this is not to say that were not *other* air actions going on over the British Isles at the same time. Such other actions described below were unrelated to Convoy Peewit, or else they were related only indirectly or tenuously to the convoy's passage down the Channel.

At 09.30, and just as the first air action over Peewit was coming to an end, the Luftwaffe began further activity in the eastern reaches of the English Channel. Between that time and 10.30, small enemy formations were detected constantly patrolling over the French side of the Straits, with one such group of aircraft approaching as far as the Goodwin Sands before almost immediately retiring. However, by 10.38 another force had crossed the coast near Dover and flown inland, but cloud cover meant that the observer corps was unable

Sgt (air gunner) Francis Keast was one of the crew of three on board a Blenheim of 600 Squadron shot down into the sea off Ramsgate during the morning of 8 August 1940.

to track its subsequent course overland although the German formation evidently steered a north-easterly course from Dover. Spitfires of 65 Squadron had, in fact, been patrolling Manston since 10.15 and it was sometime just around 11.45 that the squadron was engaged by enemy fighters. Here, over Manston, two Spitfires were swiftly despatched by Messerschmitt 109s, probably those of III./JG 26. In the engagement, Oblt Schöpfel, Oblt Müncheberg and Fw Gryzmalla each made claims for a British fighter and Sgts Kirton and

133

Phillips were both shot down and killed whilst another 65 Squadron Spitfire was damaged but made it back to RAF Hornchurch, its pilot having had a lucky escape. Meanwhile, at Manston, two Blenheims of 600 Squadron had not long been off on an airborne interception (AI radar) practice, having taken off at 11.25. The 600 Squadron operations record book takes up the story:

The pilot of the Blenheim was Fg Off D N Grice. *The East Kent Times* reported the incident in detail under the headline "A Very Gallant Gentleman": "As it roared towards the town flames were spouting from it in all directions, but, silhouetted against the glare could be seen the pilot wrenching at the controls. 'It seemed certain' said one eye witness 'that the aircraft would crash into a row of houses near the cliff edge, but the pilot succeeded in making the plane swerve off so that it crashed into the sea. When it exploded the surface of the water was covered with furiously burning petrol. I saw what I at first thought was a piece of wreckage near the burning oil, but looking through some field glasses I could see that this was the head of a man. He disappeared, however, in a few seconds.'"

"In the morning Fg Off Boyd (BQ-B) and Fg Off Grice (BQ-A) set off on an AI practice. They were to fly between base and Ashford at 6,000ft. Two minutes after they had taken off, the air raid sirens sounded and Fg Off Smith heard an aircraft diving overhead and so he ran to his operations room where he ordered the VHF tender to instruct the pair of Blenheims to land immediately. Both aircraft acknowledged at 11.34 and Fg Off Boyd dived straight into the clouds from where he was over the aerodrome and heard firing over the R/T. He landed safely. What happened to Fg Off Grice is not known as he was next seen diving out of the clouds towards Ramsgate with both engines on fire. According to reports from sources in Ramsgate, civil and naval, Fg Off Grice skilfully pulled his aircraft up out of its dive just before it would have hit the main shopping centre, avoided the harbour and crashed into the sea. One wing touched first and it turned over and sank, burning. The witnesses from Ramsgate are full of praise for Fg Off Grice's gallantry."

Fg Off Dennis Grice, along with his air gunner Sgt Francis Keast and AI operator, AC1 John Warren, were all killed in the crash and had fallen to the guns of Oblt Gerhard Schöpfel of 9./JG 26 who claimed what he called a 'Handley' in exactly this location and at this time. There can be no doubting that Schöpfel was the victor despite his slightly dubious aircraft recognition. Thus far in the morning engagements over Kent the Luftwaffe had had the upper hand, and 65 Squadron's losses had been sustained without any claim being made by that squadron to redress the balance.

No sooner had 65 Squadron landed than there were again unmistakable signs that the Luftwaffe would be over again, and by 12.00 at least another four enemy formations, each between ten and twenty aircraft strong, were detected in the Dover Straits. They appeared to be manoeuvring independently of one another but as each formation was too strong to be ignored the 11 Group controller ordered patrols over Manston and Hawkinge, with 41 Squadron covering Manston and 64 Squadron, who were using Hawkinge as their forward operating base, to cover that airfield. A further three German formations crossed in over the coast whilst 41 and 64 Squadrons

Messerschmitt 109 pilot Oblt Gerhard Schöpfel of 9/JG 26.

were in the air. One of these came in near Dungeness at 11.25 and after making a sweep as far as Maidstone, retired again. Another came in at North Foreland but was not subsequently plotted and the third came in at Pevensey at the same time and flew along the coast to beyond Beachy Head.

To counter this last threat, the Hurricanes of 615 Squadron were scrambled from Biggin Hill at 11.40 but they were too late and finally caught a glimpse of the formation as it left the coast somewhere near Brighton and although the Hurricanes chased them at 26,000ft almost all the way to France the enemy aircraft were "too fast" for them to catch. One of the 615 Squadron pilots, Fg Off R D Paxton, had a lucky escape during the pursuit when his oxygen supply failed at 26,000ft and he spun down unconscious in his out of control aircraft. Luckily, as he reached a lower altitude he came-to and pulled out of what was an otherwise terminal dive at around 3,000ft. Also chasing the same enemy formation were the Hurricanes of 145 Squadron who, like 615 Squadron, only saw their quarry in the far distance before they were vectored back westwards towards the threat approaching CW9 Peewit shortly after mid-day.

With noon approaching, further enemy formations were still being plotted around the Dover area – twenty aircraft near the Goodwins, another force near Manston and yet others off Calais. Each of these forces comprised solely groups of Messerschmitt 109s. However, the radar picture could not detect the type or composition of such formations and thus all were a potential threat and may have easily consisted of bomber formations. It was around noon that the Spitfires of 41 Squadron eventually engaged one of the groups of Me109s while 64 Squadron were attacked by another group of Me109s near Dover. Another Spitfire

Amongst the RAF fighter squadrons airborne over Kent during the Luftwaffe fighter incursions on 8 August were the Spitfires of 610 Squadron.

unit, 610 Squadron, was also up from RAF Hawkinge and became embroiled in the same combat. One of 64 Squadron's pilots was an American, Plt Off A G 'Art' Donahue who wrote a dramatic account of that action:

"The telephone rang again. The telephone orderly listened a moment and then turned to us and said 'Squadron into your aircraft and patrol base at 10,000ft!'

"Instantly we were on our feet and racing pell-mell out to our airplanes. An airman helped me on with my parachute. I climbed into the cockpit of my machine and, trembling with excitement, adjusted my straps and put on my helmet. Down the line of planes, starters whined and first one engine, then another coughed to life. I pressed my own starter button and my engine joined the chorus. There was no 'warming up', no taxiing across the field to take off into wind. Upwind, downwind or crosswind we took off straight ahead. Better a difficult take-off than give a deadly enemy a minute's extra advantage!

"We roared off like a stampeding herd of buffalo, climbing steeply and wide open. Two thousand feet, 4,000 – there were thick fluffy clouds at 5,000, and we flashed up through their misty chasms, caverns, hills and valleys; and then they were dropping away below us and forming a snowy carpet for us to look down on. The sun shone brilliantly above. New orders came over the radio from our controller. Sometimes we were over coastal towns, sometimes over the Channel, circling here, patrolling there, watching for the elusive enemy. I recalled the scene in the operations room and wondered if the girls plotting our positions were any less nonchalant now when there was a real chase on.

"Nearly an hour passed without our seeing anything. One flight (six of our twelve planes) was ordered to land, and I guessed that the trail was getting cold. Peter [Plt Off Peter Kennard-Davis] and I were in the flight remaining on patrol.

"We were about 8,000ft up, the six of us patrolling over the Channel, and for a couple of minutes we had received no new orders. The sun was very hot, and I wished I hadn't worn my tunic.

"Our only warning was the sudden whine of a transmitter and a voice shouting 'BANDITS ASTERN!!' It was blood chilling. Our squadron leader was quick on the trigger and led us in a violent turn, just in time. A myriad of grey Messerschmitts were swarming down out

American volunteer Plt Off Art Donahue who was also involved in the fighting over Kent.

of the sun, diving from above and behind and shooting as they came. 'Tal-l-ly – ho-o!' Our leader's voice was steady and strong and reassuring and in that moment filled with all his personal magnetism and strength of character. It was reassuring in its calm call to battle, and caught up shattered nerves and self-control in each of us. He led us together down into the middle of the swarm of Huns, whose speed had now carried them far down ahead of us and who were now wheeling back towards us as they came out of their dives.

"There seemed to be about thirty. It was probably a gruppe of about twenty-seven, and they simply absorbed the six of us. We picked targets and went after them and were soon completely lost from each other. One Messerschmitt was coming up in a climbing turn ahead of me, and allowing for its speed I aimed a burst of fire just ahead of its nose. I had no time to see if I hit it."

Donahue goes on in his account, telling how the dogfighting raged for many minutes until, quite suddenly, he found himself all alone in the sky. It was a not uncommon phenomenon in air fighting:

"I looked around and found no more planes of either nationality in view. I appeared to be in sole possession of this part of the battlefield. This was well out over the Channel and I knew I must be nearly out of ammunition, so I headed for the shore and our advance base [Hawkinge].

"All of our planes were already down safely when I taxied into line on the ground. Peter was 'still adrift' I learned, and it gave me a little shock. There was still plenty of time for him to show up, though."

Eventually, news came through that Peter Kennard-Davis had been shot down and had baled out, wounded, over West Langdon, Kent. He had received several bullet wounds and had lost a good deal of blood – although the hospital prognosis appeared quite optimistic. Indeed, Kennard-Davis was said to have been in wonderful spirits and keen to get back in the fray. It was therefore a great shock to Donahue to hear, two days later, that his friend had suffered a relapse and passed away in the Royal Victoria Hospital, Dover.

The engagement in which 41, 64 and 610 Squadrons had been caught up involved the Messerschmitt 109s of III/JG 51, and at least three of that unit's aircraft returned home with varying degrees of damage although with the pilots unharmed. Consequently, the claims made by Flt Lt Webster and Plt Off Wallens of 41 Squadron for three Me 109s confirmed destroyed between them would seem to be rather optimistic. As was often the case, when RAF pilots hit and damaged Me 109s, the enemy aircraft usually dived away from them, vertically, in order to escape. In so doing, the Daimler-Benz DB601 motors emitted a thick trail of black exhaust smoke and this tended to mislead RAF fighter pilots into believing that they had shot their quarry down. It is quite likely, therefore, that the three JG 51 machines that returned damaged from that combat were hit by Webster and Wallens who quite genuinely believed they had actually shot them down.

This is believed to be Spitfire P9369 of 64 Squadron, forced landed by Sgt J W C Squier at Great Couldham, Capel-le-Ferne, after combat with Messerschmitt 109s of III/JG 51. Squier was injured and the Spitfire written off. Today, Capel-le-Ferne is the site of the Battle of Britain Memorial.

A balloon of the Dover barrage is readied on the morning of 8 August. Later that day the Dover balloons were also attacked like those of CW9 Peewit.

Whilst the Luftwaffe had already given some attention that day to barrage balloons over Convoy Peewit, this was not the only time when the balloons would come under attack and they had also shot-up the balloons over Dover during the mid-day action. In fact, it was a burning barrage balloon slowly descending above Dover Castle that had initially attracted the Spitfires of 64 Squadron to the presence of enemy fighters in the area. However, apart from the offensive action against the Dover balloons none of the enemy formations that ranged over Kent and into East Sussex that morning were anything other than groups of fighters.

There were no formations of escorted bombers and the fighters seemed to have been in free-hunts to draw RAF Fighter Command into combat over the eastern Channel. Given the timings of these wide-ranging formations over Kent and the Dover Straits, and the attacks then being pressed home against shipping further west, the RAF's Air Historical Branch was led to speculate in its post-war analysis of the Battle of Britain that these forays might have been a ruse. Perhaps, speculated the Air Historical Branch, the purpose of the marauding bands of German fighters was simply to draw the defenders' attention away from the real target and, in so doing, divert at least some of the available fighter force away from the Stuka formations. There is some evidence to support this contention. Certainly, 145 Squadron had been sent off on a wild goose chase towards the incursion that had been plotted between Beachy Head and Brighton, a raid that 615 Squadron were already chasing. This had put 145 Squadron at a disadvantage and in the wrong place *exactly* when the lunch-time attack against CW9 Peewit was being launched. Flt Lt Adrian Boyd tells how it was:

"...the whole squadron was sent up at fifteen minutes to twelve to investigate a raid off Beachy Head. We went up to more than 20,000ft and saw at between 30,000 and 35,000ft no fewer than thirty-six Messerschmitt 110s. They swung round and returned to France when they saw us, and as we were unable to reach them we turned and were told over the radio telephone that a battle was going on south of the Isle of Wight. We had fifty miles to go to the convoy – it took us just about ten minutes – but although we saw the convoy, we saw no German aircraft. I think the Messerschmitt 110s we went to look at were just a blind.

I myself then led the three machines in my section to a point well south of the Isle of Wight. There we saw two separate squadrons of Messerschmitt 110s."

Whilst we have examined the input of 145 Squadron to this particular engagement in a previous chapter there can be no doubting that had the squadron, with its twelve Hurricanes, gone straight towards the convoy at 11.45 on taking off from Westhampnett, the outcome of the attacks on the shipping might have been rather different.

After the lunch-time mauling there was a short period for RAF Fighter Command to draw its breath and for the pilots of 609 Squadron to try to find some sustenance. However, at 14.10 the three Spitfires of Red Section, 234 Squadron, were ordered off from St Eval to intercept an 'X' raid at 10,000ft over Falmouth and with the plot heading steadily north-west. Eventually, the aircraft was sighted and turned out to be a solitary Junkers 88 which was immediately attacked by Plt Off E B Mortimer-Rose and Sgt A S Harker. Both pilots managed to get in a good number of hits, but ultimately the German aircraft turned back for France and

Flt Lt Adrian Boyd of 145 Squadron.

disappeared into cloud. It had been a machine of 3.(F)/123 engaged on shipping reconnaissance and although the Junkers escaped, it had been damaged in the attack and made it back to France with a seriously wounded crew member on board; Uffz T Bauer succumbing to his grievous bullet wounds the next day.

Albeit rather feebly by comparison, the RAF *did* attempt to take the war back to the Germans that day with Bomber Command sending out aircraft from No.2 Group to attack enemy airfields between 05.35 and 17.40. In all, fifteen sorties were flown and these involved aircraft from 18, 21, 82 and 105 Squadrons although twelve of these operations were aborted due to cloud cover over the target airfields. Mostly, the bombers went out as

A forced-landed Messerschmitt 110 (A2+CL) of II/ZG 2 is representative of aircraft from that unit engaged in operations against CW9 Peewit on 8 August although in fact II/ZG 2 suffered no losses or casualties that day.

singletons although some operated as pairs. Amongst the Luftwaffe bases on the target list were Schipol and Valkenburg although another operation was detailed to Caen and it is that sortie which may have been significant in the last aerial combat of the day above the English Channel.

When the final action of the day off the Isle of Wight had died away shortly after tea-time, four Blenheims took off from RAF Thorney Island; three from 235 Squadron and one from 59 Squadron. The 235 Squadron machines flew down to the mouth of the River Seine on an escort sortie at some time in the late afternoon or early evening, and although it is not clear which aircraft they were escorting it could well have been the aircraft from No.2 Group that had gone to bomb Caen. The geography would certainly make sense. The 59 Squadron machine, however, had departed at 15.50 and headed for roughly the same vicinity with instructions to patrol from Le Havre and across the Seine estuary to Cherbourg.

Exactly what happened on that flight is slightly muddled in the surviving reports although it would seem that the trio of 235 Squadron aeroplanes loitered for twenty minutes off the Seine estuary waiting for their unidentified charge to return from its duty inland. Eventually it returned, although not before fifteen Messerschmitt 110s had appeared on the scene and a running fight had ensued. Unluckily, the three Blenheims had run slap-bang into the Messerschmitt 110s of II/ZG 2, returning from their escort of the Stuka force that had taken part in the final attack of the day against CW9 Peewit.

The three Blenheims were led by Flt Lt A W Fletcher (T9446 LA-N) with Plt Off D K A Wordsworth (T1805 LA-M) and Sgt S J Hobbs (N3256 LA-K) and in the fight two of the

YEAR 1940		AIRCRAFT		PILOT, OR 1ST PILOT	2ND PILOT, PUPIL OR PASSENGER	DUTY (INCLUDING RESULTS AND REM
MONTH	DATE	Type	No.			
—	—	—	—	—	—	— TOTALS BROUGHT FOR
AUG	8	HURRICANE	E	SELF		CONVOY - "KATIES POINT"
"	"	"	"	"		"
"	"	"	"	"		"
"	"	"	"	"		"
"	9	"	D	"		AIR TACTICS
"	10	"	E	"		PATROL BRIGHTON
"	"	"	"	"		" BASE
"	11	"	"	"		OPERATIONAL TAKE OFF
"	12	"	B	"		" " "
"	13	"	"	"		" " "
"	"	"	E	"		" " " "
"	"	"	"	"		PATROL PORTLAND 20,000 ft.
"	15	"	H.	"		OPERATIONAL TAKE-OFF
"	"	"	H.	"		" " "
"	"	"	H.	"		" " "
"	16	"	H	"		" " "
"	"	"	H.	"		" " "

GRAND TOTAL [Cols. (1) to (10)]

...............Hrs..................Mins.

TOTALS CARRIED FORW

Despite being frequently airborne on 8 August 1940, pilots of 601 Squadron only engaged with the enemy once that day although the records for 601 Squadron do not show Fiske as having taken part in that action (see pages 144-5). His description of Katie's Point refers to St Catherine's Point. Despite the number of flights Fiske seems to record on 8 August it is a fact that the squadron's operations record book only gives him as being airborne once that day; from 18.20 until 18.35, when the enemy were not engaged.

SINGLE-ENGINE AIRCRAFT			MULTI-ENGINE AIRCRAFT						PASS-ENGER	INSTR/CLOUD FLYING (Incl. cols. (1) to (10))	
DAY	NIGHT		DAY			NIGHT					
PILOT	DUAL	PILOT	DUAL	1ST PILOT	2ND PILOT	DUAL	1ST PILOT	2ND PILOT		DUAL	PILOT
(2)	(3)	(4)	(5)	(6)	(7)	(8)	(9)	(10)	(11)	(12)	(13)
138.55	4.10	5.15							25	13.10	4.50
1.35			Too	early	for	fun.	"Blitz" starts. Conway attacked by 500 E/A during day.				
.40			"	late	"	"	Station got 43 conf. 9 uncorf. We never				
1.45			"	early	"	"	saw one during whole day.				
1.20			"	late	"	"	Frustration setting in badly!				
.30											
.35			E/A turned back								
.25			"	"	"	"					
1.30		Intercepted 200 + Me 110 + 109. Saw 2 probables 3 badly damaged. Sqdn. lost 4. Terrific fight. Fun						terrified too				
.50		Patrol Isle of Wight at 19,000 no E/A seen.						want to bad on a dive. Willie engine failed!			
.35		attacked two large formations Ju 88. 1 probable 1 damaged. No Sqdn. losses. 0630 AM too conf.									
.15											
.55		attacked 40 + Me 110s in defensive circle 2 probable 2 damaged. Cannon hit aileron, jammed, landed okay, no losses.									
.55											
.55											
.35											
.45											
.35											
153.35											
(2)	(3)	(4)	(5)	(6)	(7)	(8)	(9)	(10)	(11)	(12)	(13)

Blenheim's air gunners, Sgts T A Maslen and Sgt A D Maconochie (it is not known which aircraft each gunner was in) claimed to have hit and shot down in flames a single Messerschmitt 110. It has thus far proved impossible to identify the Me 110 they claimed to have destroyed as nothing appears in the Luftwaffe quartermaster's returns for the day and II/ZG 2 reported no losses. On the other hand, the Me 110s *did* claim three Blenheims destroyed, with one falling to the guns of Oblt Hermann Grasser. Since we know that the three Blenheims all returned safely we can see that there was clearly over claiming on both

Another pilot of 601 Squadron who missed the main action of the day was Flt Lt Willie Rhodes-Moorhouse DFC, although he flew on the operational take-off from Tangmere between 18.20 and 18.35 which turned out to be a non-event for the squadron. He was the son of the first aerial VC winner, Lieutenant W B Rhodes-Moorhouse, who won his award on 26 April 1915. Willie was shot down and killed over Tunbridge Wells on 6 September 1940.

sides during that action. There was, though, one Blenheim that did fail to return from its sortie in this area and at around the same time.

After having taken off, nothing further was heard from the 59 Squadron Blenheim (N3590 TR-F) and Plt Off L N Davis and Sgt G H Coulton were posted as missing. The body of Sgt B W Beaumont was eventually washed up on the French coast and buried at Hautot-sur-Mer near Dieppe. N3590 must be a strong contender for the aircraft shot down by Grasser or one of his fellow II/ZG 2 pilots and the possibility that 235 Squadron were waiting to escort this Blenheim back cannot be excluded.

Briefly, at 18.20 there was another flurry of activity for 601 Squadron with six of its Hurricanes being sent off on a scramble out to sea. Amongst the pilots involved were two whose names would later become better known in the bigger picture of the Battle of Britain: American volunteer Plt Off W L M 'Billy' Fiske and Flt Lt W H Rhodes-Moorhouse DFC. The Hurricanes were only airborne for a few minutes when they were recalled to Tangmere landing there at 18.35, exactly fifteen minutes after they had taken off. With no enemy air activity in the English Channel at this time, and no incoming raids plotted, it

Another American volunteer who flew in actions associated with CW9 Peewit was Plt Off Billy Fiske, a 601 Squadron Hurricane pilot. Fiske was shot down and badly burned on 16 August 1940 and died of his injuries the next day. A plaque in St Paul's Cathedral remembers him as "An American Citizen who Died That England Might Live".

Fg Off Richard Demetriadi, another 601 Squadron pilot, was the brother-in-law of Willie Rhodes-Moorhouse. He flew the convoy escort at 07.20 and was again operational during the engagement at mid-day on 8 August. Three days later he was shot down off Portland and killed, his body being eventually washed up on the French coast.

seems likely that there was some initial confusion as to the identity of the 235 Squadron Blenheims then out over the Channel, and 601 Squadron were ordered off on a precautionary interception.

For now, the bitter fighting that had raged so fiercely along the English Channel for almost the entire day was finally over.

Author's note: According to Royal Navy (Home Command) war diary five RN destroyers under HMS *Express* were attacked by enemy aircraft off Burnham Flats on 8 August when returning from a mine-laying operation in the Scheldt estuary. The destroyers suffered no damage and the enemy aircraft were driven off by RAF fighters. The diary is a little ambiguous and while it indicates that this occurrence was on 8 August it is entirely possible that it refers to an event a day earlier.

CHAPTER 12 Aftermath

T HE DRONE of attacking and defending aircraft and the almost incessant noise of gunfire and explosions that had punctuated large parts of the day around The Solent had finally subsided by the late afternoon. Out to sea, a relatively peaceful summer's evening had replaced the chaos of the day with 6/10 cloud now at 4,000 to 5,000ft, a light haze on the horizon and a watery sun which reflected brightly on the choppy sea with its breaking white crests. The scene, so recently a battlefield, no longer seemed anything out of the ordinary – although bodies, wreckage and survivors were still out there amongst the white-tipped crests and being gradually dispersed and spread by the tide and a freshening south-westerly wind. Rescue and salvage attempts remained ongoing and various merchant and Royal Navy vessels were limping into the shelter of port with varying degrees of damage. At RAF and Luftwaffe airfields, exhausted pilots and aircrews tried to relax after the rigours of the day's fighting and made an effort not to dwell too much on the fates of those of their colleagues who had not come home. For one RAF pilot, the experience of Convoy CW9 Peewit was just about to start.

To the north of The Solent, at RAF Gosport, a mixed bag of largely obsolete aircraft types made up the establishment of No.2 Anti-Aircraft Co-Operation Unit; a Fairey Shark, a Fairey III F, a Seal, Hawker Fury, a Hampden, Swordfish, Gladiator, Tiger Moth and Blackburn Rocs comprising at least some of the varied types on strength. Here, and with the distant funeral pyres clearly visible from over the horizon, the CO, Squadron Leader C N Carpenter, ordered one of his pilots to get airborne in one of the unit's Blackburn Roc aircraft. Pilot Officer D H 'Nobby' Clarke's duty was to help direct ships involved in attempts to rescue wrecked mariners or ditched aviators – although, in truth, some of the rescue

Plt Off Derrick Clarke of No.2 Anti-Aircraft Co-Operation Unit flew a search operation around the Isle of Wight sea area during the late afternoon of 8 August looking for survivors from the day's bitter fighting.

ships were by now in need of assistance themselves.

As Derrick Clarke walked out somewhat apprehensively to his Roc, L3131, Sqn Ldr Carpenter briefed him on the situation and told him that many ships had been dive-bombed. He added the rider: "Oh...and be careful. There are plenty of 109s around!" It didn't exactly ease Clarke's anxious state of mind, although he responded with what he hoped was a fairly chipper and unconcerned-sounding "Oh well...nice to have known you, sir," as he clambered aboard the Roc and started up. Taxiing out and pointing his aircraft into wind for take-off, Clarke was airborne at 17.05. Minutes later he was over Spithead and on his way to the scene of action. Nothing could have prepared him for what he was about to see:

"Half a dozen miles south of the Isle of Wight I found the wreckage. It stretched for miles in every direction. Tables, chairs, timber, hatches, spars, empty lifebelts, chests of drawers – debris of every sort. And coke – vast rafts of it; grey-black against the dark blue of the sea; damping the waves to gently heaving mounds. And there were patches of oil, too, silvery grey in the sun and spreading out from already sunken ships as great globs of it rose to the surface to feed each ever widening pool. There were ships in various positions of death throes. One, seemingly normal from a distance, I found to be an empty shell of red glowing coal. The shimmering heat lifted my Roc in the manner of a vicious cumuli nimbus cloud. The steel masts had crumbled into the inferno, the decks and sides showed bright cherry red through the slashes caused by bomb splinters. The bridge structure had mostly collapsed.

"There were others, too. One, upside down, showed a barnacle-encrusted bottom and part of its enormous propeller. It looked like a shark swimming past a half-tide rock. I saw another ship, seemingly undamaged, rear into the classical vertical position before it slid under, and yet another, which was burning furiously all the time I was there, was still floating when I left three hours later. But my job was to search for survivors and although I flew around at nil feet scrutinising every ship and every bit of wreckage I could not at first find a solitary human being – and neither could I see any of the so-called rescue ships.

"Then, after half-an-hour's circling, a three-star Very cartridge exploded right under my nose – so close that it almost hit the engine. I whipped over in a steep turn and there, held afloat by a strange sort of Mae West and wearing a black helmet was, what to my mind, could only be a German pilot. He waved frantically as I roared around him and I had that momentary qualm; should I do something about a Jerry – who had caused all this – or look for our own fellows? Then common decency took charge and I tried to fix the position of this solitary survivor by cross-bearings from the shore which was now about twelve miles distant. Then I set off to look for a rescue ship. I found her twenty minutes later, steaming at full speed from somewhere up Channel – grey painted, of indeterminate class and the nomenclature T68 on her sides. In relief, I headed straight for her and received a shattering welcome from the trigger-happy navy.

"I sheered away from the shell bursts and cursed their ignorance at not recognising an aircraft of their own Fleet Air Arm. I had no time to waste, so I circled to their stern and made another run at nil feet directly towards her backsides – a particularly vulnerable position for most naval ships. She twisted in an attempt to bring her guns to bear, but I turned with her. Throttling right back, lowering the flaps and opening the hood I flew past her starboard side just level with the cluster of ducking men on the bridge. As I flew slowly by I waggled two fingers in the uncomplimentary fashion of Englishmen. Winston Churchill had not yet then made the sign famous, but my recognition was achieved all the same. I grabbed a message streamer, which was weighted with a big hunk of lead, and scrawled a note 'Bloke in drink. Follow me', and lobbed it onto the deck of T68. After all, they had shot at me first! I then flew slowly back to the German pilot, who was waving feebly, and circled to mark the spot.

"While T68 was picking up the pilot, I recommenced my search and found a body in a water-logged lifeboat. Was he dead or alive? Then I found an overjoyed man on a Carley Float who waved vigorously. By this time T68 was following me around like a hungry dog behind a butcher. Something, perhaps intuition, sent me further out to sea. Thirty miles south I saw the dot of a small boat and edged towards it cautiously. It was an air force launch, badly damaged, and with her RAF ensign hoisted inverted in the universal distress signal. From 2,000ft there was no sign of T68 so I waggled my wings encouragingly and sped home. A tug from Portsmouth [sic: in fact it was Bembridge lifeboat] found her before nightfall."

Clarke landed at 20.15 with only eight gallons of petrol left after his gruelling three hours-and-ten-minutes sortie.

Apart from his unfriendly welcome by the Royal Navy, Clarke was also twice shot at by a Blenheim aircraft; once at 18.30 and again at 19.15. However, both times he managed to discourage further attacks by firing the colours of the day from his Very pistol. The only Blenheim in the air at this time was a 59 Squadron aeroplane flown by Plt Off B Van Blokland with his crew of Sgts Woodcock and Garvill, and so it seems that this must have been the attacking aircraft on each occasion. Trigger-happy gunners that day were apparently not exclusive to the Senior Service.

'Nobby' Clarke's graphic account sits exactly with the known facts of the attacks on CW9 and its aftermath; the upturned hull of Empire Crusader, the sinking Borealis, the ship marked T68 (in fact, this was HMS Basset), the shot-up HSL 116 and the rescue of Lt Müller from the sea, complete with the account of Müller firing the Very pistol – a Very pistol that was specifically mentioned in the 238 Squadron operations record book. As a graphic tale of the aftermath of the attacks on Peewit, Clarke's account is a truly superb contemporary record giving us history just as it was.

From the other side of the English Channel, the Germans were looking for their lost airmen too. Heinkel 59 seaplanes of the Seenotdienst had been out since at least early afternoon looking for Luftwaffe airmen in the water. Indeed, it was a lucky shot from the gunner on one such patrolling He 59 that had hit and crippled Sqn Ldr Fenton's Hurricane earlier in the day when both the Heinkel and Fenton were looking for downed airmen. One of those being searched for by the Luftwaffe was Hptm Werner Andres who had been hit by a pursuing RAF fighter over the Channel whilst he was escorting one of the Ju 87 Stuka attacks. With bullet strikes in the radiator, Andres' engine rapidly overheated and literally half way between the Isle of Wight and Cherbourg he found himself in the water.

Although it would be nice to be able to caption this photograph as being one of the 59 Squadron Blenheims over CW9 Peewit during the afternoon of 8 August 1940 it is, in fact, a Blenheim of 107 Squadron pictured on an entirely different occasion. Nevertheless, this is a fine representation of what Plt Off Blokland and his crew might have seen above Peewit when they reported "...some ships burning".

Supported by just his Mae West lifejacket Andres bobbed around for over two hours, vomiting and disorientated, before the overwhelming relief of being spotted and picked up by one of the searching He 59s.

After so long in the water he was almost hypothermic with cold and totally exhausted. He had quite expected to die. Land was thirty miles in either direction and he could see only the heaving sea – from horizon to horizon. Not a single ship nor any aircraft of either side was in sight for most of the time he was adrift, and the numbing cold of the English Channel, even in the middle of summer, just made him want to give up. The two hours he spent in the sea seemed like an eternity and he was beginning to hallucinate when his rescue finally came. Such was his delirious state of mind after those two hours that he couldn't even work out how he had ended up in the sea, or why.

He was one of the lucky few and despite the searches by both sides many airmen had drowned or died of exposure before the day was out. As dusk descended that evening it became clear that there would be no more survivors, either RAF or Luftwaffe, who would be coming home from the air fighting that day. Nevertheless, searches were continued the next day for any remaining survivors or bodies, including those from the wrecked ships.

59 Squadron, who had flown extensively over the convoy the day before, were ordered to carry out some of the searches. One of those sorties was flown by Blenheim (TR-Y) crewed by Plt Off R W Ayres, Sgt Roper and Sgt Webb who were detailed to 'Search derelict shipping'. Taking off at 11.05 on 9 August, Ayres and his crew searched the Selsey Bill and Isle of Wight sea areas where they saw one damaged ship off Selsey Bill and one in tow off St Catherine's Point and reported: "Wreckage seen south of The Needles. Photographs were taken." Unfortunately, no trace of the photographs that were taken by Ayres's crew exists within the squadron operations record book, nor have they yet been traced elsewhere. If they still exist, and as with the currently un-located photographs taken by other squadron aircraft actually *on* 8 August 1940, they would provide a fascinating photographic record of the attacks on CW9 Peewit.

Notwithstanding Clarke's detailed and factual account, and Werner Andres' harrowing experiences in the water, a rather different perspective on things was presented by the news media of the day. Obviously driven by propaganda and restricted by censorship, the British newspapers were both upbeat and yet guarded in what they said about Convoy Peewit and the barrage balloon ships. At the time, and aside from optimistic estimates of the numbers of aircraft destroyed over Peewit on 8 August 1940, nothing was said about the convoy itself.

On 5 January 1941, however, the *Sunday Dispatch* carried a photograph of HMS *Borealis* towing its balloon, and beneath it was the caption: "This is one of our vessels that escort the ships through the Straits of Dover under the noses of the Germans. Several balloons are flown to stop dive bombing." Whilst the caption was slightly economical with the actual truth of the matter, the article that accompanied it was rather more strident in its reportage and equally economic with the facts, stating: "On August 8th last year a convoy sailed with balloons through the Straits of Dover and reached port safely." In fact, by the time the article had appeared, HMS *Borealis* had been sitting on the bottom of the English Channel for nigh on six months, along with a goodly number of her erstwhile charges. Meanwhile, the ash from the six protective barrage balloons shot down over the convoy had long since

The Luftwaffe's last casualty associated with air actions against British Isles shipping targets on 8 August was a Heinkel 111 of I/KG 4. Until 1979 the almost complete tail section of the Heinkel still lay on the mountainside where it had crashed.

been dispersed by time and tide. Nowadays the *Sunday Dispatch* article is perhaps a form of journalism that might be called 'spin'.

When darkness fell across the British Isles that night (sunset was at 19.30 and twilight ended at 20.11) the attention of the Luftwaffe still remained, at least to some extent, focussed on shipping attacks and at some time before midnight a number of Heinkel 111s of 1/KG 4 departed their Soesterberg base in the Netherlands, detailed to carry out a mine-laying operation to the Belfast docks. At 01.30 on 9 August, one of the Heinkels, a He 111H-4, 5J+SH, slammed into the summit of Eastmans Cairn, Cairnsmore-of-Fleet in Kirkcudbrightshire and exploded. Lt A Zeiss, Uffz W Hajesch, Uffz G. Fr. von Türckheim and Uffz W Mechsner became the last casualties of action against shipping mounted by the Luftwaffe on 8 August 1940. However, the Luftwaffe perhaps still retained an interest in what was left of Convoy CW9.

In an ULTRA intercept picked up on 8 August it was learned that the Junkers 88s of I/KG 51 were to be in a state of readiness from 07.00 for attacks against shipping, with the Messerschmitt 110s of I/ZG 2 to provide escort cover. However, if the dispersed remnants of CW9 were still of interest to the Luftwaffe then that interest clearly waned. Equally, if the shipping on I/KG 51's target list *had* been the ships now in Weymouth Bay and Portland then no such operations were flown. However, there may have been a lack of clarity in the interception of the message and the date or interpretation of intent for any attack by

I/KG 51 as mentioned in ULTRA. It is possible that the shipping attacks referred to were simply held in abeyance from 9 August. Indeed, when a period of weather unfavourable for such attacks had abated, we do in fact find elements of KG 51 carrying out bombing raids on 12 August escorted by I/ZG 2. These included attacks on Portsmouth Docks and the shipping concentrated there, making it seem likely that this was the raid being referred to in the ULTRA intercept.

To an extent, the air attacks on CW9 Peewit of 8 August 1940 had signalled the end of major air assaults against shipping targets in the English Channel. Sporadic but much less concentrated bombing raids against convoys did carry on but this date was most certainly the peak of this kind of enemy air activity. From here on, the Battle of Britain moved into new phases. The battle of the convoys was all but over.

The air action of 8 August 1940 had one last hurrah for Plt Off Peter Parrott of 145 Squadron. The young pilot was physically and mentally exhausted after three operational combat sorties flying his Hurricane and his expectations were that the day was over after the last sortie. He was wrong.

"We were more than a little surprised to be ordered to send three of our number over to Tangmere [from Westhampnett] that evening for night readiness – the first time that we had been called for this duty. I was one of the three selected to go. It so happened that I had never flown a Hurricane at night, but I deemed it politic not to reveal this fact at such a late stage. It was, I suppose, inevitable that I should draw the short straw and thus be the first to go if we were scrambled. And I was. Taxiing out to the glim-lamp flarepath was another new innovation for me and was at walking speed with an airman on each wing tip to guide me. As I took off there was no visible horizon so I was forced to concentrate on the blind flying instruments. As I climbed I could see searchlight beams ahead seeking targets, and over Portsmouth there were flashes of anti-aircraft shells bursting. I next noticed that the Hurricane seemed to be gaining height rather more slowly than usual. I scanned the instruments and all was reassuringly normal with no red lights and three green-for-safety lights. Wait a minute. Three greens? *Three greens!!*

"In concentrating on the flying instruments of the blind flying panel I had omitted to raise the undercarriage. Rectifying this improved the rate of climb considerably and having reached the height ordered by the controller I levelled off and headed towards the action. I was almost immediately caught, and totally blinded, by a searchlight beam. No matter what evasive action I took I was held in the beam. I asked the controller to have the light doused, but to no avail. To lose the beam I had to get out of its range, and this I eventually did whilst worrying that I would very soon become a target for the anti-aircraft gunners as I was very nicely illuminated for them, thank you very much. Recovering my night vision took some little while and as the controller had no targets for me I was recalled after a fruitless hour. Coming into land and the Merlin coughed and crackled in the throttle-back with great glaring bright jets of bluish flame issuing from the exhaust stacks. A judicious adjustment of opening the throttle a tad and I got the same result again. It played havoc with your night vision – and just at the point when you needed it most to concentrate on a pretty hairy landing in the dark. Great! I had never enjoyed night flying and this episode confirmed my opinion that I wasn't cut out to be a night-fighter pilot. Frankly, I had had some scares and excitement that day but my flying that night certainly topped them all. By far it was a much more worrying and nerve wracking experience than fighting the Luftwaffe had ever been!"

No doubt keyed-up by the day's frenetic activity offshore, the searchlight crews of the 391st Searchlight Battery, Royal Artillery, thought their moment had come that night over Portsmouth when they held an 'enemy aircraft' in their beams for several minutes. It had been Peter Parrott's Hurricane.

On 10 August 1940, in what was a far cry from his rather tetchy memorandum subsequent to the costly 4 July debacle involving Convoy OA 178 and Portland naval base, Prime Minister Winston Churchill sent the following telegram to Sir Archibald Sinclair, Minister of State for Air:

"The war cabinet would be glad if you would convey to the fighter squadrons of the Royal Air Force engaged in Thursday's brilliant action their admiration of the skill and prowess which they displayed, and congratulate them upon the defeat and heavy losses inflicted upon the far more numerous enemy."

CHAPTER 13

8 August 1940 in Retrospect
The Sailing of Convoy CW9 Peewit

ITHERTO, EVERY published source on the Battle of Britain that makes reference to Convoy CW9 Peewit (and most books on the subject do) has stated that the convoy set sail on the *evening* of 7 August 1940 in order to creep through the Straits of Dover unseen and under the cover of darkness. This is wholly incorrect. As we have already seen, CW9 Peewit set sail from Southend-on-Sea at 07.00 on the *morning* of 7 August. There can be no doubting the correct sailing time since these are repeated in numerous admiralty reports held at The National Archives, Kew, and confirmed in naval war diaries, reports from individual ships in convoy and in corresponding RAF operations record books. Further, the simple mathematics of the speed of the convoy together with the distance travelled and the key points along its journey when specific events occurred, make it a simple task to back-track its course to the point of origin, if any further confirmation of timings were required. Therefore, we can dispense with the notion of the evening sailing on 7 August and of "creeping through the Straits of Dover under cover of darkness". It did not happen. Convoy CW9 sailed past Dover in broad daylight at around 14.00 on 7 August.

Part of the rationale for assuming that this was a night passage through the Dover Straits seems to have been based upon a supposed order that ships in convoy should be sailed by night to afford them better protection. This is a misconception possibly based upon the order set down in a tele-printer message sent on 13 August 1940 to the naval C-in-Cs at Portsmouth, Western Approaches and Rosyth and to vice-admiral Dover and the naval officers in command at Falmouth, Dartmouth, Portland and Southend-on-Sea.

In it, instructions are laid down that: "Ships to proceed by night hops in escorted small groups between <u>Falmouth and Portsmouth</u> and vice-versa," and then goes on to discuss convoys between Portsmouth and the Thames. It is possible that the wording further on in that instruction might be considered slightly ambiguous in terms of intentions for convoys sailing between the Thames and Portsmouth in either direction. However, night-time hops were not intended to be a feature of those parts of the voyage. It is also possible that some confusion has further arisen subsequently by the inclusion of this tele-printed message as an appendix to the naval war diary covering the period 1 August to 15 August 1940.

If in the past it has been assumed that this was an instruction already in place by 1 August then this overlooks the date of the instruction itself (13 August) as well as ignoring the specifics as to what the night-time order exactly referred to. However, the Admiralty's 'General Survey and Appreciation' document relating to the August convoy sailings in the English Channel is most certainly unambiguous: "The passage to the <u>west</u> (author's underlining) of Portsmouth being made by ships under the cover of darkness coast hopping from port to port." There was certainly never any intention to sail convoys through the Dover Straits by night, and if there had been any such instructions in place at the time of CW9 Peewit's departure then clearly its sailing was in flagrant breach of Admiralty orders. That was certainly *not* the case. Indeed, there were in fact very specific orders then in place that *prohibited* such navigation through the Dover Straits by night. The naval staff war diary (situation report) of 8 August states specifically in this respect:

> "C-in-C Portsmouth considers these convoys will always be vulnerable to attack by E-Boats and he advocates the fullest use of night coast hopping by small convoys capable of manoeuvre when threatened. The C-in-C Nore, however, considers destroyers afford the best protection; <u>night sailings from the Thames to Dover are not possible owing to lighting restrictions.</u>"

(Author's note: The C-in-C Portsmouth's comment overlooked the fact that the E-Boat attacks were invariably always at night, and thus night sailings were not going to offer any protection against such attacks!)

That Convoy CW9 Peewit sailed past Dover at 14.00 on 8 August is therefore beyond any doubt. The question as to how the convoy was spotted by the Germans is dealt with in the following section of this chapter. One other question needs to be addressed, however; its purpose.

As with the previously misleading information on the timings of CW9 Peewit it has often been speculated that the sailing of convoys like CW9 were merely intended to make a point to the Germans – that the English Channel was still English and still open for business. Further, that the sailing of CW9 and other convoys was a relatively pointless exercise intended merely to draw the Luftwaffe into battle. As is explored elsewhere here, none of these suppositions are accurate or anywhere near so. There was most certainly a point to the sailing of these coastal convoys – the delivery of priceless coal and goods.

German radar

The published sources referred to in the previous section, and which suggest the passage of CW9 Peewit through the Dover Straits was by night, also state that the convoy was detected by German Freya radar at Cap-Gris-Nez. Again, this is incorrect. As we have seen in a previous chapter, the convoy was spotted visually from Wissant, in daylight, and against a setting sun off Dungeness. Nevertheless, and whilst the question of radar and the part it played in the misfortunes of CW9 Peewit is irrelevant in the context of this book, it would be sensible to examine here the wider issue of Freya radar insofar as it affected British shipping traffic in the English Channel.

When the Germans had set up their long-range guns in the Pas-de-Calais during the summer of 1940, it eventually became apparent that some form of radar control may be being used to direct their fire and that this fire was not necessarily being directed by sight alone. Indeed, Lt Cdr Jonas of the Admiralty reported as follows on CW 18 (25–26 November) on 27 November 1940:

"The regularity with which CW convoys are shelled commencing at approximately No.4 Buoy, coupled with the fact that CE convoys are invariably fired upon when passing No.4 Buoy, draws attention again to the possibility of a hydrophone having been installed by the enemy near to this buoy."

In fact, and although Jonas would not have been aware of this, suspicion of radar had already brought scientist Mr N E Davis, an experienced Marconi television engineer, onto the scene with a receiver capable of a wide range of wavelength. Davis quickly determined the radiative characteristics of the transmissions and identified them as Seetakt emissions coming from a radar source. Whilst a jammer was quickly constructed, restrictions on the form of jamming modulation had to be imposed for fear that this would lead the Germans in to using an effective 'noise' against British CH transmissions. Consequently, a rather more covertly discreet jamming was implemented using a sinusoidal form. However, what does all this tell us about radar and the English Channel convoys?

Clearly, by the latter half of 1940, the British were at least aware that the

A convoy is shelled as it passes through the Straits of Dover.

Germans were using their Freya radar to spy upon shipping moving in the Channel. However, Professor R V Jones in his description of the work he carried out on German radar with British scientific intelligence is specific about Freya and Channel shipping. When the name Freya first cropped up for British intelligence during the summer of 1940 it did not take long for the connection to be made to radar, and for R V Jones to be asked to investigate and report:

"My report concluded that there were Freya stations near Cherbourg and Brest, and we learnt later that the former had detected our destroyer HMS *Delight* at a range of about sixty miles with the result that she was sunk by the Luftwaffe on 29 July 1940. Since she had neither balloons nor air escort, the Freya apparatus must have been able to detect her directly."

Nowhere in any of R V Jones's writings does he mention a Freya in situ in the Pas-de-Calais during the summer period of 1940 and he only makes reference to the radar sites at

Cherbourg and Brest, one of which had already detected HMS *Delight* with fatal results. (HMS *Delight* was sunk by the Luftwaffe after an air attack off Portland by twenty-three Ju 87 Stukas of III./St.G 2 in position 50°13' N by 2°45'W at 19.20. She exploded and sank at 21.45 after being hit by five 500kg, four 250kg and numerous 50kg bombs in yet another demonstration of the power of the Stuka as a formidable attack weapon. 147 survivors were later landed at Portland, fifty-nine of them badly injured. A total of eighteen of her crew were killed.)

Despite the lack of evidence for any Freya sets operative around the Pas-de-Calais during the high summer of 1940, there does seem to be evidence through the work of Mr N E Davis that some kind of Freya was operative in the Calais area at least by November 1940, and this may well have been a mobile set. If there was any Freya in place in the Pas-de-Calais during August 1940 then there seems to be no evidence that it was operational on 7 August 1940. Even if it was, radar certainly played no part in the misfortunes of CW9 Peewit.

Air Sea Rescue

The battles of 8 August 1940 saw the first major air fighting over the sea for both the RAF and Luftwaffe and resulted in a good many fliers of both air forces ending up in the water. Inevitably, it tested arrangements for the rescue of downed airmen by both sides and whilst the Luftwaffe system was not perfect there were serious comparable deficiencies in respect of how downed RAF fliers were rescued from the sea. In this respect, there were two key issues: (a) survival equipment for those downed in the sea; (b) arrangements for actually effecting rescue. Let us first look at the question of survival equipment.

RAF fighter pilots who had the misfortune to land in the water had only a rudimentary life jacket to keep them afloat. This was a cotton outer containing a rubber bladder that could only be inflated by the wearer through a mouthpiece. Clearly, this could be a difficult procedure for a cold, shocked and possibly wounded pilot struggling in the sea and who was almost certainly gasping for breath. If he managed to keep afloat he carried no means by which to attract the attention of ships or aircraft. He was a small dot in a very big ocean. To make matters worse his life jacket (known colloquially as a Mae West) was issued in a dark green colour which was pretty much the same colour as the English Channel or North Sea on an average day. Some pilots sensibly 'borrowed' yellow aircraft dope from the stores and painted their lifejackets for increased visibility. Other than that, pilots carried no additional survival aids. Heliograph mirrors, lamps and whistles to attract attention came much later than the Battle of Britain.

From the very outset of going into the water, the RAF airman of 1940 was at a distinct disadvantage when compared to his German counterpart. The frequent and timeless *crie de coeur* from servicemen and the news media of personnel being sent into action with inadequate or inferior kit is hardly a new one. The Luftwaffe fighter pilot in the same situation, however, was infinitely better equipped and would be supported by a state-of-the-art lifejacket or *Schwimmwest*. These were of a rubberised yellow canvas that could be automatically inflated by a small CO_2 bottle but with an additional mouthpiece to keep the air in the jacket topped-up. (Although by no means fireproof, the German lifejacket was also infinitely more resistant to flame than was the British version. There are plenty of accounts of RAF pilots finding themselves in the sea with a singed lifejacket only to face the depressing sight of long strings of bubbles emerging from the melted bladder when they blew into the inflation tube.) Other lifejackets were also used by the Germans, with some Luftwaffe crews being issued the rather more bulky kapok lifejackets that required no inflation. These had a high collar which helped to keep the wearer's head up out of the water.

The German flier would also have a pack of bright green fluorescein dye which stained the sea around him a vivid emerald green colour that was visible for many miles. He also had a yellow skull-cap to place over his flying helmet, carried 'survival' chocolate and sometimes a flare pistol that he could use to attract attention. He would also have an issue clasp knife (called a gravity knife) with which he could cut away any entangled parachute shroud lines or harness. In the case of anything more than a single-seat aircraft, the German airmen had a bright yellow rubber dinghy (with automatic inflation) equipped with paddles, flares, first aid kit, basic survival rations, compass, rum, cigarettes and matches. Undoubtedly the chances of survival for the Luftwaffe airman, and of being spotted, were significantly better than were those for an RAF flier of the same period, perhaps understandably as early Fighter Command thinking was of fighting over our homeland, and not the sea.

Significantly, the Fighter Command operations record book for 8 August 1940 makes very specific reference to the failings of survival equipment for RAF pilots:

"It is enquired whether an immediate issue of a smoke producing device cannot be made since the new type of lifejacket is not yet available for trial and it must be some time before a service issue is made. [In fact, the 'new' pattern was the 1941 lifejacket which did not come into service until much later in 1941.] Meanwhile a device is necessary to enable MTBs and other vessels to locate pilots fallen in the sea."

It was all very timely, and yet in many cases too late. Certainly it was too late for the downed RAF pilots of CW9 Peewit. Indeed, most RAF aircrew downed in the sea during the forthcoming Battle of Britain still had woefully inadequate and inferior kit, and mostly had the English Channel coloured Mae West with no marker dye. However, the request by RAF Fighter Command for the immediate issue of some additional aids to attract attention was not entirely ignored and was at least, in part, being put in place by as early as the end of August 1940.

Plt Off Jack Rose, a Hurricane pilot with 32 Squadron, recalled that on the morning of 25 August each pilot on the squadron was issued with a pack of fluorescene to sew on his lifejacket. While waiting at dispersal for the next scramble, Rose borrowed an outsize needle and passed the time sewing on the pack to his life jacket. Shortly afterwards, his flight was scrambled and six Hurricanes intercepted a formation of twelve Dorniers at 12,000ft. Rose opened fire on a bomber, but an escorting Me 109 attacked him and his aircraft was hit and became uncontrollable. He was forced to bale out, landing in the English Channel. After floating for two hours a searching aircraft from his squadron spotted the trail left by the coloured dye in the water. A ship was directed to him and he was rescued. A fellow pilot, Plt Off K R Gillman, who was shot down in the same battle had not sewn on his

German war artist Hans Liska drew this rather dramatic depiction of the German air-sea-rescue Heinkel 59 crews picking up ditched fliers – in this case an RAF crew! The He 59s performed a valuable though dangerous service saving both German and British airmen alike, although were given no quarter by British fighter pilots. On 8 August they were able to rescue several Luftwaffe aircrew from the English Channel.

fluorescence pack and also landed in the sea. Unfortunately, he was not found. Rose remained convinced that the pack had saved his life and its absence may well have resulted in his friend's death.

Whilst Rose's experience was an impressive demonstration of the value of this marker dye, the packs did not become widely available for the pilots of RAF Fighter Command during the Battle of Britain and it was not until December of that year that they started to become standard issue equipment. However, the speed of implementation of this equipment from its first suggestion on 8 August 1940 to when it was supplied to 32 Squadron is commendable given the inevitable time taken to develop, test, source and manufacture the materials before actually issuing and placing them in service.

Once they were in the sea, however, it was something of a lottery as to whether RAF or Luftwaffe airmen would be picked up alive. The odds for that lottery were stacked rather more favourably during the Battle of Britain on the German side because of their far superior rescue organisation – although it is important to point out that both sides would clearly rescue aircrew of either nationality and frequently did so. Survival could also sometimes come at a price – captivity.

As we have seen, the Luftwaffe had in place a fleet of Heinkel He 59 seaplanes belonging to Seenotflugkommando 1 that operated in the English Channel with the purpose of rescuing downed Luftwaffe aircrew and some of these aircraft were certainly operational on 8 August. Initially painted white overall and bearing the Red Cross emblem and civilian aircraft registration codes, it had obviously been hoped by the Germans that these aircraft would be afforded immunity from attack by the enemy. It was not to be. On 9 July one such He 59 was intercepted by Spitfires of 54 Squadron over the English Channel and forced down onto the Goodwin Sands, its crew captured. The RAF air intelligence report into the downing of the He 59 was comprehensive:

"The aircraft, which was unarmed, landed as soon as it was attacked by Spitfires. It suffered no damage apart from a broken petrol feed or tank. It has since been brought ashore near Walmer lifeboat station.

"The men were unarmed and whatever else they may or may not have been doing they seem to be genuine sea-

The unarmed and Red-Cross-marked He 59 rescue seaplane brought down on the Goodwin Sands on 9 July.

rescue Red Cross workers. This crew saved Sqn Ldr Doran and his observer from the sea off Stavanger. The aircraft was equipped with stretchers, a rubber dinghy, oxygen apparatus and other medical stores.

"They had ordinary two-way radio equipment which was, they stated, used solely for navigation and receiving messages in connection with their job. The crew stated that they had definite instructions not to report any points of operational significance. They stated that their names were registered with the International Red Cross authorities and they were glad to have an opportunity of explaining their organisation. The crew said that there were between twelve and fifteen of these He 59s and these were moved about fairly considerably. This particular crew have in recent months been to Bergen, Stavanger, Amsterdam, Cherbourg and Boulogne."

The downing of this rescue seaplane gave cause for some deliberation by the Air Ministry over what should be done if further such craft were encountered. Should they be regarded as operating as ambulance craft and thus given protection under the Geneva Convention? Or should they be treated as hostile like any other Luftwaffe aircraft? It did not take the Air Ministry too long to make up its mind. On 14 July 1940 it issued Air Ministry Order 1254:

"It has come to the notice of His Majesty's Government in the United Kingdom that enemy aircraft bearing civil markings and marked with the Red Cross have recently flown over British ships at sea and in the vicinity of the British coast, and that they are being employed for purposes which HM Government cannot regard as being consistent with the privileges generally accorded to the Red Cross.

"HM Government desires to accord ambulance aircraft reasonable facilities for the transportation of the sick and wounded, in accordance with the Red Cross convention, and aircraft engaged in the direct evacuation of sick and wounded will be respected, provided that they comply with the relevant provisions of the convention.

"HM Government is unable, however, to grant immunity to such aircraft flying over areas in which operations are in progress on land or at sea, or approaching British or Allied territory, or territory in British occupation, or British or Allied ships.

"Ambulance aircraft which do not comply with the above requirements will do so at their own risk and peril."

It was very much at "risk and peril" that the He 59 shot at by Sqn Ldr Harold Fenton off the Isle of Wight on 8 August had entered the combat zone to carry out a search and rescue mission. However, although the He 59 downed on 9 July was unarmed we certainly had a case of the He 59 encountered by Fenton being armed with at least one MG 15 machine gun. Doubtless the Luftwaffe had by now realised that their air-sea-rescue craft would not be granted any form of immunity. Shots from the He 59 had, in fact, resulted in Fenton's ditching although there is some doubt that Fenton actually shot down the He 59 he attacked. (See Appendix C.)

A German high speed launch rescued a He 111 crew of 8/KG 55 on 26 August 1940 from the Solent.

On the same day, Spitfire pilot Sgt Cyril Babbage was shot down into the sea off Bognor Regis and also rescued – by rowing boat!

Whatever the He 59 crews may or may not have been doing in addition to rescuing downed aircrew is uncertain, but it is an undeniable fact that the service they gave resulted in a considerable number of airmen, British *and* German, being plucked from an otherwise watery grave. The RAF had no comparable service and continued searching along the English Channel by the He 59 crews during the Battle of Britain was undoubtedly courageous. On 8 August alone they were responsible for rescuing at least four Luftwaffe airmen from the sea.

In terms of reliance upon marine craft for the rescue of downed RAF fliers, this was very much a hit and miss affair during 1940. On 8 August there were two RAF high speed launches operating in the sea around the Isle of Wight, looking for downed airmen. These were from the marine craft unit at RAF Calshot and although they were at sea for many hours they failed to find either survivors or bodies. However, the formal organisation of an RAF air sea rescue service was not in place until February 1941 and during the Battle of Britain there was a mixed reliance upon a variety of vessels for rescuing downed RAF fliers. These included the RNLI and Royal Navy MTBs and launches although the RAF did have at its disposal thirteen HSLs, of which ten covered the North Sea and English Channel and came under naval control. However, as early as 22 July 1940, HSL 100 had arrived at Newhaven and established an air sea rescue base, and on 9 August, just the day after CW9 Peewit, the RAF's HSL 121 arrived at Newhaven to become part of 28 ASRMCU. (HSL 121 had been one of the two craft engaged off the Isle of Wight during the CW9 Peewit operations).

The lack of any proper formalised air sea rescue service that was properly integrated within the organisation of the RAF was clearly an impediment to the effective rescue of ditched RAF aircrew during the Battle of Britain, and during the official period of the battle (10 July to 30 October) no less than 179 RAF aircrew were posted as missing and no trace of them was ever found. This was exactly one third of the total casualties sustained by the RAF during the Battle of Britain. The overwhelming majority of these were lost over the sea, although it is impossible to say how many of them might have been saved if they had had better survival kit and an effective and integrated air sea rescue organisation to rely upon.

Aside from the He 59 seaplanes operated by the Luftwaffe, the Germans also had in place a high speed rescue launch service to pluck airmen from the sea, and this organisation was operating in the English Channel during the Battle of Britain. Contrasting the differences between the rescue organisations of the two services was the rescue of an He 111 crew from the sea, just off the Isle of Wight on 26 August 1940, right from under their enemy's noses. As it happened, 26 August also saw the highest number of RAF aircrew rescued from the sea around Britain during 1940, with six men being taken from the water by various means. Not many miles from the successful snatching of the Heinkel crew, Spitfire pilot, Sgt Cyril Babbage of 602 Squadron landed by parachute in the sea off Bognor Regis. He too was rescued – by two fishermen and two soldiers in a rowing boat.

German War Aims and CW9 Peewit

From his headquarters on 1 August 1940, Hitler had issued Directive No.17 for the conduct of air and sea warfare against England. In it, he set out his plans and intentions for the furtherance of his war aims, and shaped the way the air and sea war would unfold over the coming days and weeks:

"In order to establish the necessary conditions for the final conquest of England I intend to intensify air and sea warfare against the English homeland. I therefore order as follows:

1) The German air force is to overpower the English air force with all the forces at its command, in the shortest time possible. The attacks are to be directed primarily against flying units, their ground installations, and their supply organisations, but also against the aircraft industry, including that manufacturing anti-aircraft equipment.

2) After achieving temporary or local air superiority the air war is to be continued against ports, in particular against stores of food, and also against stores of provisions in the interior of the country. Attacks on the south coast ports will be made in the smallest possible scale, in view of our own forthcoming operations.

3) On the other hand, air attacks on enemy warships and merchant ships may be reduced except where some particularly favourable target happens to present itself, where such attacks would lend additional effectiveness to those mentioned in paragraph 2, or where such attacks are necessary for the training of crews for further operations.

4) The intensified air warfare will be carried out in such a way that the air force can at any time be called upon to give adequate support to naval operations against suitable targets. It must also be ready to take part in full force in Operation *Seelöwe*.

5) I reserve for myself the right to decide on terror attacks as measures of reprisal.

The intensification of the air war may begin on or after 5 August. The exact time is to be decided by the air force after completion of preparations and in the light of the weather. The navy is authorised to begin the proposed intensified naval war at the same time.

Adolf Hitler   1st August 1940

Quite apart from the direct orders of the Führer as set out in this directive, it is also necessary when considering the background of the attacks on CW9 Peewit to examine the wider remit of the Luftwaffe battle plan at that time.

Within the combined plans of the German armed forces for the invasion of the British Isles, the task of the German air force was twofold: in the middle of July orders by the German air force operations staff to the various Luftflotten (air fleets) made clear their two specific aims as follows:

(a) To eliminate the Royal Air Force both as a fighting force and in its ground organisation;

(b) To strangle the supply of Great Britain by attacking its ports and its shipping.

In relation to the attacks on CW9 Peewit it can therefore be seen that both of these war aims were, at least in part, being met. Further, Adolf Hitler's Directive No.17 of 1 August was carefully being followed by operations staff when planning the 8 August attacks. Direct attacks on south coast ports were avoided (see point 2 of the directive) and, additionally, the drawing of RAF Fighter Command into battle could be seen as furthering the stated war aim of overpowering the RAF and striving towards the eventual achievement of air superiority. It was clearly not, though, the main objective and in that context we also need to examine Air Chief Marshal Sir Hugh Dowding's dispatch to *The London Gazette* of 11 September 1946. In it, he stated that:

"....the weight and scale of the attack(s) indicates that the primary object was rather to bring our fighters to battle than to destroy the hulls and cargoes of the small ships engaged in the coastal trade."

In respect of the attacks on CW9 Peewit, however there is absolutely no evidence whatsoever that the primary German objective in carrying out these major assaults was in any way to bring the RAF to battle. The object was to destroy the convoy of merchant ships, a battle aim perceived to be in line with the general war aims of the Luftwaffe operations staff.

To wit: *"To strangle the supply of Great Britain by attacking its ports and its shipping."* True, Hitler's 1 August directive had shifted a degree of emphasis away from attacks on shipping and had laid the foundation stone for the next phase of the assault which would be aimed largely at destroying the RAF. However, within Hitler's directive was still embodied the intent to continue attacks on British merchant shipping. To wit: *"Air attacks on enemy warships and merchant ships may be reduced <u>except where some particularly favourable target happens to present itself.</u>"* Clearly, in the case of CW9 Peewit a particularly favourable target had indeed presented itself. Thus the shipping strikes mounted on 8 August helped move towards the fulfilment of both the Führer's directive *and* the war aims of the Luftwaffe operations staff. Whilst drawing the RAF into battle that day might indeed have marginally furthered the intended aim of eliminating the RAF it was, nevertheless, a by-product of the shipping assaults and not the primary purpose of them as Dowding had later supposed.

Embodied, too, within Adolf Hitler's Directive No.17 was the very specific statement that: *"The intensification of the air war may begin on or after 5 August."* There can certainly be no doubting that 8 August saw an intensification of the air war, although it is almost certainly the case that this statement within the directive was a specific reference to the planned all-out offensive against the RAF that was ultimately launched on 13 August 1940 – *Adler Tag* (Eagle Day). Very clearly, Luftwaffe offensive weaponry was amassed, ready and waiting for the word to go all along the northern coast of France; the men, the aircraft, the equipment and the ordnance had all been put in place and were prepared for the launch of Eagle Day. Consequently, when CW9 Peewit presented itself as a "particularly favourable target" there was no shortage of resources to deal with it.

The Commencement of the Battle of Britain

As indicated elsewhere in this work there was initially some confusion over the dates between which the Battle of Britain had been fought. As we have seen, Dowding retrospectively varied the date of commencement back from 8 August to 10 July although, in doing so, he added the rider about there being some merit to the choice of 8 August. Indeed, such merit might well have been that that day saw the heaviest air fighting of the war thus far. Dowding added that the revised choice for the date of commencement (10 July) was somewhat arbitrary but referred to it as having seen "…the first really big formation (seventy aircraft) intended primarily to bring our fighter defence to battle on a large scale".

With the benefit of historical hindsight one might question the validity of that statement on two counts. Again, we have a day in the German air campaign that was directed largely at convoy targets – there being no less than eight convoys at sea around the British Isles on 10 July 1940. However, in the days leading up to 10 July RAF Fighter Command had countered a good dozen raids of fifty or more aircraft. RAF losses had already been high in fighter aircraft and pilots, to the extent that on the very day that the Battle of Britain was later declared to have begun, the operations record book for 54 Squadron (Spitfires) stated: "As a result of the first phase of the Battle of Britain the squadron could only muster eight aircraft and thirteen pilots." So far as 54 Squadron were concerned, the Battle of Britain had *already* started – and long before 10 July, too.

Clearly, and as Dowding had stated, his decision about dates was arbitrary. However, not only must his assessment that the 10 July saw the first raids "intended to draw the RAF into battle" be questioned but so must his statement about the numbers of aircraft involved. In that respect, not so much the actual numbers involved but what benchmark might he have set for determining just how many aircraft in a raid signalled that battle had been joined? One swallow might not make the summer, but equally how many aircraft were needed to make the battle? Given that at least some seventy-five aircraft had taken part in the two-pronged Portland attack on 4 July is it not surprising that *this* day failed to be selected as the first day of the Battle of Britain? Indeed, in his dispatch of September 1946 Dowding made a tacit acknowledgement of the Portland raid but

Air Chief Marshal Sir Hugh Dowding, C-in-C RAF Fighter Command during the Battle of Britain.

even although the numbers of aircraft involved then were at least more than, equal to or comparable with the numbers he quoted for involvement on 10 July he still did not select that date. The reason is clear.

On 4 July RAF Fighter Command had not put in an appearance over Portland and the enemy aircraft had attacked unhindered. It would surely have been singularly inappropriate (and ultimately embarrassing) to have chosen *that* particular day as being the commencement of battle notwithstanding the weight of the German air assaults that took place.

Interestingly, in his memoirs, Generalfeldmarschal Albert Kesselring made specific reference to the German air assault against the British Isles as having got underway on 8 August. Of course, and with his memoirs written whilst still in captivity at the end of the war it may well have been that Kesselring had access to the 1941 HMSO publication on the Battle of Britain, which as we know gave the same day as the commencement of the battle and all-out German air attacks. It may well be, therefore, that Kesselring's statement may have no greater historical accuracy than the HMSO publication as regards to dates and he may well have been *intending* anyway to refer to Eagle Day on 13 August. If this is not the explanation then it is difficult to see from where else Kesselring might have drawn that date, or the basis of his reliance upon it.

Of course, whichever day had been settled upon, the dates ultimately set for the Battle of Britain were entirely 'artificial' and gave some shape by way of time-frames to a battle that didn't really have one. In truth, the battle just faded in, reached a crescendo, and then faded out again. In that respect, one could equally question the cut-off of 31 October, since there was certainly fierce and frequent daylight air activity continuing way beyond that date

Generallfeldmarschal Albert Kesselring.

and on into November and December. For example, on 14 November 1940, a heavy Junkers 87 Stuka raid was launched against Convoy CE16 Booty in the Dover Straits and a fierce battle involving Spitfires of 66, 74 and 603 Squadrons and Hurricanes of 46 and 249 Squadrons ensued with the Ju 87s and their escorting Messerschmitt 109s of JG 26 and JG 51. It was a huge melee. But the Battle of Britain had officially ended two weeks earlier.

It had not been the author's initial intention to set out to suggest any alternative date for the start or finish of the Battle of Britain and neither is the author necessarily suggesting that any one date has more merit than another. However, since this book focuses upon the actions of 8 August 1940, and since that date was *originally* and very pointedly laid down by the Air Ministry as the date upon which the battle had started, then it was inevitable that commentary on the question of dates should be made here. When deliberating over what time frame he should set, Dowding was faced with an almost insurmountable problem. The dates he finally settled upon are now set in stone – quite literally.

Looking retrospectively at some of the dates Dowding had to choose from, how his decision might have been reached, and why, is a legitimate exercise in the context of this book. It is not a revisionist challenge to what are now historically accepted dates. The Battle of Britain will officially remain in history as having taken place between 10 July and 31 October 1940. That those dates should have alone been chosen by Dowding, who led his 'fighter boys' to victory, is entirely appropriate – howsoever he reached that conclusion.

An Overview of the English Channel Convoys

Elsewhere in this work we have looked at the importance of coal, both as a vital war commodity and its significance as a coastal (English Channel) cargo. However, it is also necessary to examine the vital work of the convoys to the British war effort, most especially due to the fact that the value and purpose of sailing these coastal collier convoys has often been questioned and challenged.

As mentioned earlier, some authors and commentators have, in the past, suggested that these coastal convoys were being run unnecessarily and merely as 'bait' to bring the Luftwaffe into battle but nothing could be further from the truth. Equally, it is quite unlikely that the Luftwaffe were attacking the convoys to draw the RAF to battle as Dowding later supposed. As we have seen, the intent of the German attacks was *to strangle the supply of Great Britain by attacking its ports and shipping*" and in this respect the Germans certainly had a very clear appreciation of the significance of the coastal convoys and of Britain's sea trade, generally. In fact, the Luftwaffe fighter arm would probably have rather had it that RAF Fighter Command stayed away from its attacks against Channel shipping. They were no doubt pleased when the RAF failed to show, for example, when HMS *Delight* was bombed and sunk on 29 July, or when Convoy OA 178 and Portland were hit heavily on 4 July 1940.

Indeed, this period of German air attacks against maritime assets was purely about destroying shipping. The war aims directed at destroying the RAF in the air and on the ground did not come into play until after 8 August with the launch of Eagle Day five days later, which heralded the purposeful and sustained attempt to bring the RAF to its knees by attrition over a long period of operations.

It is also necessary to look at the sometimes contentious issue of RAF fighter cover (patrols) above the convoys. Very often there were complaints from the Royal Navy and merchant mariners that there was either insufficient cover or no cover above the convoys as they traversed the English Channel. Whilst the case of Convoy OA 178 hit off Portland is perhaps a little unfair to use as an example (it was very far out and beyond the normal distance escorted by the RAF, anyway) it is certainly the case that CW10 had no cover – at least, according to the Royal Navy report (see Appendix H) and one could argue, perhaps, that the cover over CW9 was at times insufficient or late. However, the difficulties associated with providing some kind of air-umbrella at all times have already been stated although, of course, we do know that Churchill was concerned about the air cover question in the aftermath of the 4 July Channel attacks. Coincidentally though, Dowding had been pressed on the question of convoy protection just the day before.

Dowding made it clear that if his command was to be heavily committed to the defence of targets inland then he would be unable to protect coastal convoys. For this reason he stated that he looked forward to a time when all ocean convoys were passed around the north of Scotland (this actually came into play after the OA 178 attack) and that the English Channel should be restricted to coastal convoys of small ships "…so that the south coast traffic does not much matter". The latter remark is singularly hard to comprehend, since it beggars belief that Dowding would have considered the south coast traffic of relative inconsequence. That the Channel traffic mattered very much indeed is a fact that is beyond either doubt or question.

Two weeks after the 3 July conference, Dowding gave further notice to the Air Ministry that if he was to protect shipping efficiently then he must have more squadrons – but Dowding knew that there *were* no more squadrons and it was thus an impossible request. He pointed out that recent attacks on shipping were not being made by one or two bombers, as was the case in the previous autumn and winter, but by strong and escorted formations of bombers. In his opinion, three squadrons per sector were needed for no other task than for the protection of shipping if the job was to be done properly. In that assessment Dowding was most probably correct, and although he knew that no such 'extra' squadrons could be made available to him, he was probably just covering his back in the event of any failure to protect future convoys adequately. Quite likely the stinging criticisms of the inability of Fighter Command to protect either OA 178 or Portland naval base during the 4 July attacks were still fresh and raw. However, and although the convoy protection issue would not go away, the actual attacks on convoys would ease after 8 August. That said, the convoys that continued to sail of course still needed protective air cover.

A more detailed examination of the Channel convoys is neither appropriate nor possible within the context of this book since the work is aimed at examining the events relating principally to one day and to one convoy. Readers who might wish to explore further and in more detail the bigger picture of naval and maritime warfare in the English Channel are directed to the excellent *Coastal Convoys 1939-1945* by Nick Hewitt and *Naval Warfare in The English Channel 1939-45* by Peter C Smith This author commends both titles as essential reading.

A Question of Medals

Notwithstanding any controversy that might linger on about the battle's actual dates, to set them for any conflict or battle is absolutely necessary within Britain's system for establishing participation in such military confrontations by the issue of an appropriate medal or award. However, and whilst it is most unlikely that this matter was foremost in Dowding's mind when he came to consider the dates of the Battle of Britain, it is a fact that the beginning and cut-off dates of the battle have meant that only those aircrew of RAF Fighter Command who flew at least one operational sortie between 10 July and 31 October 1940 would qualify for the award of the coveted Battle of Britain bar to their 1939-45 Star. This was a clasp that was to be worn on the full medal ribbon of the star, or represented by a gilt rosette if just the medal ribbon was worn. However, quite apart from the requirement to have flown at least one operational sortie, the qualifying aircrew member must also have served on an accredited squadron.

To this end, the Air Ministry drew up Order AMO A.741/1945, a list of RAF Fighter squadrons who were deemed to have participated in the fighting of the Battle of Britain with the result that a total of 2,917 men qualified for the award and were drawn from seventy-one squadrons and units. Whilst we have seen, for instance, that men like Sqn Ldr George Lott (shot down on 9 July) were denied a Battle of Britain bar or a RAF Fighter Command pilot killed, say, on 1 November 1940 was not considered a casualty of the Battle of Britain, there was another controversial issue regarding qualification for the bar that so happens to relate to a squadron heavily involved over CW9 Peewit on 8 August 1940 – 59 Squadron.

Clearly and specifically included within that official list detailed above is 59 Squadron. Consequently, this meant, for example, that all of the pilots and aircrew from that squadron who participated in the actions on that day would have qualified for the award of the bar. Indeed, one such was Plt Off C M M Grece who had flown on a search operation over CW9 Peewit during the morning of 8 August and who was subsequently awarded the bar in line with the requirements laid down under the Air Ministry order. On 12 July 1954 Grece was tragically killed in a flying accident in a private light aircraft at Southampton (Eastleigh) Airport whilst serving as station commander of RAF Middle Wallop. Then a group captain, Grece was certainly the recipient of a Battle of Britain bar at the time of his death.

Another such recipient was Plt Off P A Womersley who flew another search that morning with 59 Squadron. Indeed, Pat Womersely certainly took part in a good many other operations with 59 Squadron during the Battle of Britain period, which would also have been considered to be qualifying operational sorties. However, Womersley, Grece and every other

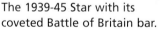

The 1939-45 Star with its coveted Battle of Britain bar.

Squadron Leader George Lott. By a matter of hours he was denied the status of being a Battle of Britain pilot.

pilot or aircrew who flew with 59 Squadron would ultimately have their entitlements revoked – and this included Plt Off L N Davis, Sgt G H Coulton and Sgt B W Beaumont of the same Squadron who had all paid with their lives for their participation over CW9 Peewit.

On 9 November 1960, the RAF issued a revised list of those squadrons considered to qualify for the Battle of Britain bar and 59 Squadron was no longer on it. At a stroke, or arbitrarily as Dowding might have put it, all of those to whom the award had originally been issued on 59 Squadron were told to take down the bar forthwith and to duly return them to the RAF medals branch. Further, any subsequent claims for the award by those who had served on 59 Squadron during the qualifying period, but who had not yet received their award, would not have their applications entertained. Under the circumstances it all seems exceptionally harsh.

What led to this reversal of entitlement for the aircrew of 59 Squadron might be explained by the fact that it was a Coastal Command squadron as opposed to a Fighter Command squadron. That said, however, 59 Squadron fell under the control of Fighter Command during the Battle of Britain as did 235 Squadron – another Blenheim squadron in the same position. 235 Squadron flew broadly similar operations throughout the battle to those flown by 59 Squadron and it also participated in the actions of 8 August. Unlike 59 Squadron however, its aircrew rightfully continue to be recognised as Battle of Britain participants, are entitled to wear the bar and rosette and also have their names recorded on

As a Blenheim pilot with 59 Squadron, Plt Off Pat Womersley flew operationally over CW9 Peewit and was awarded the Battle of Britain bar. Later, it was withdrawn from him and other 59 Squadron aircrew on the basis that the squadron was "ineligible".

the official Battle of Britain roll. As one 59 Squadron pilot later put it, when writing of the withdrawal of the award: "….the feelings about this change ran pretty high at the time, I can tell you!" The question remains, why exactly was 59 Squadron singled out?

For Cpl W G Will, the former barrage balloon handler on HMS *Borealis*, there was also a bone of contention about medal awards. Of course, for him there was no question of a Battle of Britain bar but the unnecessary irritation related instead to his qualification (or otherwise) for the Atlantic Star. This medal was awarded mainly to Royal and Commonwealth navies for a period of not less than six months afloat between 3 September 1939 and 8 May 1945 in the Atlantic or home waters. The medal was also awarded to army or RAF personnel afloat and on active service with either the Royal or Merchant Navy, but in this case the qualifying period was reduced to two months. Whilst there was clearly a case for the award to Cpl Will and his men who had served the requisite period and met the qualifying conditions, the Air Ministry clearly thought otherwise. They wrote to Will on 15 October 1946 as follows:

"In considering whether a special application [for the Atlantic Star] should be made on their behalf, Balloon Command advise that it is most unlikely that any barrage balloon vessel personnel would have succeeded in completing the necessary qualifying period of service at sea in open waters."

In fact, in the case of Will, he most certainly *had!* That he saw the suggestion his service might have been unworthy of reward was understandably distressing for him and he was angered to think that he had had to go cap in hand to request his due medal entitlement. Indeed, Cpl Will had already been awarded the British Empire Medal for his service at sea with the RAF water-borne barrage balloon units. His 1941 citation had stated:

"This airman has been continuously employed as a barrage balloon operator on the Channel convoy from Sheerness to Southampton and return. He has made fourteen return trips during which there has been considerable enemy activity by shelling from the French coast, dive bombing and E-Boat attacks. When balloons have been destroyed he has helped the naval ratings with the operation of the various guns and assisted in every possible way in a co-operative effort between the RAF and the Royal Navy."

Somewhat grudgingly, it seems, the Air Ministry finally conceded to Cpl Will's claim for his Atlantic Star. Exactly as was the case with 59 Squadron, this was not about a claim for a right or an entitlement, *per se*. It was more to do with justifiable pride and the due and appropriate recognition, rightfully given, for valiant service.

The Channel Guns

By the summer of 1940 the Germans were establishing long-range guns on the French coast with particular concentrations around the Pas-de-Calais. These guns were capable of shelling Dover, Folkestone and beyond – and frequently did. Equally, they had the capacity to strike at shipping in the Straits of Dover including convoys. In fact, many of the convoys passing through the Straits did come under German shellfire, although no ship was ever hit

SECRET.

h6/46.

FORM E

COMBAT REPORT.

76

Sector Serial No. .... (A) ....

Serial No. of Order detailing Flight or Squadron to
Patrol .... (B) A 45

Date .... (C) 8/8/40.

Flight, Squadron .... (D) Flight: "B" Sqdn.: 238.

Number of Enemy Aircraft .... (E) 40 +

Type of Enemy Aircraft .... (F) ME 110's + ME 109's.

Time Attack was delivered .... (G) 12.35

Place Attack was delivered .... (H) 6 miles S. of Needles.

Height of Enemy .... (J) about 11,000 ft.

Enemy Casualties .... (K) 1 ME109 unconfirmed.

Our Casualties .... Aircraft .... (L) NIL.

.... Personnel .... (M) NIL.

GENERAL REPORT .... (R)

I was Green 2 and the Section was ordered to patrol convoy + intercept raid. We were approximately 6 miles W. of the convoy when ordered to "gate" and fly E. Green Leader gave order line astern and dived to approx. 11,000 ft from 15,000 ft. The E/A adopted no formation and I broke away to attack a ME 109 which climbed in a southerly direction. I fired one short burst (2 secs.) from astern at 250 yards. He continued to climb in a gentle light hand turn. I took a long burst (approx. 7-8 secs.) from about 200 yards on deflection and E/A let off smoke increasing in volume + dived at about 60° + not full throttle. I followed him down firing the rest of my ammunition at about 150 yards from astern, and compelled to break off attack at 5000 feet as 2 ME 109's were attacking me. These I evaded by half rolling and I turned and made for home. Landed at Middle Wallop 1305. Number of rounds fired 2400 rounds.

Signature

O.C. { Section GREEN
Flight "B"
Squadron   Squadron No. 238

P/O F.N. CAWSE

(8567—1611) Wt. 27885—2553 850 Pads 9/39 T.S. 700 FORM 1151

The combat report filed by Cawse for his action on 8 August.

or sunk in these attacks which came from a concentration of what would eventually be no less than seventy-two guns in five battalions which the Germans eventually established on the coast. Primarily, the original objective was to help protect the flanks of the German invasion of the British Isles. However, none of the guns were operative by 8 August 1940 and the first ranging shots were not fired until some while later. Thus explaining why CW9 Peewit was not troubled by the German cross-channel guns.

Claims and Losses

Detailed aircraft claims and losses tables for both sides are submitted at Appendix (C) (D) (E) and (F) although some commentary is necessary in respect of these.

Whilst the aircraft loss tables are believed to be as comprehensive and accurate as possible, it is the case that some caution needs to be exercised in relation to the various fighter claims. Indeed, it is important to view them

Plt Off Frederick Cawse of 238 Squadron was one of the pilots who claimed an enemy aircraft destroyed in the fighting over CW9 Peewit on 8 August. He was shot down and killed three days later.

exactly as that; in other words, *claims* rather than accurate representations of aircraft actually destroyed. Identifying accurately the pilots and aircrew of both sides who made claims that day is a difficult task, but those listed are as near as possible a comprehensive tally of the pilots and aircrew who submitted claims they felt to be substantiated.

In terms of ships lost, these are also detailed at Appendix B along with the maritime roll of honour.

In total, twenty-three Luftwaffe aircrew were killed or missing in the operations on 8 August and twelve wounded with three POWs. Coincidentally, a total of twenty-three RAF pilots and aircrew were killed or missing (twenty-six if including a bomber crew lost off Holland) and four wounded. The Luftwaffe lost some twenty-four aircraft and the RAF lost twenty-two, this against some forty-one or so claimed as destroyed by the Luftwaffe and eighty-four originally claimed as destroyed by the RAF.

It should be noted that the Stuka losses were surely a severe blow to the Luftwaffe, such that Reichsmarschall Hermann Göring felt obliged to report on 15 August 1940:

"The fighter escort defences of our Stuka formations must be re-adjusted as the enemy is concentrating his fighters against our Stuka operations. It appears necessary to allocate three fighter gruppen to each Stuka gruppe, one of these fighter gruppen remaining with the Stukas and dives with them to the attack; the second flies over the target at medium altitude and engages the fighter defences; the third protects the whole attack from above. It will also be necessary to escort Stukas returning from attack over the Channel."

YEAR 1940		AIRCRAFT		PILOT, OR	2ND PILOT, PUPIL	DUTY
MONTH	DATE	Type	No.	1ST PILOT	OR PASSENGER	(INCLUDING RESULTS AND RE
—	—	—	—	—	—	— TOTALS BROUGHT FO
AUG.	9	SPITFIRE	K	SELF		HAWKINGE.
	8		K	"		PATROL.
	8		K	"		PATROL.
	9		D	"		LOCAL
	9		B	"		PATROL
	10		B	"		HAWKINGE.
	10		B	"		SCRAMBLE
	11		B	"		RET. KENLEY.
	11		B	"		PATROL
	11		B	"		SCRAMBLE.
	12		K	"		LOCAL.
	13		K	"		TO HAWKINGE.
	13		K	"		PATROL
	13		E	"		KENLEY.
	14		G	"		TO HAWKINGE.
	14		K	"		FROM
	14		K	"		PATROL
	14		B	"		FROM "
	15		D	"		TO HAWKINGE.
	15		E	"		RET.
	16		E	"		LOCAL.
	17		E	"		SCRAMBLE.
	18		E	"		LOCAL.

GRAND TOTAL [Cols. (1) to (10)]

.... Hrs .... Mins.

TOTALS CARRIED FC

Compiling accurate and meaningful claims lists for fighter actions is a difficult task, which is complicated yet further by often conflicting records. Here, 64 Squadron Spitfire pilot Plt Off J J O'Meara's log book records claims for three He 111s damaged in fighting over Kent that day. In fact, no Heinkels (or Luftwaffe bombers of any description) were operational over Kent on 8 August and the entries provide us with a good example of the anomalies often thrown up when researchers try to make sense of what is sometimes recorded.

SINGLE-ENGINE AIRCRAFT				MULTI-ENGINE AIRCRAFT						PASS-ENGER	INSTR.-CLOUD FLYING [incl. in cols. (1) to (10)]	
DAY		NIGHT		DAY			NIGHT					
DUAL	PILOT	DUAL	PILOT	DUAL	1ST PILOT	2ND PILOT	DUAL	1ST PILOT	2ND PILOT		DUAL	PILOT
(1)	(2)	(3)	(4)	(5)	(6)	(7)	(8)	(9)	(10)	(11)	(12)	(13)
8.50	287.20	1.55	8.40	3.20	208.45	35.35		21.45	2.10	9.10	11.20	26.15
	.20											
	1.00				✠ 3 HE 111 K					DAMAGED		
	✠		1.20	HEARD ON R/T: ACHTUNG, ACHTUNG, SPITFIEREN. HIER KOMMEN SIE								
	.30											
	▬		.50									
	.50											
	.30				✠ 1 ME 110					DAMAGED.		
	.25											
	1.00				✠ 1 ME 109					ON FIRE		
	.30				✠ 1 ME 109					PROBABLE		
	1.20											
	.25											
	1.10				✠ 1 HE 109					PROBABLE		
	.55											
	.20											
	50											
	1.10				✠ 1 ME 109					CONFIRMED		
	.35											
	.30											
	.30											
	1.10											
	1.20											
	.55											
8.50	346.50	1.55	10.50	3.20	208.45	35.35		21.45	2.10	9.10	11.20	26.15

CHAPTER 14 Seventy Years On

O N 5 AUGUST 2009 the author was privileged to be aboard Dave Wendes's dive-boat *Wightspirit* sailing during the early morning from Lymington in Hampshire out to the position of the wreck of HMS *Borealis* south of St Catherine's Point. The purpose of the voyage was to send down two divers onto the wreck, which sat thirty-eight metres beneath the English Channel, on the scattered gravel of a hard and flat chalk sea bed. The divers, part of a team assembled by the TV production company 360 Productions, were to locate and film the wreck as part of a series of BBC1 television documentary programmes called "Dig 1940". These programmes would be shown during 2010 to mark the seventieth anniversary of the Battle of France, Dunkirk and the Battle of Britain.

Whilst the exploration of *Borealis* was hardly a 'dig', the dive was in fact intended to bring to the surface a few tangible relics of the ship that might help tell the story for television. Intrepid divers Rob Allen and Dave Robbins were tasked for the job, as a film crew waited on board *Wightspirit* with the programme presenter, Jules Hudson, for the pair to reach the wreck and start filming. When they did, the images that came back from the deep were ghostly pictures of a moment frozen in time from 1940.

Borealis, although quite badly damaged and ravaged by the usual decay that one would associate with English Channel wrecks, was relatively intact and identifiable for the ship she once was. Although she had been explored by divers before, this expedition had something more of a purpose to it. Within the framework of the eventual programme, the wreck of *Borealis* would help contextualise the story of Convoy CW9 Peewit into the overall picture of events during 1940 and, specifically, the Battle of Britain.

Therefore, the author was asked what specific aspects of the ship might be searched for on the dive with the object of filming those particular features. Of course, the discovery of something that related directly to the barrage balloon was certainly desirable and it seemed possible that the winch or the hydrogen cylinders might still be at the wreck site. Consequently, they were at the top of the list for Rob and Dave to seek out – if they could.

Next, perhaps some evidence of the concrete block protection placed around the bridge and wheelhouse might have survived and would make for potentially interesting imagery. A final item on the 'wish list' of things to look for was any evidence of the ropes and hawsers used in the attempts to tow *Borealis* before she had eventually succumbed to her attacks.

It was a tall order to hope or expect that any of the items on the list might still be there. When Rob and Dave went over the side of *Wightspirit*, the best that the film crew could hope for was that they actually managed to find *Borealis* – although confidence in the expertise of Dave Wendes and his two diving companions was more than high. These men knew the wreck, were familiar with the immediate sea area and also knew the optimum time and tides to catch in order to maximise chances of good visibility.

Recovered by divers were these portholes from *Borealis*, one of them holed by a German bullet.

To say that all expectations were surpassed by the results of the filming would be an understatement, with just about everything on the list ticked-off and filmed: the protective concrete blocks, the towing cables and hawsers, a winch and the hydrogen cylinders. Of the latter, these were still grouped together and some had clear impact damage and holes from shrapnel strikes. Clearly, Lieutenant Arthur Hague's assessment that the cylinders may have been holed when he came to re-board the ship had been an accurate one. Whilst some had badly split, and therefore the gas would have immediately escaped, others may have been holed by tiny splinters or possibly their valves and pipes may have been disrupted or damaged allowing the gas to escape. Here was the evidence that the cylinders had certainly been hit. As for the concrete blocks, these could still be seen in a collapsed heap where they had fallen, as Hague described, after being demolished in the bomb blast. Some had probably been cracked or broken, too, by the shock of *Borealis* settling on the sea bed.

When the wreck of HMS *Borealis* was dived on during August 2009 for the BBC mini-series "Dig 1940" the barrage balloon hydrogen cylinders were still in evidence.

These mooring bollards on the wreck of *Borealis* provide an interesting comparison to the photograph of Lt Arthur Hague sitting on them on 8 August 1940!

The ropes and cables were also a fascinating find – still fixed fast to the stern where her would-be salvagers had tried to tow her to port during the afternoon of that fateful day. Nearby, a pair of bollards presented an interesting sight since a photograph exists of a rather forlorn-looking Arthur Hague seated in that same place. Tin-hatted, Hague is sitting on these very bollards surveying the wreckage of his vessel scattered around him – the photograph having been taken shortly before *Borealis* was finally abandoned.

When Rob Allen and Dave Robbins surfaced they brought with them a nylon mesh 'finds' bag containing three relic items for the TV crew; a chunk of the concrete protection, a battery that was found to be dated 1940 and a broken china tea cup marked with the crown and anchor symbol of the Royal Navy on its barnacle-encrusted bottom. Arthur Hague's tea cup, perhaps? Whoever might have last drunk from the cup in 1940 these tangible relics of CW9 made good television for an animated Jules Hudson to describe enthusiastically, and for the cameras to film.

Small relics they may have been, but a real connection nonetheless to Convoy Peewit. Although they didn't tell us anything we didn't already know about *Borealis* or CW9 – save that the cylinders had certainly been holed in the last Stuka attack – the recovered relics and the sea bed images were powerful reminders of what had happened that day. Whilst no lives had been lost on board *Borealis* the connection with Convoy Peewit certainly made sight of the wreck a sobering image. They gave good cause to reflect on the many lives that *were* lost that day; Royal Navy sailors, merchant seamen of several nations, RAF and Luftwaffe crews – all of whom had died in the battle that had ultimately sunk this little ship.

Sadly, Arthur Hague and William Will had passed away several years prior to the dive and filming, else it would have been fascinating to have had them on board. It is hard to say what either veteran might have thought or what they might have said about sight of their old ship.

The captain's tea cup? This broken relic was brought to the surface by divers from the August 2009 exploration having been found in the wreckage of the bridge. It is quite likely that it was Arthur Hague's tea cup, since the other ranks on board would have used china or enamel mugs – not cups and saucers! During the writing of this book this fortunate discovery sat on the author's desk as a tangible link to CW9 Peewit.

Whatever their reactions might have been, this fascinating expedition in 2009 had resulted in the story of CW9 Peewit being told for a wide and prime-time BBC television audience and it also triggered subsequent work that led to the production of this book.

If it might be possible to attach an epitaph retrospectively to the loss of HMS *Borealis* then it surely ought to be in recognition of the determination and fortitude of all the mariners who became involved, one way or another, with CW9. Their courage has been virtually overlooked until now, although the epic that was the Channel convoy story is an important aspect of the Battle of Britain. Most especially we should recognise the bravery of so many Royal Navy gunners on 7 and 8 August 1940. The record stands to show these men for the heroes they truly were. They were undaunted by overwhelming odds and were men who stood at their posts on ships that were burning, sinking, being bombed, torpedoed or machine-gunned. Many refused to leave their posts until they were wounded, dead, or else literally forced to abandon ship when it finally sank beneath

More than fifty years after the event, captain of HMS *Borealis* Arthur Hague (left) met another combatant from CW9 Peewit, former Hurricane pilot Peter Parrot at Tangmere Military Aviation Museum.

them. All of them, to a man, were unsung and unknown heroes of the Battle of Britain. Let this book stand as a tribute to that handful of brave souls whilst not forgetting those pilots of RAF Fighter Command who also fell in defence of CW9. The last word must go to Arthur Hague. Writing almost sixty-five years after HMS *Borealis* had been sunk from under him, he said:

"As I celebrate my 83rd birthday I remember with gratitude the sacrifice of those gallant young men who made it possible for me to do so."

Arthur Hague and the men of HMS *Borealis* had very much been party to some of the opening shots of the Battle of Britain – whatever date one might choose to accept as marking that battle's commencement.

APPENDIX A

The Merchant Vessels of Convoy CW9

Name	Tonnage	Build Date
AJAX (Dutch)*	942	1923
ALACRITY (British)	554	1940
ALT (British)	1,004	1911
AUDUN (Norwegian)	1,304	1925
*BALMAHA**		
BETSWOOD (British)	1,051	1936
COQUETDALE (British)*	1,597	1923

The ship's record card for the SS *Coquetdale*.

Name	Tonnage	Build Date
CRASTER (British)	733	1935
DE RUYTER (Dutch)	458	1931
EMPIRE CRUSADER (British)	1,042	1925
FIFE COAST (British)	367	1933
GLADONIA (British)	360	1939
HOLME FORCE (British)	1,216	1930
JOHN M (British)	500	1937
LESRIX (British)	703	1924
LONDON QUEEN (British)	781	1933
MARSWORTH (British)	366	1925
NATO (Dutch)	399	1939
OMLANDIA *		
OUSE (British)	1,004	1911
PATTERSONIAN (British)	315	1915
POLGARTH (British)	794	1920
POLLY M (British)	380	1937
RYE (British)	1,048	1924
SCHELDT *		
SPARTA (British)	708	1900
SURTE *		
TRES (Norwegian)	946	1917
VEENENBURGH (Dutch)	400	1927
WHITLEY (British)	1,196	1924

Author's note: Those vessels marked * were the six ships that sailed from St Helen's Road on the morning of 8 August intending to meet CW9 Peewit off the Isle of Wight.

Merchant Navy and Royal Navy Casualties Associated with CW9 Peewit

Merchant Navy

Quartermaster Edgar BROWN*	HMS *Wilna*	Lymington Cemetery
Able Seaman Alfred Percy FULLICK*	HMS *Wilna*	Haslar Naval Cemetery
Carpenter Samuel Phillips KEAT*	HMS *Wilna*	St Endellion Churchyard, Cornwall
2nd Eng Officer John ROBSON	MV *Fife Coast*	Tower Hill Memorial
Able Seaman Percy Horace WRIGHT	MV *Fife Coast*	Tower Hill Memorial
Ch Eng Officer Leonard YOUNG	MV *Fife Coast*	Tower Hill Memorial
Able Seaman Thomas MARSHALL	MV *Fife Coast*	Boulogne Eastern Cemetery
2nd Officer John William Pounder BOWMAN	SS *Empire Crusader*	Portsmouth (Milton) Cemetery
Master Frederick William SPENCER	SS *Empire Crusader*	Calais Southern Cemetery
Master William COUSINS	SS *Holme Force*	Tower Hill Memorial
2nd Officer Frederick Robert MERCER	SS *Holme Force*	Tower Hill Memorial
Cook William THOMAS	SS *Holme Force*	Tower Hill Memorial

*These seamen were all serving as naval auxiliary personnel (Merchant Navy) aboard a Royal Navy vessel.

Author's note: Those Merchant Navy casualties from CW9 Peewit who were not found are commemorated on the Tower Hill Memorial, London, where the names of almost 24,000 seamen with no known grave and who were lost during World War II are remembered.

Foreign Merchant Naval Services

Cook Bjarne ARNSTEN (Norwegian)	SS *Tres*	Died of injuries 13 August 1940
Stoker D J Baaij (Dutch)	SS *Ajax*	Dutch War Cemetery, Mill Hill, London. Died of injuries 10 August 1940
1st Eng J B Smit (Dutch)	SS *Ajax*	Dutch War Cemetary, Mill Hill, London.
Sailor P Spaans (Dutch)	SS *Ajax*	Buried at sea
Sailor A Toet (Dutch)	SS *Ajax*	Dutch War Cemetery, Orry-la-Ville, Senlis, France

Author's note: The four Dutch seamen listed above served with the Koninklijke Nederlandsche Stoomboot Mij (Royal Dutch Steamboat Company).

Royal Navy

Seaman Isaac Charles BOWLES	HM Trawler *Cape Palliser*	Haslar Naval Cemetery
Engineman Fred PILE	HM Trawler *Cape Palliser*	Grimsby Scartho Rd Cemetery
Ordinary Signalman Peter John TURNER*	HMS *Pembroke IV*	Chatham Naval Memorial
Able Seaman Thomas George WELLSPRING**	HMS *President III*	Portsmouth Naval Memorial
Able Seaman Richard John COMPTON-COOK	SS *Holme Force*	Chatham Naval Memorial
Able Seaman Charles GORMAN	SS *Holme Force*	Chatham Naval Memorial
Able Seaman Maurice Henry IRONMONGER	SS *Holme Force*	Chatham Naval Memorial
Cook Jeffrey William HINTON	HM Trawler *Cape Palliser*	Haslar Naval Cemetery
Commander John Kenneth Beafoy BIRCH***	HM Trawler *Rion*	Haslar Naval Cemetery

*Ordinary Signalman Turner was one of the signallers for the convoy commodore and served on board the commodore ship for CW9 Peewit the SS *Empire Crusader*, although his parent unit was HMS *Pembroke IV*.

**Able Seaman Wellspring was a DEMS gunner on board the MV *Fife Coast* although his parent unit was HMS *President III*.

***Commander Birch died on 14 August 1940 of wounds received on 8 August.

Author's note: Those Royal Navy casualties who were not found and have no known grave are commemorated on the Royal Naval memorials at Chatham and Portsmouth.

APPENDIX C

Luftwaffe Losses on 8 August 1940 – Operations over Britain

8./JG26	Me 109E-4	12.00	Shot down in combat with Spitfires of 41 and 64 Squadrons and crashed in sea east of Margate. Possibly claimed by Webster and Wallens of 41 Squadron. Oblt Willi Oehm missing.
I./JG27	Me 109E-1		Shot down in combat and abandoned 35 km south of Isle of Wight. Pilot baled and rescued by Seenotdienst.
1./JG27	Me 109E-3		Shot down in combat 50 km south of Isle of Wight. Lt Igor Zirkenbach killed.
1./JG27	Me 109E-3		Shot down in combat 35 km south of Isle of Wight. Lt Karl-Heinz Bothfeld killed.
Stab II./JG27	Me 109E-4	16.25	Shot down by Hurricanes of 43 Squadron south of Isle of Wight during escort for Ju 87s of II./StG77. Hptm Werner Andres rescued by Seenotdienst.
II./JG27	Me 109E-4	16.25	Shot down by Hurricanes of 43 Squadron south of Isle of Wight during escort for Ju 87s of II./StG77 and abandoned by pilot who was rescued unhurt by Seenotdienst.
II./JG27	Me 109E-2	16.30	Damaged by Hurricanes of 43 Squadron south of Isle of Wight during escort for Ju 87s of II./StG77 but returned to base, pilot unhurt.
5./JG27	Me 109E-4	16.30	Shot down by Hurricanes of 43 Squadron south of Isle of Wight during escort for Ju 87s of II./StG77 and abandoned off Cherbourg. Oberfw Erich Krenzke baled out and rescued wounded.
5./JG27	Me 109E-4	16.25	Shot down by Hurricanes of 43 Squadron south of Isle of Wight during escort for Ju 87s of II./StG77 and abandoned by pilot. Uffz Edgar Schulz missing.
6./JG27	Me 109E-1	16.30	Shot down by Hurricanes of 43 Squadron south of Isle of Wight during escort for Ju 87s of II./StG77 and Uffz Heinz Uebe rescued wounded.
7./JG27	Me 109E-1		Returned damaged after combat north of Cherbourg. Gefr Ernst Nittmann slightly wounded.
9./JG27	Me 109E-4		Shot down in sea 20 km north west of Cherbourg. Uffz Ludwig Girrbach missing.
III./JG51	Me 109E		Forced landing at St Omer-Wizernes due to engine failure during combat with Spitfires of 41 and 64 Squadrons off Dover at 12.00. Pilot unhurt.
8./JG51	Me 109E-4		Forced landing at St Omer-Wizernes due to engine failure during combat with Spitfires of 41 and 64 Squadrons off Dover at 12.00. Pilot unhurt.
9.JG51	Me 109E-4	11.50	Badly damaged in combat over Channel with Spitfires of 41 and 64 Squadrons. Returned to base. Pilot unhurt.

Stab I./StG3	Ju 87B-1	15.10	Shot down by Hurricanes of 145 Squadron south of Isle of Wight. Oblt Martin Müller rescued by HMS *Basset* but Uffz Josef Krampfl killed. The body of Krampfl was later washed ashore on French coast at Veules-les-Roses.
2./StG3	Ju 87B-1		Forced landing at Théville after damage by Hurricanes of 145 Squadron 20 km south of the Isle of Wight at 15.10. Pilot unhurt. Uffz Josef Bösenecker badly wounded and admitted to hospital in Valonges.
2./StG3	Ju 87B-1	15.10	Shot down by Hurricanes of 145 Squadron south of Isle of Wight. Fw Friedrich Zschweigert and Fw Herbert Heinrich both missing.
2./StG3	Ju 87B-1	15.10	Shot down by Hurricanes of 145 Squadron south of Isle of Wight. Uffz Rudolf Kleinhans missing and Uffz Karl Quante killed.
3./StG3	Ju 87B-1		Crash-landed at Wuilly-le-Tessin airfield after combat with Hurricanes south of Isle of Wight at 15.10. Pilot unhurt. Fw Valentin Grossmann badly wounded and admitted to hospital in Falaise.
Stab II./StG77	Ju 87B-1	16.20	Shot down by Hurricanes of 43 and 145 Squadrons south of the Isle of Wight. Hptm Waldemar Plewig captured wounded and Fw Kurt Schauer missing.
II./StG77	Ju 87B-1		Damaged by Hurricanes of 43 and 145 Squadrons at 16.20 south of Isle of Wight and landed damaged at Bougy. Crew unhurt.
II./StG77	Ju 87B-1		Forced-landing at Deauville after damage by Hurricanes of 43 and 145 Squadrons south of Isle of Wight at 16.20. Crew unhurt.
II./StG77	Ju 87B-1		Crash-landing at Bougy after damage by Hurricanes of 43 and 145 Squadrons south of Isle of Wight at 16.20. Crew unhurt.
II./StG77	Ju 87B-2		Forced-landing at Bougy after damage by Hurricanes of 43 and 145 Squadrons south of Isle of Wight at 16.20. Crew unhurt.
4./StG77	Ju 87B-1	16.20	Shot down by Hurricanes of 43 and 145 Sqns south of Isle of Wight. Hptm Horst-Henning Schmack and Obgfr Rudolf Wuttke both missing.
4./StG77	Ju 87B-1	16.20	Fuel lines damaged in attack by Hurricane flown (W.Nr 5600) by Fg Off P L Parrott of 145 Squadron south of Isle of Wight and forced-landed at St Lawrence, Isle of Wight. Uffz Fritz Pittroff captured unhurt and Uffz Rudolf Schubert killed. (Aircraft codes: S2+LM)

Messerschmitt 110 L1+FH of 13.(Z)/LG1 flown by Uffz Lammel and Fw Datz participated in the escort operations flown in support of attacks directed at CW9 Peewit on 8 August. The pair were shot down in this aircraft over the English Channel on 13 August 1940.

5./StG77	Ju 87B-1		Forced-landing at Cherbourg after combat with Hurricanes of 43 and 145 Squadrons south of Isle of Wight at 16.20. Pilot unhurt. Uffz Helmut Umlauft badly wounded.
II./JG53	Me 109E-4		Crash-landed at Dinan following combat south of Swanage at 16.10 with Hurricanes of 43 Sqn and Spitfires of 152 Sqn. Pilot unhurt.
V.(Z)/LG1	Me 110C		Damaged in combat south of the Isle of Wight with Hurricanes of 145 and 238 Sqns and Spitfires of 609 Sqn at 12.30. Crew unhurt.
V.(Z)/LG1	Me 110C		Damaged in combat south of the Isle of Wight with Hurricanes of 145 and 238 Sqns and Spitfires of 609 Sqn at 12.30. Crew unhurt but aircraft written-off.
V.(Z)/LG1	Me 110C		Damaged in combat south of the Isle of Wight with Hurricanes of 145 and 238 Sqns and Spitfires of 609 Sqn at 12.30. Crew unhurt but aircraft written-off.
13.(Z)/LG1	Me 110C-2		Damaged in combat south of the Isle of Wight with Hurricanes of 145 and 238 Sqns and Spitfires of 609 Sqn at 12.30. Lt Günther Beck and Uffz Paul Busch badly wounded and admitted to hospital in Caen.
13.(Z)/LG1	Me 110C	13.10	Badly damaged in combat south of the Isle of Wight with Hurricanes of 145 and 238 Sqns and Spitfires of 609 Sqn at 12.30 and crashed 3 km east of Cherbourg-Théville. Fw Gerhard Jentzsch killed and Uffz Alfred Dieckmann badly wounded and admitted to hospital in Valognes. Aircraft written-off. Aircraft codes: L1+EH.
14.(Z)/LG1	Me 110C		Shot down in combat with Hurricanes of 145 and 238 Sqns and Spitfires of 609 Sqn south of Isle of Wight at 12.30. Fw Alfred Sturm and Fw Helmut Brunner both missing.
8./StG1	Ju 87B-1		Returned damaged after engagement south of Isle of Wight at around 09.00, probably after attack by Hurricanes of 145 Sqn. Oblt Klaus Ostmann badly wounded and admitted to hospital in Valognes. Gunner believed unhurt.
9./StG1	Ju 87B-1		Returned damaged after engagement south of Isle of Wight. Uffz Roland Reitter and Obgfr Bernhard Renners both slightly wounded and admitted to hospital in Valognes.
9./StG1	Ju 87B-1		Shot down by fighters south of Isle of Wight and crashed in Channel. Fw Herbert Torngrind and Gefr Heinrich Bauer both missing.
9./StG1	Ju 87B-1		Shot down by fighters south of Isle of Wight and crashed in Channel. Gefr Ernst Walz and Gefr Robert Schütz both missing.
I./StG2	Ju 87B-1		Crash-landed at Wuilly-le-Tessin airfield after engagement south of Isle of Wight. Both crew unhurt.
II./StG2	Ju 87B		Returned to base damaged after being attacked south of Isle of Wight, probably by Spitfire flown by Flt Lt J H G McArthur of 609 Sqn. Crew both believed to have been slightly wounded.
3.(F)/123	Ju 88A-1	14.36	Returned damaged after attacks by Plt Off E B Mortimer-Rose and Sgt A S Harker of 234 Sqn over Falmouth. Uffz Theodor Bauer badly wounded and died the next day.

Author's note: Some published sources have stated that a Luftwaffe air-sea-rescue Heinkel He 59N (W.Nr 0540) of Seenotstaffel 2 was shot down into the English Channel on 8 August 1940. According to Luftwaffe researcher, the late Heinrich Weiss, the crew were rescued from their dinghy by an unspecified German naval vessel twenty-five miles south-south-west of the Isle of Wight. However, nothing exists in the Luftwaffe quartermaster general's returns for aircraft losses that day to substantiate that this loss actually occurred. Given Sqn Ldr H A Fenton's claim to have attacked an aircraft of this type over the Channel on 8 August and its inclusion in other published lists, it was felt appropriate to mention it by way of this footnote.

APPENDIX

D

RAF Losses on 8 August 1940

Fighter Command

Author's note: The RAF losses contained within this list cover the 24 hour period of 8 August 1940 and are mainly those of Fighter Command. Many, although by no means all, are associated with operations over (or related to) Convoy Peewit. Whilst 59 Squadron was a Coastal Command squadron it fell under the control of RAF Fighter Command.

Blenheim	L1448 YP-K	23 Squadron	23.48	Plt Off C F Cardell Sgt C Stephens	Crashed on night patrol. Both crew killed.
Hurricane	P3267	43 Squadron	16.40	Plt Off H C Upton	Engine seized in combat with Ju 87. Forced-landed at Ford Fm, Whitwell, IOW. Pilot unhurt.
Hurricane	P3466	43 Squadron	16.40	Sgt C A L Hurry	Returned damaged from combat. Pilot unhurt.
Hurricane	P3781	43 Squadron	16.45	Plt Off J Cruttenden	Shot down by enemy aircraft ten miles south of IOW. Pilot missing.
Hurricane	P3468	43 Squadron	16.45	Plt Off R S Oelofse	Shot down by enemy aircraft ten miles south of IOW. Pilot killed.
Hurricane	P3202	43 Squadron	16.45	Flt Lt R F Carey	Port wing damaged by fire from Me 110. Pilot wounded in arm but returned safely.
Hurricane	P3214	43 Squadron	16.45	Plt Off C A Woods-Scawen	Damaged in combat with Me 110s south of IOW. Pilot wounded by shell splinters but returned to base.
Blenheim	N3590 TR-F	59 Squadron		Plt Off L N Davis Sgt G H Coulton Sgt B W Beaumont	Took off at 15.50 for Channel patrol. Failed to return. Crew missing, although Sgt Beaumont washed ashore and buried at Hautot-sur-Mer, Dieppe.
Spitfire	P9369	64 Squadron	11.10	Sgt J W C Squier	Shot down by Me 109 and forced-landed at Great Couldham, Capel-le-Ferne. Pilot injured.
Spitfire	L1039	64 Squadron	12.05	Plt Off P F Kennard-Davis	Shot down in flames by Me 109 north of Dover. Pilot baled out at West Langdon but died on 10 August 1940.
Spitfire	K9911 YT-E	65 Squadron	11.40	Sgt D I Kirton	Shot down in flames by Me 109 and crashed near RAF Manston. Pilot killed.

Sgt Marian Domagala was a Czech pilot flying with 238 Squadron who made a victory claim during the fighting on 8 August 1940.

Sgt David Ian Kirton, a Spitfire pilot with 64 Squadron, was one of the casualties of the fighting over Kent on 8 August 1940.

Spitfire	K9905	65 Squadron	11.45	Flt Sgt N T Phillips	Shot down in flames by Me 109 and crashed at Westwood, Kent. Pilot killed.
Spitfire	L1094	65 Squadron	11.55		Damaged by Me 109 Over Manston. Returned to base. Aircraft damaged but pilot unhurt.
Hurricane	P2955	145 Squadron	09.05	Plt Off L A Sears	Failed to return after combat south of IOW. Pilot missing.
Hurricane	P3381	145 Squadron	09.15	Sgt E D Baker	Failed to return after combat south of IOW. Pilot missing.
Hurricane	P2957	145 Squadron	16.40	Plt Off E C Wakeham	Shot down in action to south of IOW. Pilot missing.
Hurricane	P3163	145 Squadron	16.40	Fg Off Lord R U P Kay-Shuttleworth	Shot down in action to south of IOW. Pilot missing.
Hurricane	P3545	145 Squadron	16.45	Sub Lt F A Smith	Shot down in action to south of IOW. Pilot missing.
Spitfire	K9894	152 Squadron	16.15	Sgt D N Robinson	Shot down south of Swanage by Me 109 and crash-landed at Bestwall, Wareham. Pilot unhurt.
Spitfire	R6811	152 Squadron	16.20	Plt Off W Beaumont	Shot down south of Swanage by Me 109 and crash-landed at Spyway Farm, Langton Matravers. Pilot unhurt.
Spitfire	N3278	234 Squadron	10.15	Sgt J Szlagowski	Ran out of fuel during patrol. Crashed at Pensilva. Pilot unhurt.
Hurricane	P3823	238 Squadron	12.45	Flt Lt D E Turner	Shot down south of IOW. Pilot missing.
Hurricane	P3617	238 Squadron	12.50	Fg Off D W MacCaw	Shot down south of IOW. Pilot missing.

Hurricane	P2947	238 Squadron	13.40	Sqn Ldr H A Fenton	Shot down searching for two missing pilots of squadron. Pilot rescued from sea off IOW with injuries.
Hurricane	P2981	257 Squadron	12.00	Flt Lt N M Hall	Shot down by Me 109 off St Catherine's Point. Pilot killed.
Hurricane	R4094	257 Squadron	12.00	Sgt K B Smith	Shot down off St Catherine's Point. Pilot missing.
Hurricane	P3058	257 Squadron	12.05	Fg Off B W J D'Arcy-Irvine	Shot down by Me 109 off St Catherine's Point. Pilot killed.
Hurricane	R4100 RF-N	303 Squadron		Sgt M Belc	Crashed on landing with undercarriage raised after training flight. Pilot unhurt.
Hurricane	V7235 RF-M	303 Squadron		Sgt J Frantisek	Crashed on landing with undercarriage raised after training flight. Pilot unhurt.
Blenheim	L8665	600 Squadron	11.55	Fg Off D N Grice Sgt F J Keast AC1 B W Warren	Shot down by Me 109 off Ramsgate. Crew all killed.
Spitfire	P9322	609 Squadron	12.40	Plt Off M J Appleby	Damaged by Me 110 over IOW. Aircraft returned to base and pilot unhurt.
Spitfire	L1082	609 Squadron	13.05	Plt Off C N Overton	Forced-landed at Christchurch. Pilot unhurt.
Spitfire	R6765 DW-T	610 Squadron	11.30		Damaged by Me 109 over Hawkinge. Pilot unhurt.
Spitfire	L1045 DW-G	610 Squadron	11.20		Forced landing near Wittersham after combat with Me 109. Pilot unhurt.

Bomber Command

Blenheim	L9472	18 Squadron	17.00 approx	Sgt V R T Land Sgt J H Saville Sgt J F Parvin	Presumed lost to flak and crashed in sea after operation to bomb Schipol and Valkenburg. Parvin buried at Bergen op Zoom, Saville and Land missing.

Author's note: One further RAF Fighter Command aircrew casualty is shown on the Battle of Britain Roll of Honour with a date of death recorded as 8 August 1940. He was Plt Off John Cecil Bull of 25 Squadron. However, Bull did not die as the result of active service but through a shooting accident whilst on leave.

Luftwaffe Fighter Claims Over England for 8 August 1940

APPENDIX E

Oblt Gerhard Schöpfel	9./JG 26	11.34	Spitfire	W. Canterbury
Oblt Gerhard Schöpfel	9./JG 26	11.35	Blenheim	S. Ramsgate
Fw Gerhard Gryzmalla	8./JG 26	11.40	Hurricane	NE. Margate/Canterbury
Oblt Joachim Müncheberg	Stab.III/JG 26	11.55	Spitfire	Margate
Uffz Hans Sippel	1./JG 27	09.05	Hurricane	S. Isle of Wight
Ltn Igor Zirkenbach	1./JG 27	09.10	Spitfire	S. Isle of Wight
Oblt Rudolf Krafftschick	1./JG 27	12.45	Spitfire	S. Isle of Wight
Hptm Eduard Neumann	Stab.I./JG 27	12.55	Spitfire	40km S. of Needles
Ltn Helmut Strobl	5./JG 27	16.25	Hurricane	S. Isle of Wight
Ofw Hans Umbach	9./JG 27	09.05	Hurricane	15km S. Isle of Wight
Uffz Karl Born	7./JG 27	12.25	Hurricane	S. Isle of Wight
Oblt Ludwig Franzisket	7./JG 27	12.25	Hurricane	S. Isle of Wight
Ofw Hans Umbach	9./JG 27	12.28	Hurricane	S. Isle of Wight
Uffz Karl Born	7./JG 27	16.20	Hurricane	S. Isle of Wight
Ofw Hans Richter	8./JG 27	16.20	Hurricane	S. Isle of Wight
Uffz Albert Kurz	8./JG 27	16.30	Hurricane	S. Isle of Wight
Fw Franz Blazytko	8./JG 27	16.30	Hurricane	S. Isle of Wight
Uffz Erich Clauser	8./JG 27	–	Hurricane	S. Isle of Wight
Oblt Max Dobislav	9./JG 27	–	Barrage Balloon	Isle of Wight
Oblt Josef Fözö	4./JG 51	11.35	Spitfire	SE. Folkestone
Hptm Hannes Trautloft	Stab.III./JG 51	11.48	Spitfire	Dungeness
Oblt Otto Kath	Stab.III./JG 51	11.50	Spitfire	S. Dover
Ltn Fritz Stendel	8./JG 51	11.50	Spitfire	S. Dover
Uffz Maximilian Mayerl	8./JG 51	11.55	Spitfire	Dover
Oblt Hans Kolbow	9./JG 51	11.55	Spitfire	SW. Dover
Hptm Günther von Maltzahn	Stab.III./JG 53	16.05	Spitfire	S. Swanage
Oblt Richard Vogel	4./JG 53	16.10	Hurricane	S. Swanage
Hptm Heinz Bretnütz	6./JG 53	16.15	Spitfire	S. Swanage
Uffz Karl Witton*	Stab.II./St.G 77	16.30	Hurricane	English Channel
Oblt Helmut Müller	13.(Z)LG 1	12.25	Spitfire	20-30km from Needles
Oblt Joachim Glienke	13.(Z)LG 1	12.28	Hurricane	20-30km from Needles

Ltn Ernst Gorisch	13.(Z)LG 1	12.30	Spitfire	20-30km from Needles
Fw Georg Klever	13.(Z)LG 1	12.30	Spitfire	20-30km from Needles
Ofw Rudolf Korbert	13.(Z)LG 1	12.32	Spitfire	20-30km from Needles
Oblt Helmut Müller	13.(Z)LG 1	12.35	Spitfire	20-30km from Needles
Fw Hans Datz	3.(Z)LG 1	12.40	Spitfire	20km from Needles
Oblt Joachim Glienke	13.(Z)LG 1	12.45	Hurricane	20-30km from Needles
Fw Hans Datz	3.(Z)LG 1	12.48	Spitfire	35km from Needles
Oblt Helmut Müller	13.(Z)LG 1	12.50	Hurricane	20-30km from Needles
Ltn Karl Goetze	13.(Z)LG 1	16.27	Hurricane	20-30km from Needles
Ltn Hans Schmid	II./ZG2	16.30	Spitfire	S. Isle of Wight
Oblt Emil Schnoor	II./ZG2	16.30	Spitfire	S. Isle of Wight
Oblt Helmut Grasser	II./ZG2	17.30	Blenheim	Off Cherbourg

* Author's note: Uffz Karl Witton was the bordfunker (radio operator/air gunner) on board one of the Stukas of Stab II./St.G 77 engaged in the 16.30 attack on Convoy CW9. Thus, this claim is by a rear gunner. He usually flew with Oblt Heinz Sonntag as his pilot. The pair were lost ten days later during the attack on RAF Ford.

APPENDIX F

RAF Fighter Claims Over England for 8 August 1940

The following comprises a list of claims made by individual fighter pilots of RAF Fighter Command for 8 August 1940. It includes confirmed claims, but not probable or damaged claims, although the overall totals for confirmed and probables are included in the table at the end of this appendix. That an individual pilot's claim was 'confirmed' does not necessarily reflect an actual German loss, since post-war research clearly indicates that pilots over-claimed significantly. This was true of the entire war and not just 8 August. It was also a feature of claims from pilots of all combatant nations and air arms.

Total Claims by Pilot:

41 SQUADRON

Flt Lt J T Webster	Me 109 Destroyed	12.00	Manston/Calais
Plt Off R W Wallens	Me 109 Destroyed	12.00	Manston/Calais
Plt Off R W Wallens	Me 109 Destroyed	12.00	Manston/Calais

43 SQUADRON

Sqn Ldr J V C Badger	Me 109 Destroyed	16.00	N. of Cherbourg
Sgt H J L Hallowes	Me 109 Destroyed	16.30	40 miles S. of Swanage
Flt Lt T F D Morgan	Ju 87 Destroyed	16.20	S. of IOW
Plt Off H C Upton	Ju 87 Destroyed	16.20	7 miles off Ventnor
Plt Off H C Upton	Ju 87 Destroyed	16.20	7 miles off Ventnor
Plt Off C A Woods-Scawen	Me 110 Destroyed	16.25	St Catherine's Point

145 SQUADRON

Fg Off G R Branch	Ju 87 Destroyed	09.00	3 miles S. of IOW
Plt Off A N C Weir	Me 109 Destroyed	12.45	S. of IOW
Plt Off P W Dunning-White	Me 110 Destroyed	12.45	S. of IOW
Sqn Ldr J R A Peel	Me 109 Destroyed	15.10	S. of St Catherine's Point
Fg Off A Ostowicz	Me 109 Destroyed	15.10	S. of IOW
Plt Off J E Storrar	Ju 87 Destroyed	15.12	S. of IOW
Fg Off A H Boyd	Ju 87 Destroyed	15.15	S. of IOW
Plt Off P W Dunning-White	Ju 87 Destroyed	15.15	S. of IOW
Plt Off P L Parrott	Ju 87 Destroyed	15.15	St Catherine's Point

152 SQUADRON

Fg Off E S Hogg	Me 109 Destroyed	16.07	10 miles S. of Swanage
Fg Off E S Hogg	Me 109 Destroyed	16.07	10 miles S. of Swanage
Plt Off D C Shepley	Me 109 Destroyed	16.07	10 miles S. of Swanage

213 SQUADRON

Flt Lt J E Sing	Me 109 Destroyed	17.35	15 miles N. of Guernsey

235 SQUADRON

Sgt T A Maslen	Me 110 Destroyed (1/2)	16.30	Off Seine Estuary
Sgt A D Maconochie	Me 110 Destroyed (1/2)	16.30	Off Seine Estuary

238 SQUADRON

Sgt E W Seabourne	Me 109 Destroyed	12.35	6 miles S. of The Needles
Sgt M Domagala	Me 109 Destroyed	12.35	6 miles S. of The Needles
Plt Off C T Davis	Me 110 Destroyed	12.35	6 miles S. of The Needles
Fg Off D P Hughes	Me 110 Destroyed	12.35	6 miles S. of The Needles

257 SQUADRON

Plt Off A C Cochrane	Me 109 Destroyed	12.30	Mid-Channel
Plt Off K C Gundry	Me 109 Destroyed	12.30	Mid-Channel

601 SQUADRON

Plt Off J K U B McGrath	Me 109 Destroyed	12.30	S. of St Catherine's Point

609 SQUADRON

Flt Lt J H G McArthur	Ju 87 Destroyed	12.40	Off IOW
Flt Lt J H G McArthur	Ju 87 Destroyed	12.40	Off IOW
Sqn Ldr H S Darley	Me 110 Destroyed	12.40	Off IOW
Plt Off J M Appleby	Me 110 Destroyed	12.40	Off IOW
Plt Off J Curchin	Me 110 Destroyed	12.40	Off IOW

Author's note: The assembly of any definite listing of claims is made problematical by the varying information contained between combat reports, operations record books and pilots log books. The list offered here is not necessarily fully representative of all claims filed or granted to RAF aircrews, but covers those that have thus far been established.

APPENDIX G

Convoy CW9 Peewit Timeline of Principal Events 7-8 August 1940

7 AUGUST 1940

07.00	Convoy CW9 sails from Southend-on-Sea.
14.30	Convoy off Dover.
18.30	Convoy sighted off Dungeness from Wissant.
19.34	Sunset.
20.00	Four E-Boats depart Cherbourg headed for CW9.

8 AUGUST 1940

02.00	E-Boats attack convoy off Beachy Head/Newhaven SS *Holme Force*, *Fife Coast* and *Ouse* all sunk.
04.15	E-Boats break off engagement with CW9.
04.30	Six merchant vessels leave St Helen's Road to rendezvous with CW9 off the Isle of Wight.
04.34	Sunrise.
06.20	Reconnaissance Dornier 17 spots convoy off Selsey Bill.
07.18	The six vessels that departed at 04.30 arrive at rendezvous off St Catherine's Point but do not find Convoy CW9, which is some hours astern of schedule.
08.30	Fifty-seven Junkers 87 Stukas depart Cherbourg peninsula en-route to attack CW9.
08.30	Hurricanes of 145 Squadron depart Westhampnett to patrol CW9.
08.40	Ventnor chain home radar station picks up raid headed for CW9.
09.00	Stukas attack the six ships off Isle of Wight that had failed to join CW9. Air battle ensues. SS *Ajax* and *Coquetdale* sunk, remaining four all damaged.
09.10	Two RAF high speed launches leave RAF Calshot to search for downed aircrew.
10.00	Shore battery on Isle of Wight opens fire on RAF launches.
11.45	Forty-nine Junkers 87 Stukas depart Cherbourg peninsula to attack CW9.
12.19	CW9 attacked by the Stukas. Barrage balloons all shot down. HMS *Borealis* hit and badly damaged. SS *Empire Crusader* sunk. SS *Tres*, *Pattersonian* and *John M* all damaged. Large air battle over CW9.
14.00	Sqn Ldr Harold Fenton shot down south of Isle of Wight whilst conducting a sea search. Picked up by HMS *Basset*.
15.30	Eighty-two Stukas depart Cherbourg peninsula to attack CW9.
16.15	Stukas attack concentration of small naval craft at sea to assist casualties of CW9. HMS *Borealis* hit again.

16.30	RAF high speed launch 116 shot up by German aircraft.
16.40 (approx)	RAF Blenheim shot down off Cherbourg by returning Me 110 escort fighters.
16.45	English Channel clear of all significant enemy activity.
17.15	Bembridge lifeboat launched to assist aircraft in distress.
17.20	HMS *Borealis* sinks.
18.00 (approx)	Remnants of CW9 dispersing west and into Weymouth Bay.

APPENDIX H

Secret Report on Convoy CW9

Be pleased to lay before their Lordships the report from the commanding officer of HMS *Astral*.

The following is an extract from the report from the senior officer mobile balloon barrage (HMS *Astral*). The use of balloons is in abeyance at the moment, but the experience gained by HMS *Astral* should be useful if balloons are again used. (*)

"As a result of experience gained in the action, the following points are submitted: If large convoys are to be sailed at night then greater protection against E-Boats is essential. A close escort of suitable ships, armed with weapons large enough to stop or destroy them is required and illuminants should be used in such a way so as to light up the convoy as little as possible. (**) Ships of the convoy should be armed with a larger low-angle machine gun.

"Experience shows that the mobile balloon barrage is no deterrent on a clear day with high or no clouds. It is possible that it would be effective after the summer, when low cloud at about 1,000ft may be expected, with the balloons flown just below the cloud.

"It is possible that if a much larger number of balloons were employed, the time required to destroy them might delay the bombers sufficiently long enough to allow the fighters to arrive in time to break up the attack.

"If it is intended to proceed with the mobile balloon barrage scheme it is submitted that, quite apart from the above reason, it is desirable to have at least ten balloons to cover a convoy of twenty-five ships sailing in two columns, especially as the coastal convoys usually become spread out over a much longer distance than the two cables (***) per ship as ordered in the routeing instructions.

"It is desirable that mobile balloon barrage vessels should be more heavily armed in both LA and HA weapons. It is submitted that French vessels which already carry larger guns should have them brought into working order and supplied with the appropriate ammunition. The commanding officer of HMS *Elan II*, which is fitted with a 75mm gun, reports that he saw an E-Boat stopped at point blank range, and considers that he could have destroyed it if his gun had been in operation, and he had any ammunition.

The commander-in-chief, Portsmouth."

Author's notes:

* After the debacle of the balloons on 8 August 1940, the use of them in the mobile balloon barrage was suspended with immediate effect. According to an Admiralty signal dated 13 August 1940: "Ships in convoy are to fly kites. Balloon barrages will not be used but balloon barrage vessels fitted with kites and extra guns will reinforce the escorts." However, they were soon reinstated. (See Appendix I)

** See Chapter 4. It will be noted that the masters of various merchant vessels were of the impression that the flares were fired by the attacking E-Boats, although the statement in this report by the commanding officer of HMS *Astral* implies that they may have been pyrotechnics utilised by the defending Royal Navy ships, rather than by the attackers.

*** Two cables: a measurement equivalent to 2/10 of a nautical mile.

Although the following report does not relate to CW9, its content and recommendations in respect of CW10 (30 to 31 August) contains a great deal of relevance. Most of the points covered were equally applicable to CW9.

SECRET REPORT AND REMARKS ON CONVOY CW10

1) **Fighter Escort.** This is considered essential. It is particularly true to say of the CW and CE convoys, that where the convoy is, enemy bombers will also be found. As proof of this, ninety bombers were seen and many more heard, but not one single British fighter was sighted during the twenty-four hours that the convoy was at sea.

2) **Searchlights.** The convoy was silhouetted from the south east almost continually while passing from Dover to Dungeness by a large number of searchlights in use on the coast. [Author's note: by the date of CW10's sailing the evenings had been drawing in, such that it was between dusk and dark between these points.] There was no AA fire to warrant the use of searchlights. It is suggested that when one of the convoys passes through the Straits of Dover, the military authorities should be requested to keep the number of searchlights in use down to a minimum.

3) **Lack of 'Own Intelligence'.** HMS *Fernie* was ordered to leave the convoy and was not available for protection for one hour while investigating two armed trawlers sighted southwards and steaming east. Had the Portsmouth command patrols been included in the sailing orders, or otherwise communicated to the senior officer (Escorts), this would have been avoided.

4) **Alterations in Number and Type of Escorts.** The Hunt Class destroyers are considered the model type for this work, and four is the ideal number, as it would then be possible to give full anti-aircraft and anti-submarine protection to the convoy by stationing them as follows:- one ahead, one astern and one on each beam of the convoy. There is little doubt that the Germans will eventually base a destroyer force in the northern French ports and this will probably take effect from the time the destroyers driven ashore or scuttled at Narvik are re-fitted and become available for service.

5) **Anti-Submarine Trawlers.** With this probability in mind, it is not understood what useful purpose is served by the three trawlers detailed for the CW and CE convoys, as

there is nothing they can do that cannot be done better by the Hunt Class. Further to this, in action with surface forces (destroyers and/or E-Boats) the trawlers become a liability, owing to their low speed and unmanoeuvrability.

6) **Motor Anti-Submarine Boats.** From the knowledge pooled in the last three channel convoys it is considered that the motor a/s boats are a menace to themselves and the convoy. This opinion is heartily endorsed by the masters of the merchant vessels I met and talked to at Southend. The reasons for this statement are as follows:-

   a) Inability to perform at low speed.
   b) Their perpetual booming roar, clearly audible four miles away, draws all enemy forces towards the sound and incidentally the convoy.
   c) Due to their speed, they leave a clear white wake which acts as a magnet to the enemy and night flying aircraft.
   d) Referring to (a) and (b) above, they interfere with the escort's anti-submarine look outs and listeners.
   e) Their frequent appearance amongst the convoys stretches taut nerves to the limit and there is no doubt that there will be a regrettable incident sooner or later, and probably sooner.
   f) Motor anti-submarine boats are not the best craft for this type of work. In the event of an action with anything but an E-Boat, they are of no assistance to the Hunt Class.

7) **Motor Torpedo Boats.** With reference to (f) above, it is considered that MTBs are superior to motor anti-submarine boats for this type of work for the following reasons:

   (i) They are fitted with a cruising engine which is silent.
   (ii) They can keep the speed of the convoy without showing a wake.
   (iii) They are fitted with two torpedo tubes, which in the event of action with enemy destroyers, would be an invaluable help to the Hunt Class who carry NO torpedoes.
   (iv) They are at least equal, if not superior, in fighting efficiency to the E-Boats.

SUMMARY: It is recommended that the convoy escort should consist of four Hunt Class destroyers, assisted by five MTBs, which would join the convoy before dark and leave before daylight.

Vice-Admiral, Nore Command.

Secret Report
Channel Mobile Balloon
Barrage

1) A meeting was held at the Admiralty on Sunday 25 August to discuss the operation of the Channel mobile balloon barrage.

2) The basis of the discussion was that the barrage should include two flotillas each, consisting of six ships fitted to fly balloons or kites, with two ships in reserve. The operational control of the mobile barrage is to be under the commander-in-chief, The Nore, Sheerness. A flotilla will sail the round trip from Sheerness to St Helens and return, and then give leave and refit as necessary. The second flotilla sailing the round trip with the next convoy and so on. The reserve ships are to be based at Southampton and available as required.

3) After discussion, the following recommendations were agreed:

   (i) To enable the barrage to function effectively, two complete balloon barrage flotillas under control of commander-in-chief, The Nore in Sheerness are essential. (Reserve ships to be based on Southampton.) Naval channel of communication with 952 Barrage Balloon Squadron, RAF, to be through commodore, Sheerness.

   Owing to the arduous nature of the service and in view of the advent of winter conditions, the ships must be seaworthy, have a necessary speed of a minimum of 12 knots, adequate accommodation for full crew and effective anti-aircraft and light-artillery armament manned by permanent RN personnel. The present ships of the small tug type are too small, unseaworthy and have insufficient accommodation and cooking facilities for their crews and should be withdrawn from this service and replaced by large and effective vessels.

   The anti-aircraft armament of each ship to be at least one Oerlikon gun and two AA Lewis guns behind cover. Anti E-Boat armament should also be provided.

   (ii) No difficulty should be experienced in flying balloons from balloon barrage vessels and kites from merchant ships* in the convoy in accordance with the laid down plan. Both balloons and kites to be lethal. To ensure proper control of balloons and kites, an RAF balloon officer and a RN kite officer to be accommodated in the ship of the senior officer mobile balloon barrage flotilla.

(iii) Balloon barrage vessels to fly balloons except when they have been shot down, when kites will be flown.

(iv) At night, kites will not be flown except, subject to Air Ministry concurrence, between Sheerness and St Helens only. Kites will be flown by day and night if all balloons have been shot down.

(v) Maximum height of balloons to be 2,500ft, observing that they must be below effective gun range, which in the case of Oerlikon and twelve-pounder guns is 3,000ft. Balloons to be flown at cloud base if this is lower than the maximum height recommended.

(vi) There are at present eight vessels in the Channel mobile balloon barrage, three at Sheerness, four at Southampton and one at Falmouth. Six additional craft are required. The three vessels at Sheerness, have, to date, accompanied every convoy and therefore it is proposed that they should accompany convoy CW10 sailing from Sheerness to St Helens then proceed to Southampton to give leave and re-store. Convoy CE10, sailing from St Helens, to be accompanied by the four ships present at Southampton. Subsequent orders for the whole Channel mobile balloon barrage to be given by commander-in-chief, The Nore.

NOTE: Present Location of Channel Mobile Balloon Barrage Vessels.

Rene Le Benerais	Sheerness
Gatinais	Sheerness
Elan II	Sheerness
Pingouin	Southampton
Astral	Southampton
Mamouth	Falmouth
Fratton	Southampton
Pintade	Southampton

Pingouin & *Mamouth* undergoing refit having broken down.
Pintade not yet fitted out.

Author's notes: *Kites: Most merchant ships were fitted with anti-aircraft kites, but these were not always flown and were very unpopular with the RAF. Equally as lethal as balloon cables, the kites could not be seen easily and thus their cables were a greater hazard.

Of the existing vessels at the time of this report, *Pingouin, Mamouth* and *Pintade* were all tugs and thus fell within the category of vessels deemed unsuitable for the task.

List of Channel Convoys During 1940

CE Convoys = Channel Eastbound

CW Convoys = Channel Westbound

Convoy Number	From	To	Sailed	Arrived
CE1	St Helen's Road	Southend		
CE2	St Helen's Road	Southend		
CE3	St Helen's Road	Southend		
CE4	St Helen's Road	Southend		
CE5	St Helen's Road	Southend	18 July	19 July
CE6	St Helen's Road *Bosom*	Southend	20 July	22 July
CE7	St Helen's Road	Southend	22 July	24 July
CE8	Falmouth	Southend	31 July	5 Aug
CE9	St Helen's Road	Southend	21 Aug	22 Aug
CE10	St Helen's Road	Southend	3 Sept	4 Sept
CE11	St Helen's Road	Southend	18 Sept	19 Sept
CE12	St Helen's Road	Southend	3 Oct	4 Oct
CE13	(CANCELLED)			
CE14	St Helen's Road	Southend	11 Oct	12 Oct
CE15	St Helen's Road	Southend	1 Nov	2 Nov
CE16	St Helen's Road	Southend	13 Nov	14 Nov
CE17	St Helen's Road *Booty*	Southend	21 Nov	22 Nov
CE18	St Helen's Road	Southend	29 Nov	30 Nov
CE19	St Helen's Road	Southend	18 Dec	19 Dec
CE20	St Helen's Road	Southend	26 Dec	27 Dec
CW1	Southend	Yarmouth Road	6 July	7 July
CW2	Southend	Yarmouth Road	8 July	9 July
CW3	Southend *BREAD*	Yarmouth Road	10 July	11 July
CW4	Southend	Yarmouth Road	12 July	13 July
CW5	Southend	Falmouth	14 July	16 July
CW6	Southend	Falmouth	17 July	19 July
CW7	Southend	Falmouth	20 July	22 July

Convoy Number	From	To	Sailed	Arrived
CW8 *Booty*	Southend	Falmouth	25 July	29 July
CW9 *Peewit*	Southend	Yarmouth Road	7 Aug	8 Aug
CW10	Southend	Yarmouth Road	30 Aug	31 Aug
CW11 *Peewit*	Southend	Yarmouth Road	11 Sep	12 Sep
CW12	Southend	Yarmouth Road	28 Sep	29 Sep
CW13	(CANCELLED)			
CW14	Southend	Falmouth	11 Oct	14 Oct
CW15	Southend	Yarmouth Road	25 Oct	26 Oct
CW16	Southend	Yarmouth Road	6 Nov	7 Nov
CW17	Southend	Yarmouth Road	17 Nov	18 Nov
CW18	Southend	Yarmouth Road	25 Nov	26 Nov
CW19	Southend	Yarmouth Road	5 Dec	6 Dec
CW20	Southend	Yarmouth Road	21 Dec	22 Dec
CW21	Southend	Yarmouth Road	31 Dec	1 Jan

Author's note: Convoys CE13 and CW13 were both cancelled. There seems to be no operational reason for this and it may well be that 13 was skipped for purely superstitious reasons.

St Helen's Road is an anchorage point off the north eastern tip of the Isle of Wight that was used as an assembly point for vessels forming CE convoys, or those joining CW convoys.

Yarmouth Road is an area at the opposite (western) end of The Solent which became the official dispersal point for CW convoys.

A Channel convoy passes through the Straits of Dover during the summer of 1940 as an escort destroyer lays a protective smoke screen.

APPENDIX K

The BBC Broadcasts a Live Luftwaffe Attack

POSSIBLY ONE of the most dramatic BBC radio broadcasts of the war (and possibly the most controversial) was that made by Charles Gardner from the cliff tops at Dover on Sunday 14 July 1940, as he was giving a running commentary on a Luftwaffe attack against Convoy CW5. His pre-war pedigree as a sports commentator becomes self evident when listening to the original recording. So famous is this broadcast, that it would be remiss of any book dealing with the Channel convoys not to cover it. By any standards, it was an extraordinary broadcast that became renowned for the: "Oh boy! I've never seen anything so good as this!" remark as Gardner watched the dogfighting. The following is a verbatim transcript:

"Well now... the Germans are dive bombing a convoy out at sea. There are one, two, three, four, five, six, seven German dive bombers, Junkers 87s. There's one going on its target now. A bomb! No!... there... he's missed the ship! He hasn't hit a single ship. There are about ten ships in the convoy but he hasn't hit a single one and you can hear our anti-aircraft guns going at them now. There are one, two, three, four, five, six... about ten German machines dive bombing the British convoy, which is just out to sea in the Channel.

"I can't see anything. No! We thought he had got a German one at the top then, but the British fighters are coming up. Here they come! The Germans are coming in an absolutely steep dive, and you can see their bombs actually leave the machines and come into the water. You can hear our anti-aircraft guns going like anything. I am looking round now. I can hear machine-gun fire, but I can't see our Spitfires. They must be somewhere there. Oh. Here's a plane coming down. Somebody's hit a German and he's coming down with a long streak...coming down completely out of control.... a long streak of smoke and now a man's baled out by parachute. The pilot has baled out by parachute. It's a Junkers 87 and he's going slap into the sea... and there he goes now... *SMASH!*... a terrific column of water and there was a Junkers 87. Only one man got out of it by parachute, so presumably there was only a crew of one in it.

"Now then... oh, there's a terrific mix up over the Channel! It's impossible to tell which are our machines and which are German. There's a fight going on, and you can hear the little rattles of machine-gun bullets. [loud explosion] That was a bomb, as you

BBC reporter Charles Gardner makes his famous broadcast as he watches an attack on a Channel convoy.

may imagine. Here comes one Spitfire. There's a little burst. There's another bomb dropping – it has missed the convoy again. You know, they haven't hit the convoy in all this. The sky is absolutely patterned with bursts of anti-aircraft fire and the sea is covered with smoke where the bombs have burst, but as far as I can see there is not one single ship hit and there is definitely one German machine down. And I am looking across the sea now. I can see the little white dot of the parachute as the German pilot is floating down towards the spot where his machine crashed with such a big fountain of water about two minutes ago.

"Well now, everything is peaceful again for the moment. The Germans, who came over in about twenty or twenty-five dive bombers delivered their attack on the convoy and I think they made off as quickly as they came. Oh yes... I can see one, two, three, four, five, six, seven, eight, nine... ten Germans haring back towards France for all they can go....and here are our Spitfires coming after them. There's going to be a big fight, I think, out there, but it will be too far away for us to see. Of course there are a lot more Germans up there. Can you see, Cyril? Yes... there are one, two, three, four, five, six, seven on the top layer, one, two, three... there's two layers of German machines. They are all, I think, I could not swear to it, but they were all Junkers 87s. There are two more parachutists I think... no... I think they are seagulls.

"You can hear the anti-aircraft burst still going. Well... that was a really hot little engagement while it lasted. No damage done except to the Germans who lost one machine and the German pilot, who is still on the end of his parachute, although appreciably nearer to the sea than he was. I can see no boat going out to pick him up, so he'll probably have a long swim ashore.

"Well...that was a very unsuccessful attack on the convoy I must say.

"Oh... there's another fight going on, away up, about 25 or even 30,000ft above our heads and I can't see a thing of it. The anti-aircraft guns have put up one, two, three, four, five, six bursts but I can't see the aeroplanes. There we go again... oh... what? Oh, we have just hit a Messerschmitt! Oh, that was beautiful! He's coming right down... you hear those crowds? He's finished! Oh, he's coming down like a rocket now. An absolutely steep dive. Let us move round so we can watch him a bit more... No, no, the pilot's not getting out of that one. He's being followed down. What? There are two more Messerschmitts up there? I think they are all right. No... that man's finished. He's going down from about 10,000ft , oh, 20,000 to 2,000ft and he's going straight down. He's not stopping! I think that's another German machine that's definitely been put paid to. I don't think we shall actually see him crash, because he's going into a bank of cloud. He's smoking now. I can see the smoke although we cannot count that as a definite victory because I did not see him crash. He's gone behind a hill. He looked certainly out of control.

"Now we are looking up to the anti-aircraft guns. There's another! There's another Messerschmitt. I don't know whether he's down or whether he's trying to get out of the anti-aircraft fire which is giving him a very hot time. There's a Spitfire! Oh, there's about four fighters up there, and I don't know what they are doing. One, two, three, four, five fighters... fighting right over our heads. Now there's one coming right down on the tail of what I think is a Messerschmitt and I think it's a Spitfire behind him. Oh, darn! He's turned away and I can't see. I can't see. Where's one crashing? Where? No... I think he's pulled out. You can't watch fights like these very coherently for long. You just see about four twirling machines, you just hear little burst of machine gunning and by the time you have picked up the machines they are gone.

"Hello? Look, there's a dogfight going on up there. There are four, five, six machines all whirling and turning around. Now... hark at those machine guns going. Hark! One, two, three, four, five, six; now there's something coming right down on the tail of another. Here they come. Yes, they are being chased home! There are three Spitfires chasing three Messerschmitts now. Oh boy! Look at them going! Oh boy... that was really grand. There is a Spitfire behind the first two. He will get them. Oh, yes! Oh boy! I've never seen anything so good as this! The RAF fighters have really got these boys taped. Our machine is catching up the Messerschmitts. He's got the legs of it, you know.

"Now... right in the sights. Go on, George! You've got him. Bomb! Bomb! No, no... the distance is a bit deceptive from here. You can't tell, but I think something definitely is going to happen to that first Messerschmitt. Oh yes, just a moment... I think I wouldn't like to be him. Oh, I think he's got him. Yes? Machine guns are going like anything. No there's another fight going on... no... they've chased him right out to sea. I can't see but I would think the odds would be on that first Messerschmitt catching it. Oh look. Where?

Where? I can't see them at all. Just on the left of those black shots. See it? Oh yes, oh yes… I see it. Yes, they've got him down too. Yes, the Spitfire has pulled away from him. Yes, I think that first Messerschmitt has been crashed on the coast of France all right."

Author's note: After Gardner's report was broadcast there was quite widespread disquiet about the reporting of a life or death battle "…along the lines of a football match". However, his words very much captured the spirit of the moment and reflected how the public viewed the air battles going on above them at this time, and often relished such jingoistic accounts of an apparent enemy rout. Unfortunately, however, one of the aircraft that Gardner so enthusiastically described as smashing in to the sea turned out to be a Hurricane of 615 Squadron flown by Plt Off Michael Mudie who died of his injuries the next day. Also, and despite Gardner's belief that not a single ship was hit, two were damaged and the coaster SS *Island Queen* was sunk.

Selected Bibliography

The following books and publications were referred to by the author during the preparation of this work.

Bungay, Stephen	*The Most Dangerous Enemy*	(Aurum 2001)
Crook, Flt Lt D M	*Spitfire Pilot*	(Grub Street 2009)
Donahue, A G	*Tally-Ho! Yankee in a Spitfire*	(Macmillan & Co 1942)
Franks, Norman	*Wings of Freedom*	(William Kimber 1980)
Franks, Norman	*Frank 'Chota' Carey*	(Grub Street 2006)
Goss, Chris	*Luftwaffe Bombers Battle of Britain*	(Crécy 2000)
Goss, Chris	*Brothers in Arms*	(Crécy 1994)
Hewitt, Nick	*Coastal Convoys 1939-1945*	(Pen & Sword 2008)
HMSO	*British Coaster*	(HMSO 1947)
HMSO	*British Vessels Lost At Sea 1939-45*	(PSL 1980)
HMSO	*The Battle of Britain*	(HMSO 1941)
Hurd, Sir Archibald	*Britain's Merchant Navy*	(Odhams 1946)
Gretzyngier, Robert	*Poles in Defence of Britain*	(Grub Street 2001)
Halley, James J	*Squadrons of the RAF*	(Air Britain 1998)
Jones, R V	*Most Secret War*	(Hamish Hamilton 1978)
Mason, Frank	*Battle Over Britain*	(McWhirter Twins 1969)
McKee, Alexander	*Strike From The Sky*	(Souvenir 1960)
McKee, Alexander	*The Coal Scuttle Brigade*	(Souvenir 1957)
McMillan, Capt Norman	*The RAF In The World War*	(Harrap 1944)
Minifie, James M	*Eastbound Channel Convoy*	(*Harpers* Magazine, Jan 1941)
Overy, Richard	*The Battle*	(Penguin 2000)
Ponting, Clive	*Churchill*	(Sinclair-Stevenson 1994)
Probert, Air Cdre Henry	*The Rise and Fall of the German Air Force 1933-45*	(Arms & Armour Press 1983)
Ramsey, Winston G	*Battle of Britain Then and Now*	(After The Battle 1980)

SELECTED BIBLIOGRAPHY

Ramsey, Winston G	*Blitz Then and Now (Vol.1)*	(After The Battle 1987)
Saunders, Andy	*No 43 "Fighting Cocks" Squadron*	(Osprey 2003)
Smith, Peter C	*Luftwaffe Ju 87 Dive Bomber Units*	(Classic 2006)
Smith, Peter C	*Naval Warfare in the English Channel 1939-1945*	(Pen & Sword 2007)
Smith, Peter C	*Stuka Squadron*	(PSL 1990)
Sutherland, Jon and Canwell, Diane	*The RAF Air Sea Rescue Service 1918-1986*	(Pen & Sword 2005)
Vasco, John J and Cornwell, Peter D	*Zerstörer*	(JAC 1995)
Von Eimannsberger, Ludwig	*Zerstörer Gruppe*	(Schiffer 1998)
Weir, Fg Off A N C and Wood, Derek	*Verses of a Fighter Pilot*	(Faber & Faber 1941)
Dempster, Derek	*The Narrow Margin*	(Arrow Books 1969)
Wynn, Kenneth	*Men of the Battle of Britain*	(CCB 2000)
Ziegler, Frank H	*The Story of 609 Squadron*	(Macdonald 1971)

Index

GERMAN PERSONNEL